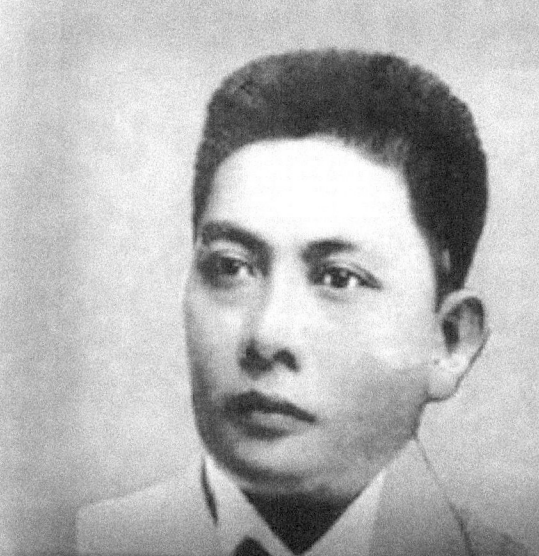
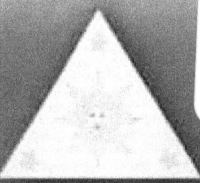

BORN: JULY 25, 1872
DIED: OCTOBER 30, 1930
BIRTHPLACE: IMUS, CAVITE
OCCUPATION: STUDENT
FACTION: MAGDIWANG

SANTIAGO ALVAREZ

BRIGADIER GENERAL

BATTLES:	DATE:	RESULT:
NOVELETA	AUGUST 30, 1896	FILIPINO VICTORY
BINAKAYAN-DALAHICAN	NOVEMBER 9 - 11, 1896	FILIPINO VICTORY

Santiago Alvarez, also known as Kidlat ng Apoy, was born in Imus, Cavite on July 25, 1872. His early education was interrupted by the 1896 revolution; in peacetime, he enrolled in the University of Santo Tomas, but obtained his Bachelor of Arts from the Colegio de San Juan de Letran. He then took up law in Liceo de Manila. Alvarez was a founder and honorary president of the first directorate of the Nacionalista Party, during the establishment of the American civil government. Alvarez died in San Pablo City on October 30, 1930.

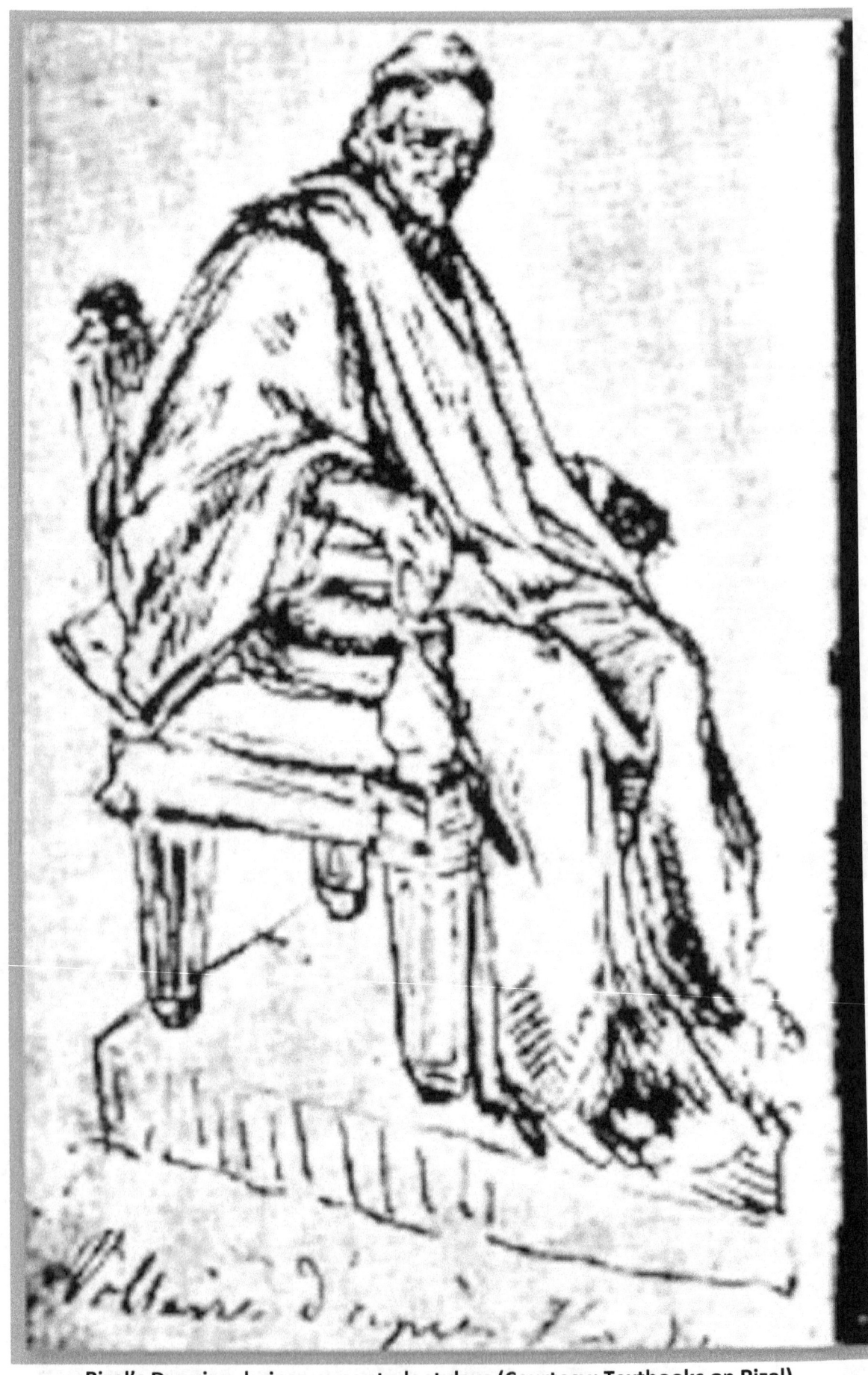

Rizal's Drawing during young student days (Courtesy: Textbooks on Rizal)

WELCOME! Thank you for viewing these heritage or nostalgic pictures of famous individuals, places and events in the history of our beloved country, The Philippines. They say, a picture is worth a thousand words. But more info about the person/event can easily be searched in the internet. These old pictures are available in galleries, museums, magazines, and other forms of media. We record them as archives in this format for posterity. This book can be displayed as coffee table book for family and guests. Each picture can be cut and framed, by buying extra copies. This book is suitable for libraries and schools in Philippines and USA. It is ideal reference material for study of history and celebrities. It is suitable as gift for any occasion. It's a collector's item. Heirs of those shown in pictures may want to own this book for their own families. Pictures are arranged in no particular order. Browse at random.

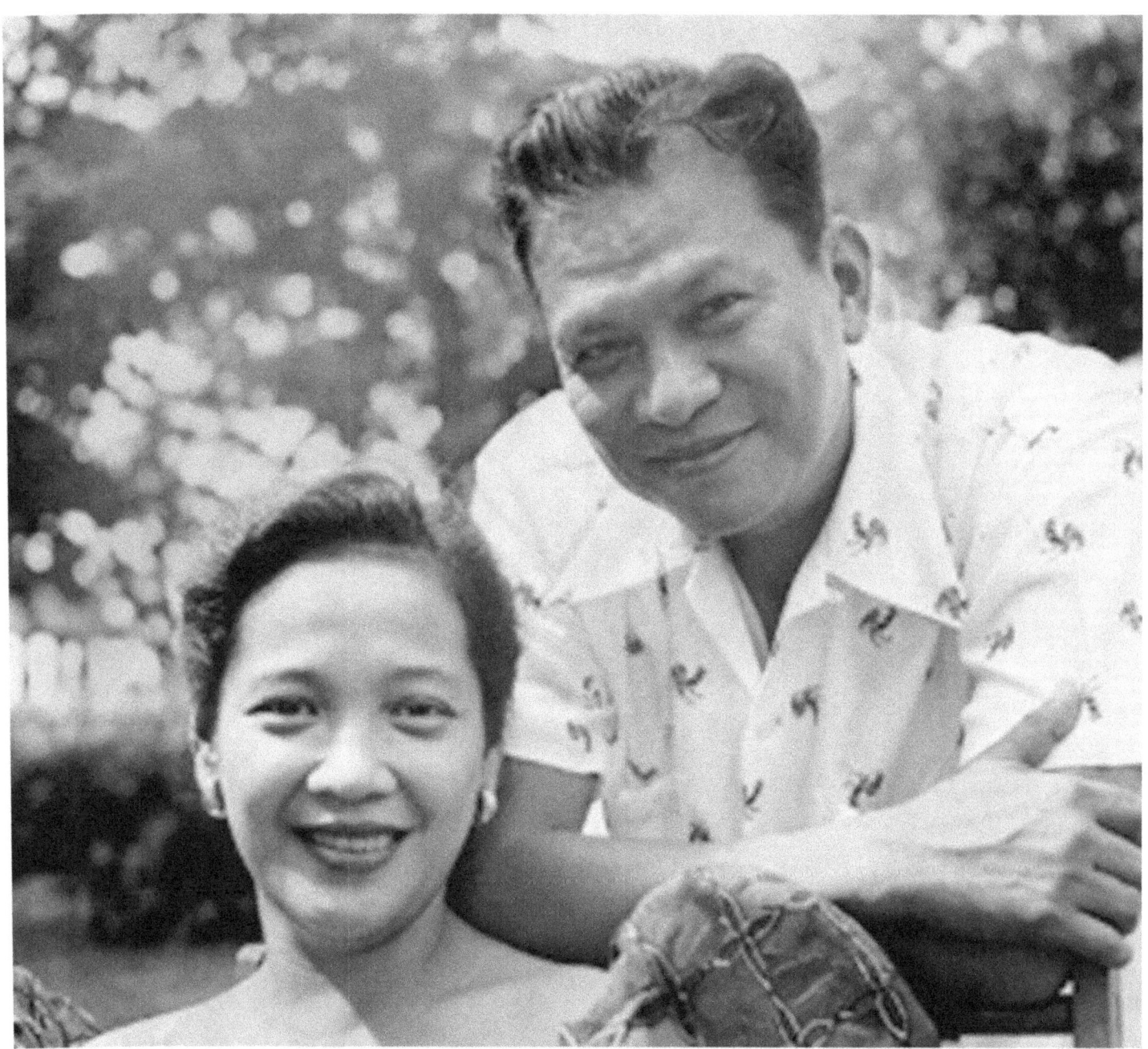

President Ramon (The Guy) Magsaysay and First Lady Luz Banzon-Magsaysay (Courtesy: Phil. Museum)

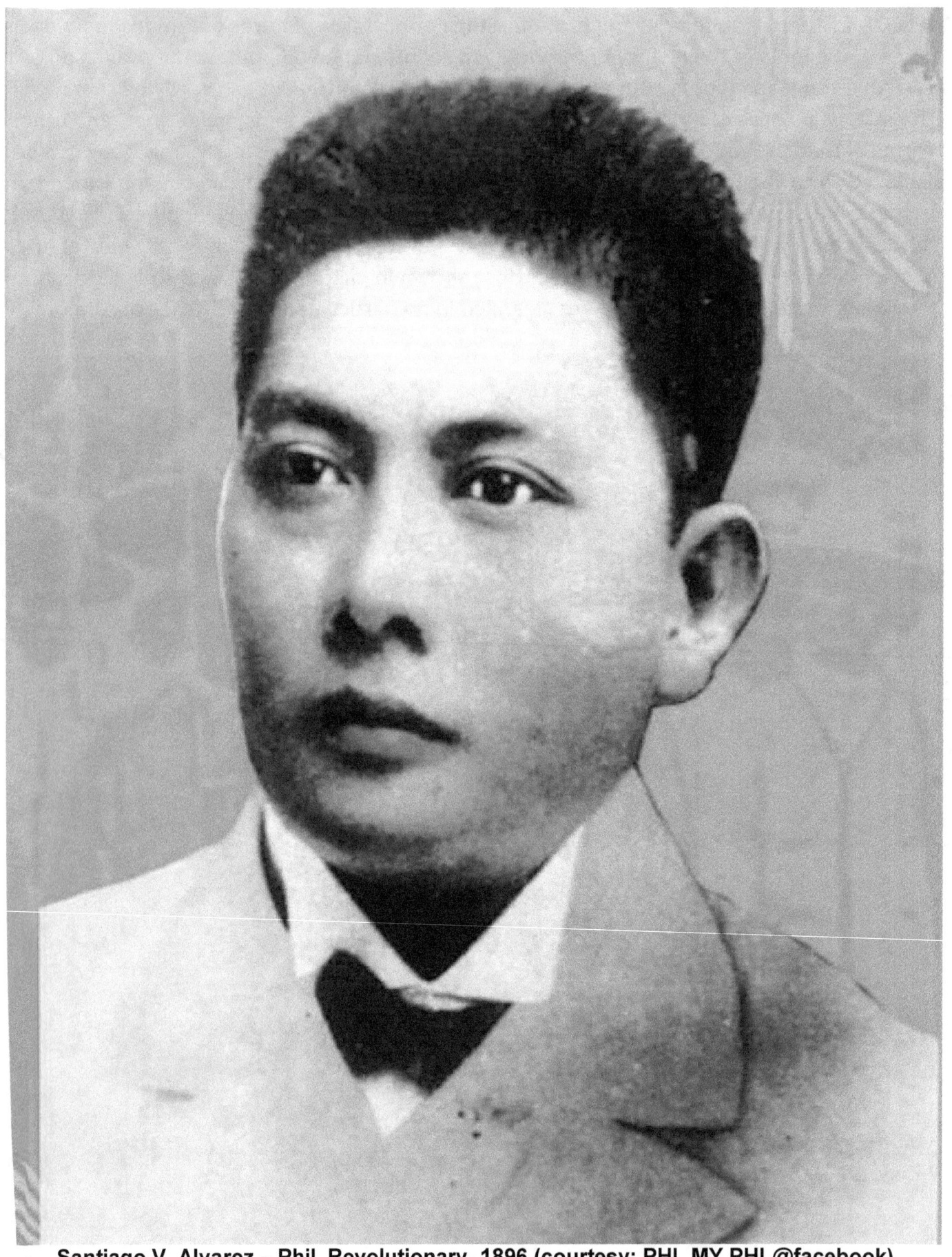

Santiago V. Alvarez – Phil. Revolutionary, 1896 (courtesy: PHL MY PHL@facebook)

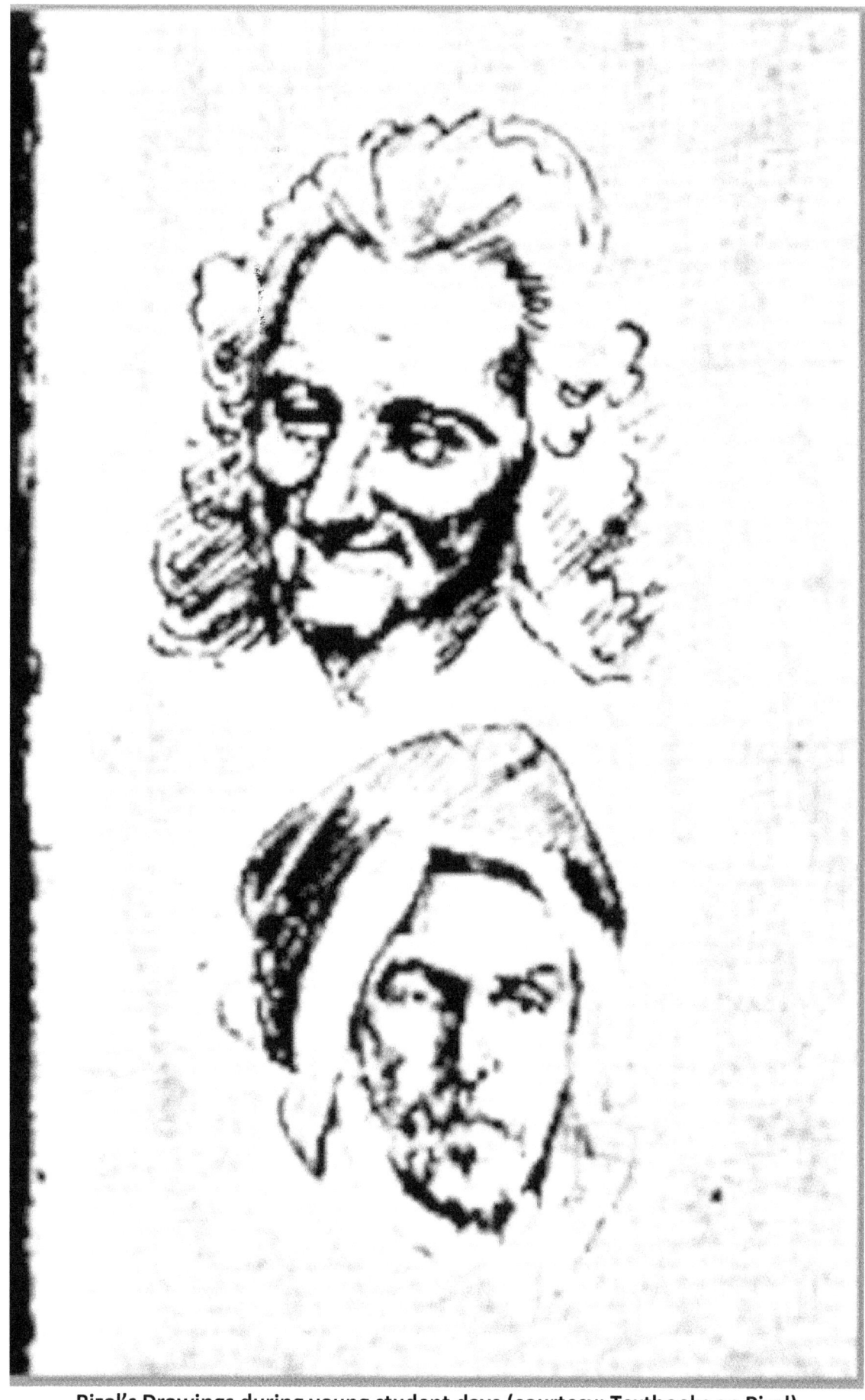

Rizal's Drawings during young student days (courtesy: Textbooks on Rizal)

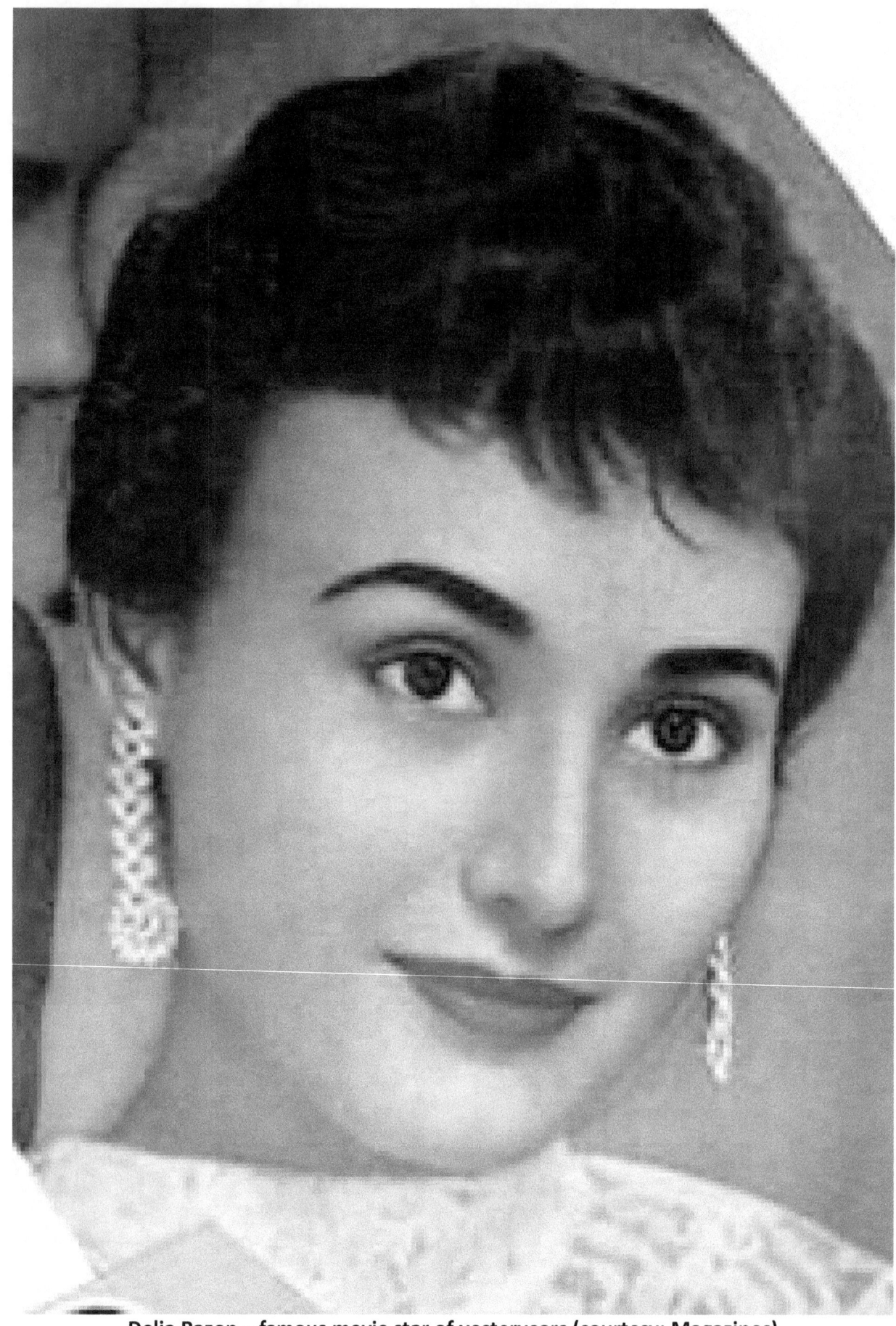

Delia Razon – famous movie star of yesteryears (courtesy: Magazines)

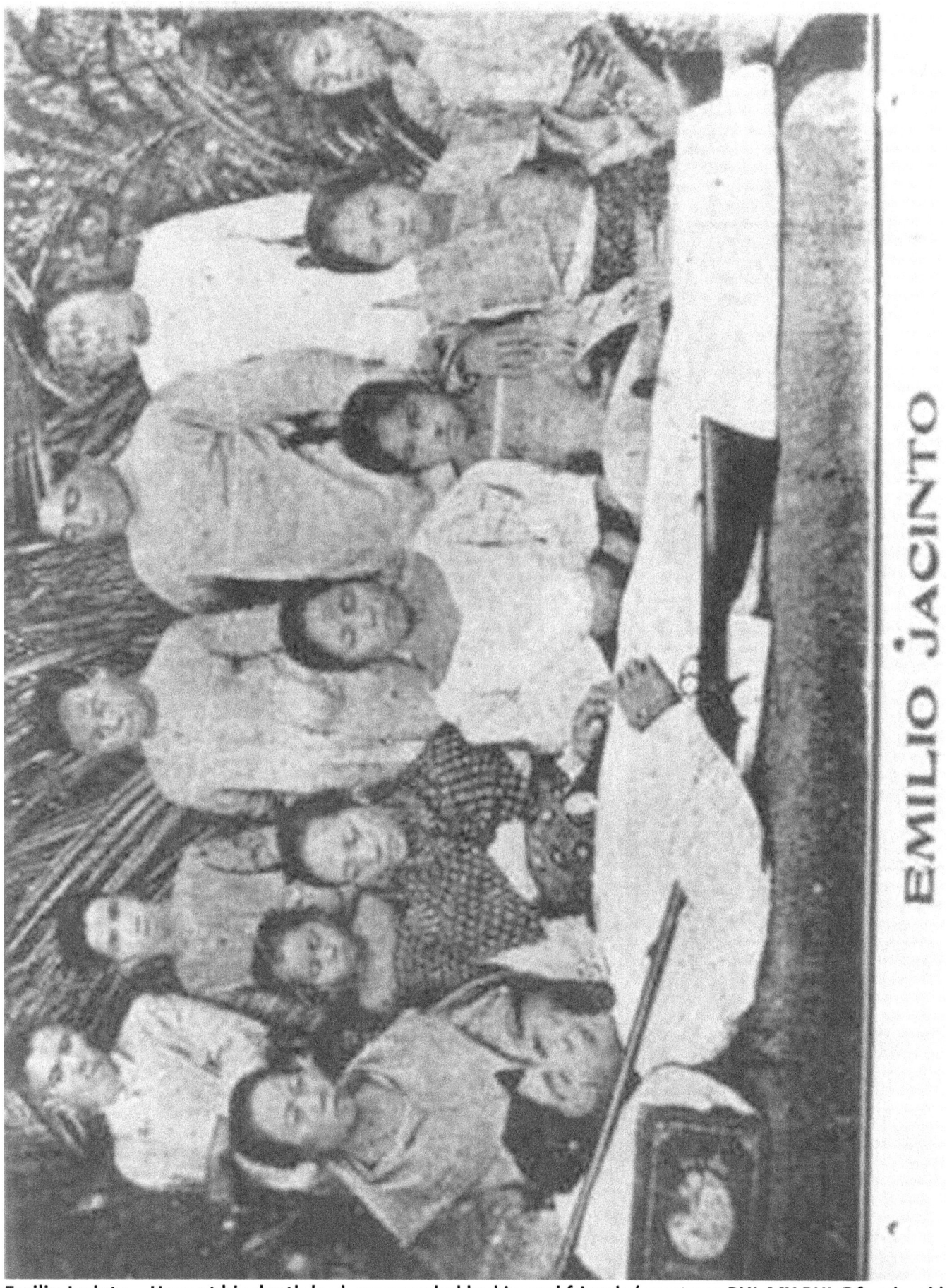

EMILIO JACINTO

Emilio Jacinto – Hero at his death bed, surrounded by kin and friends (courtesy: PHL MY PHL@facebook)

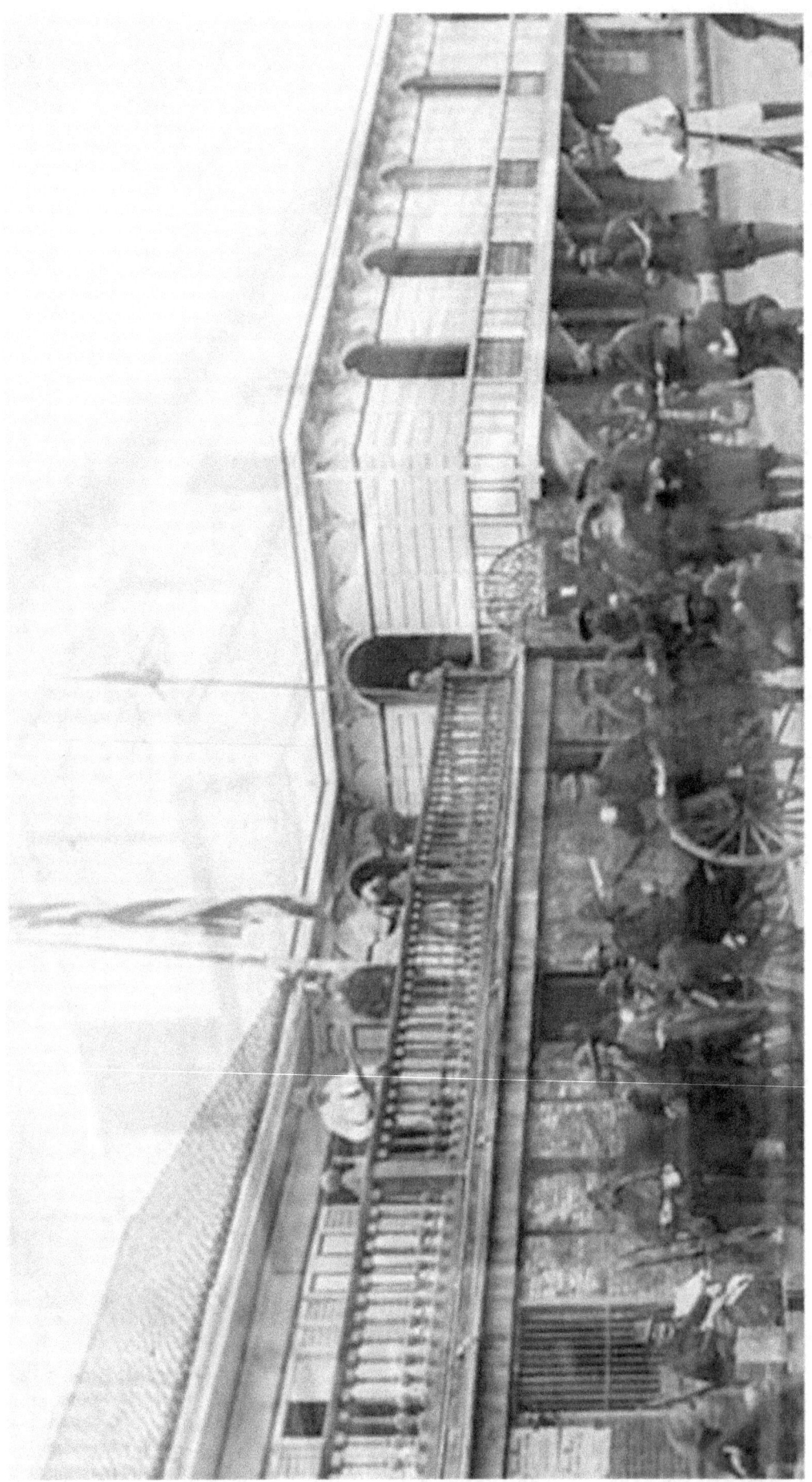

American Soldiers-Occupiers in Manila, 1900 (courtesy: PHL MY PHL@facebook)

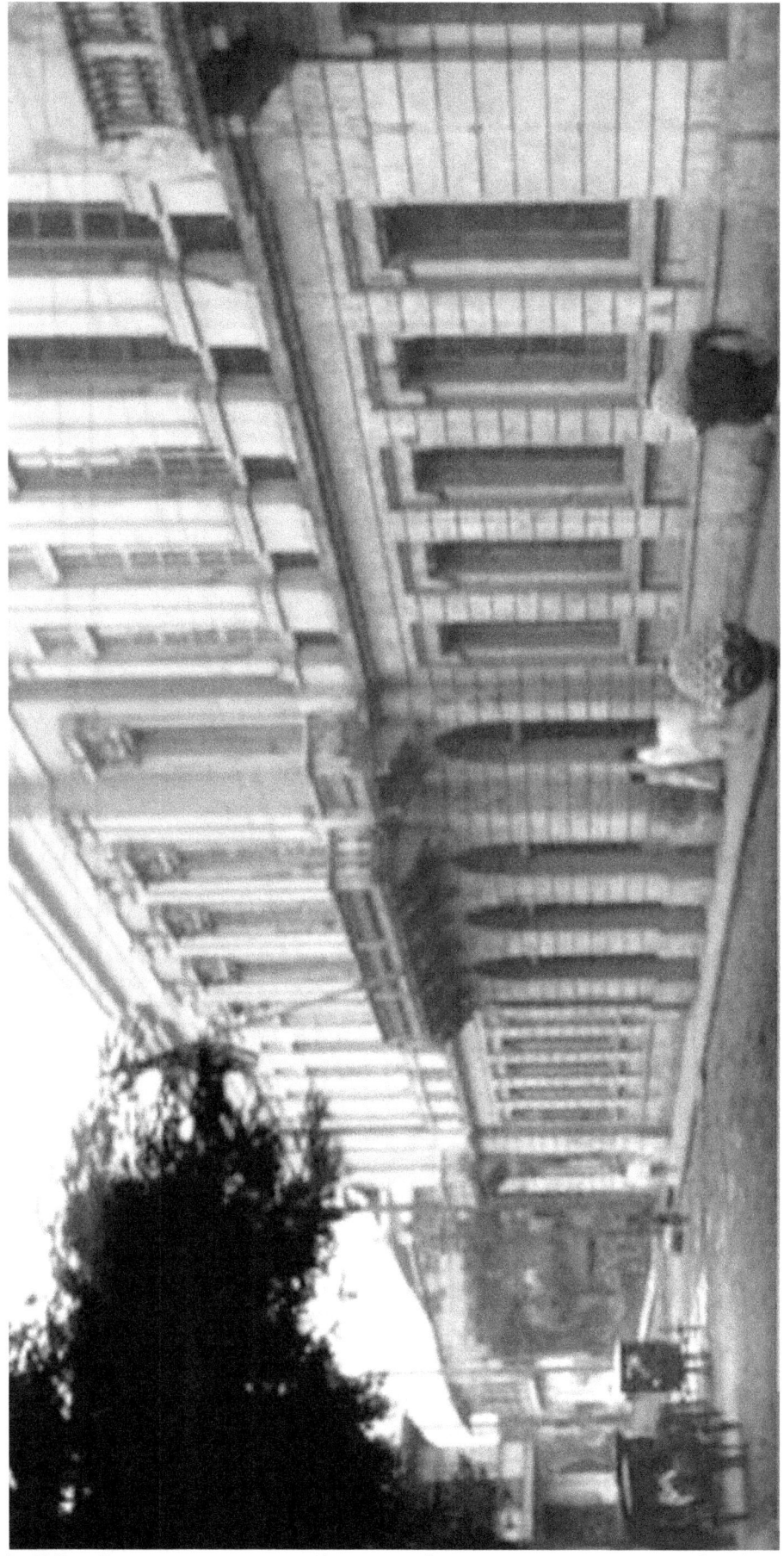

A building in Intramuros, Manila, 1900s (courtesy: PHL MY PHL@facebook)

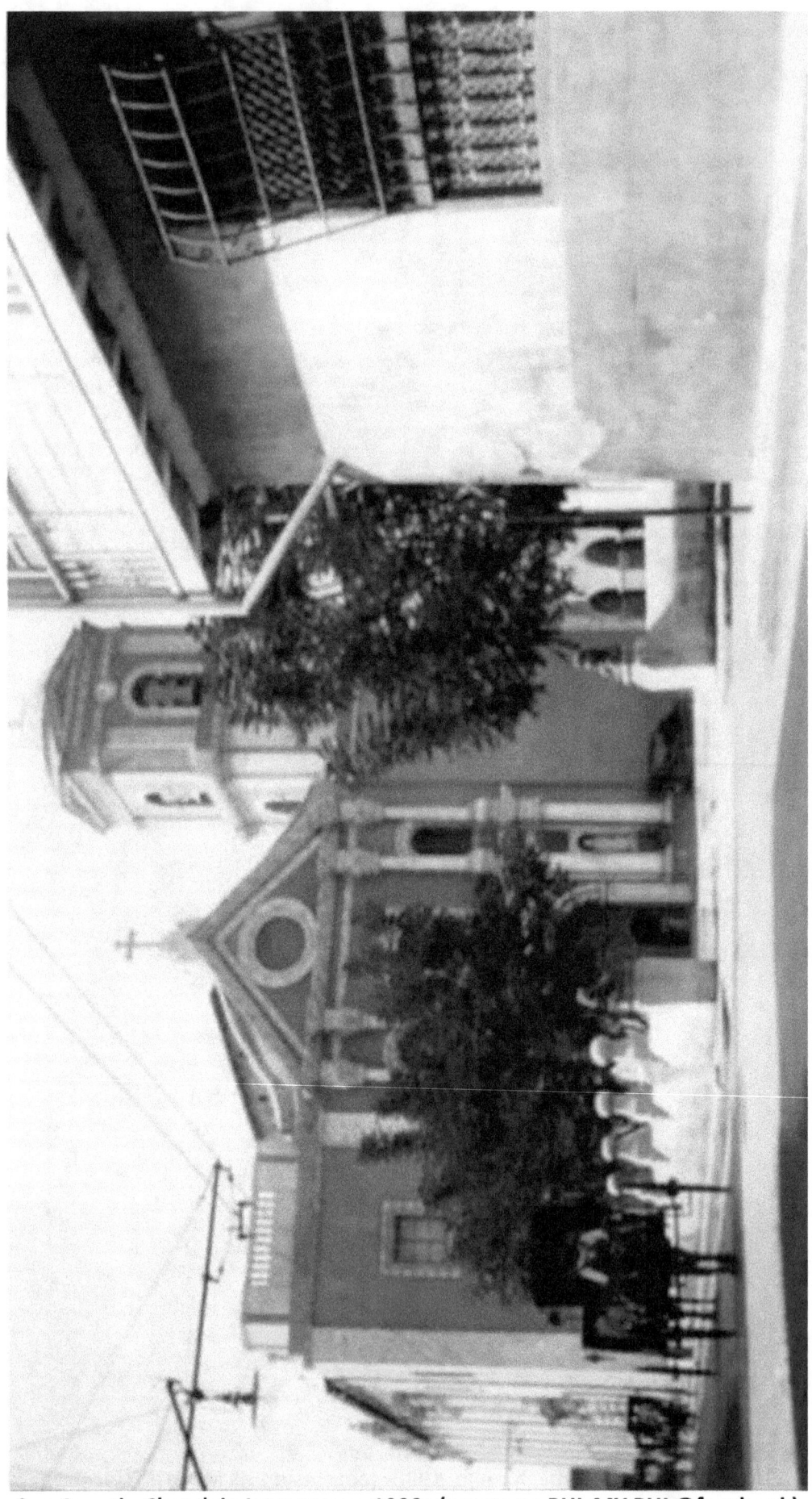

San Agustin Church in Intramuros, 1900s (courtesy: PHL MY PHL@facebook)

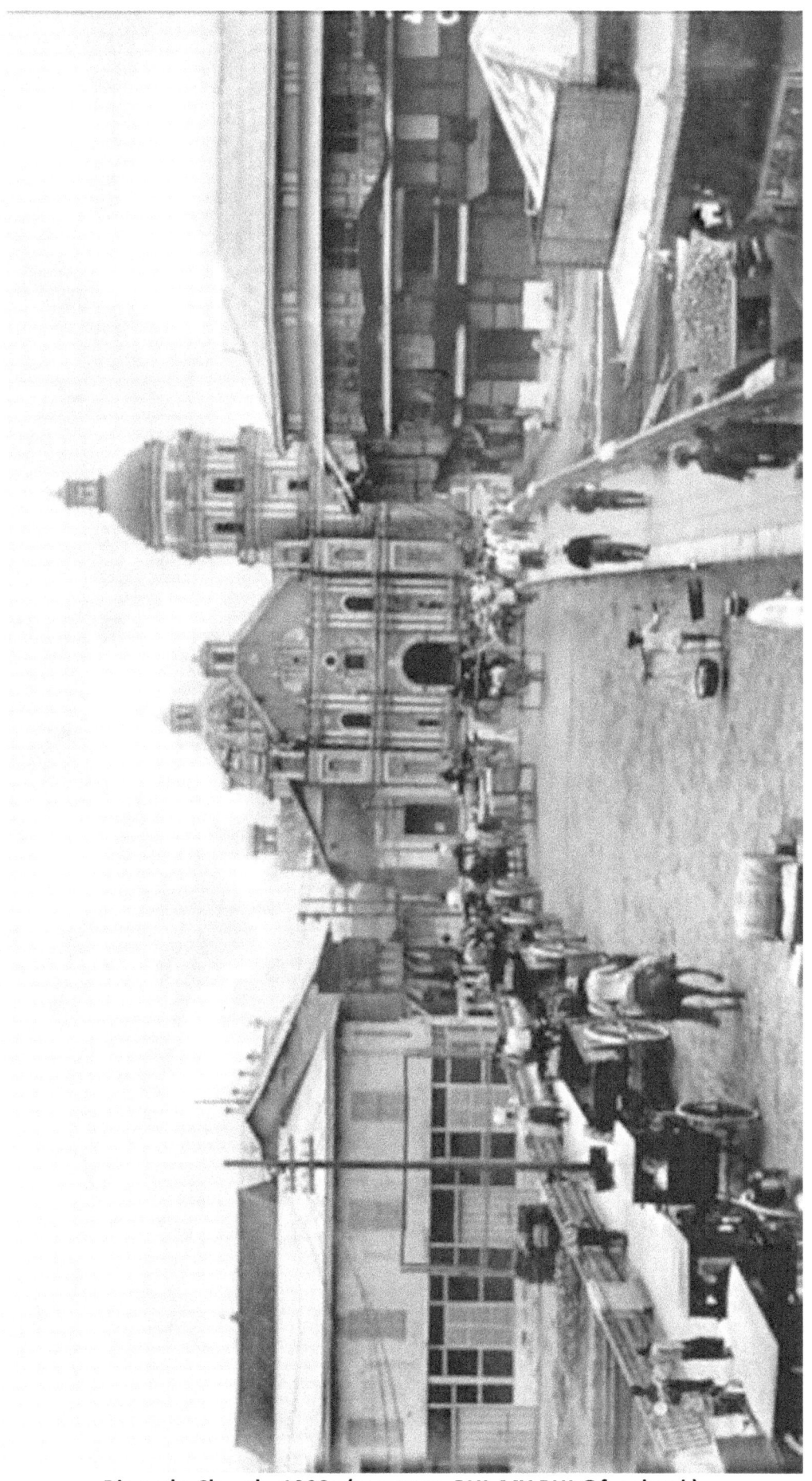

Binondo Church, 1900s (courtesy: PHL MY PHL@facebook)

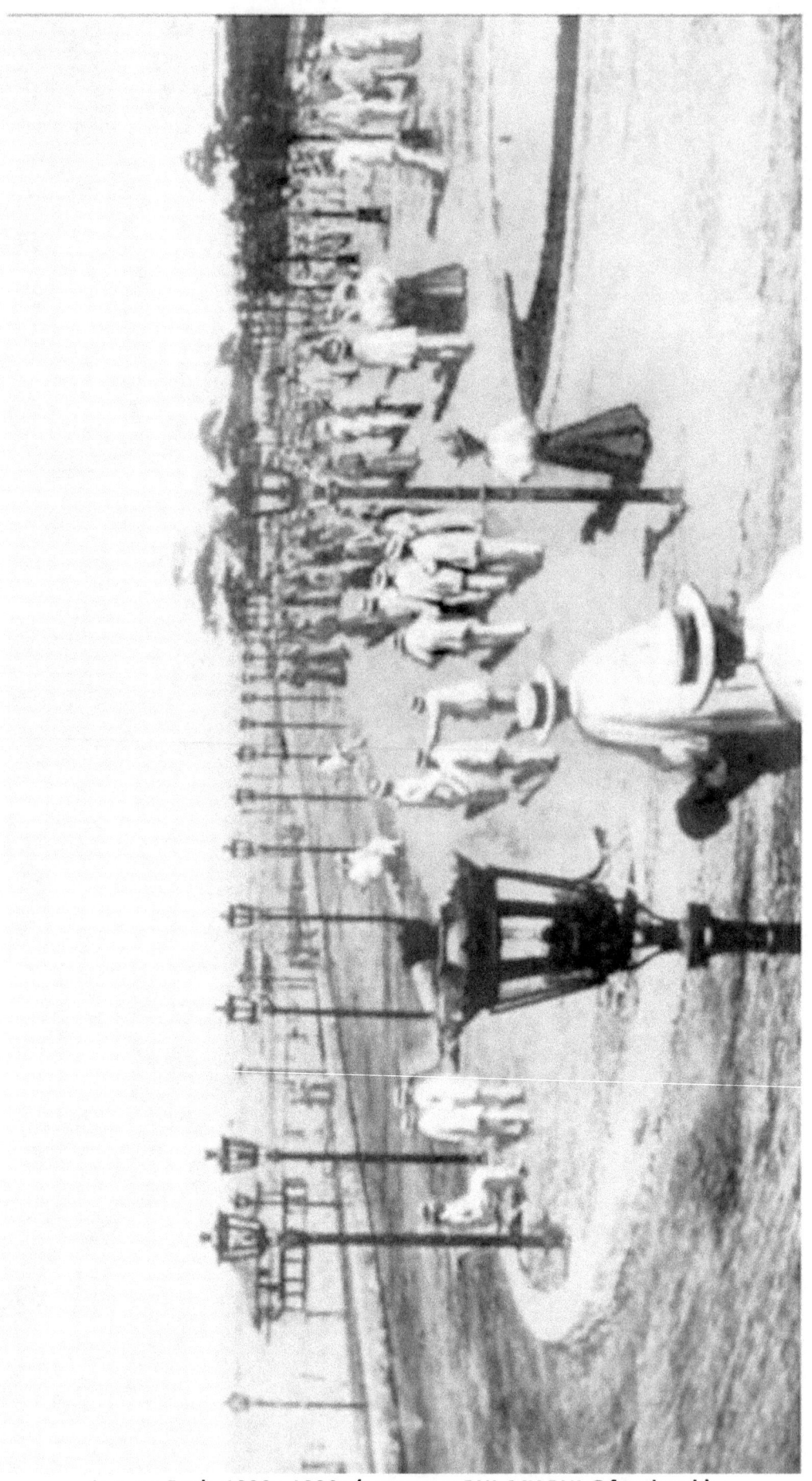

Luneta Park, 1800s-1900s (courtesy: PHL MY PHL@facebook)

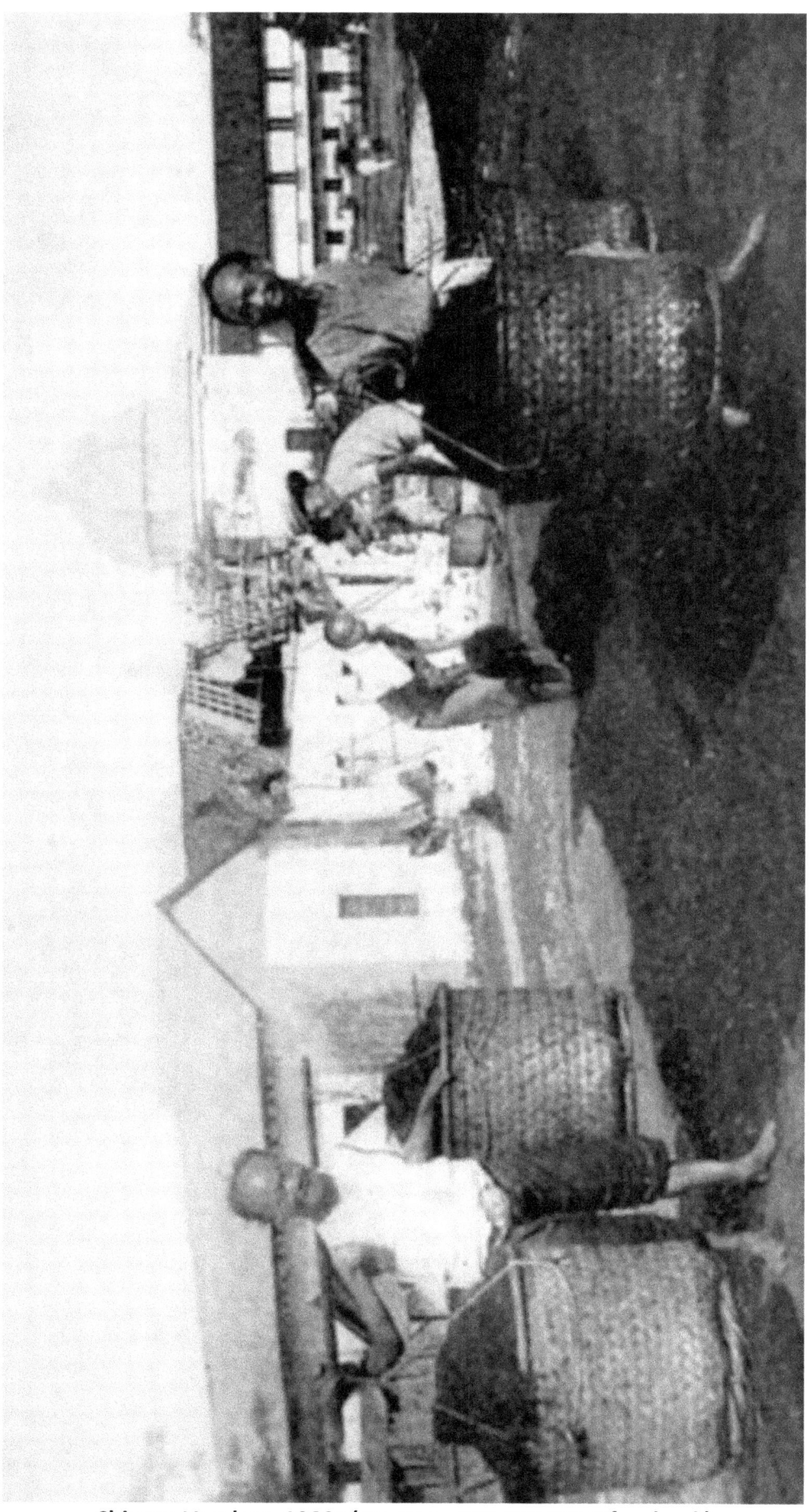

Chinese Vendors, 1900s (courtesy: PHL MY PHL@facebook)

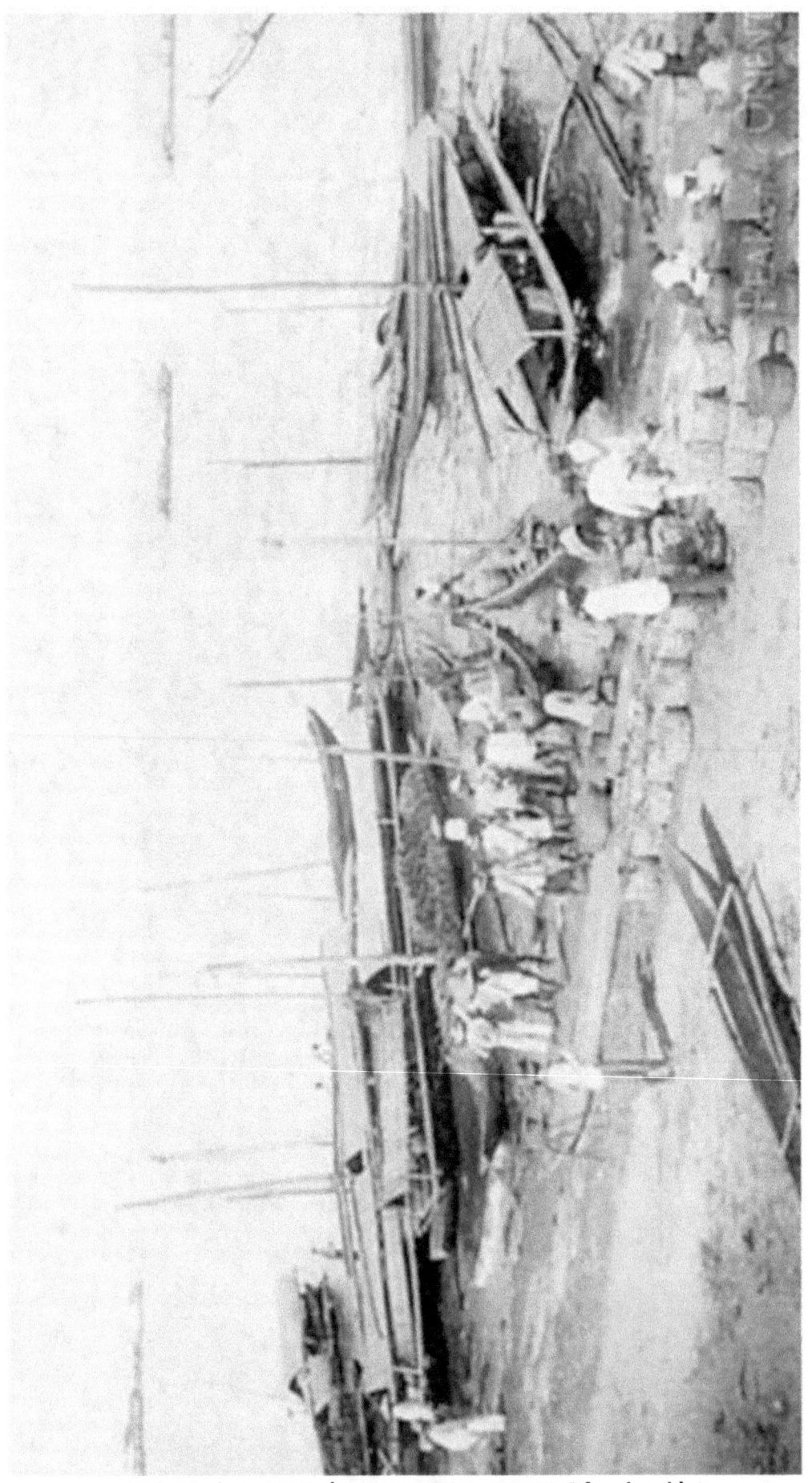

Fish Market, 1900s (courtesy: PHL MY PHL@facebook)

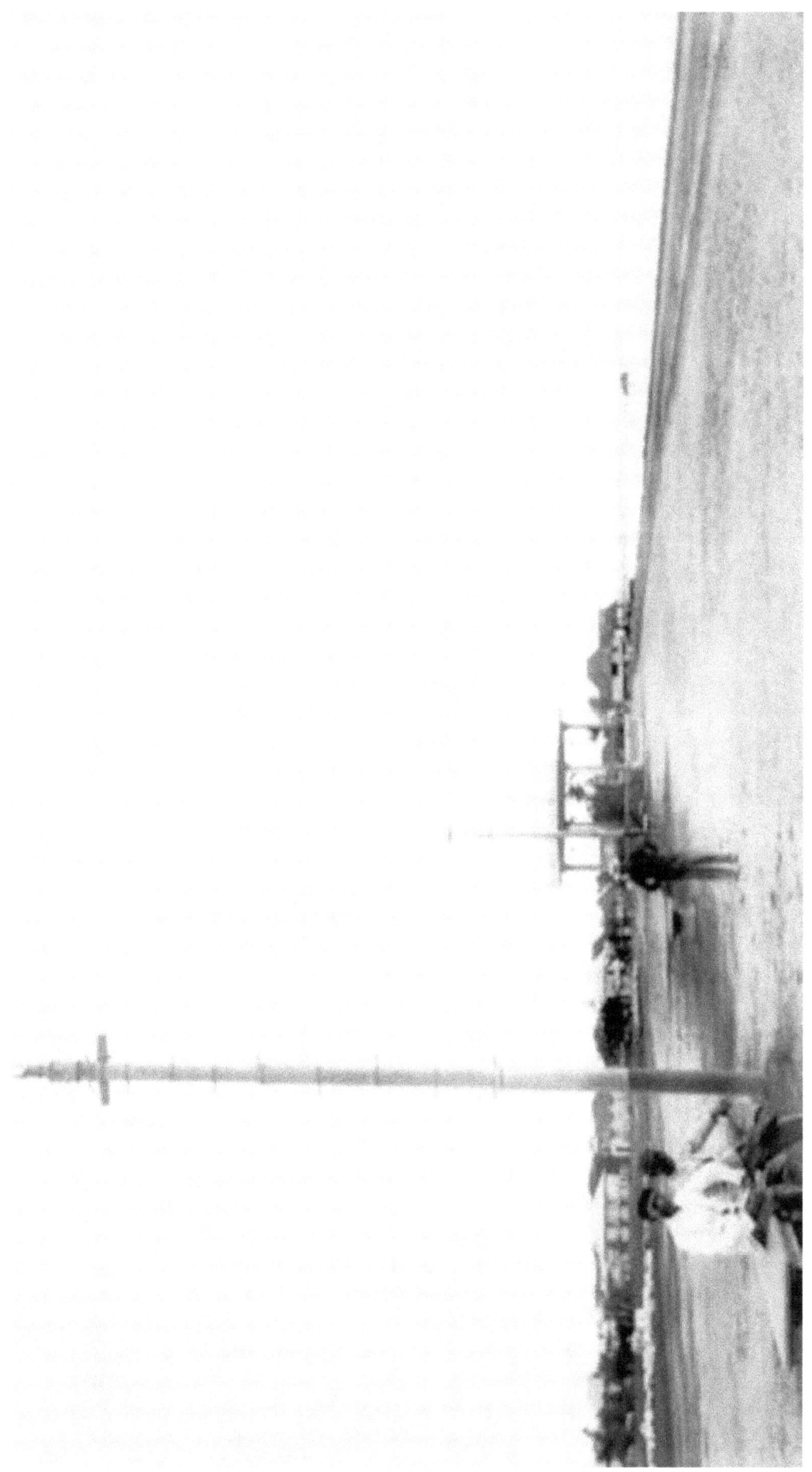

Luneta Park, near the breakwater, 1900s (courtesy: PHL MY PHL@facebook)

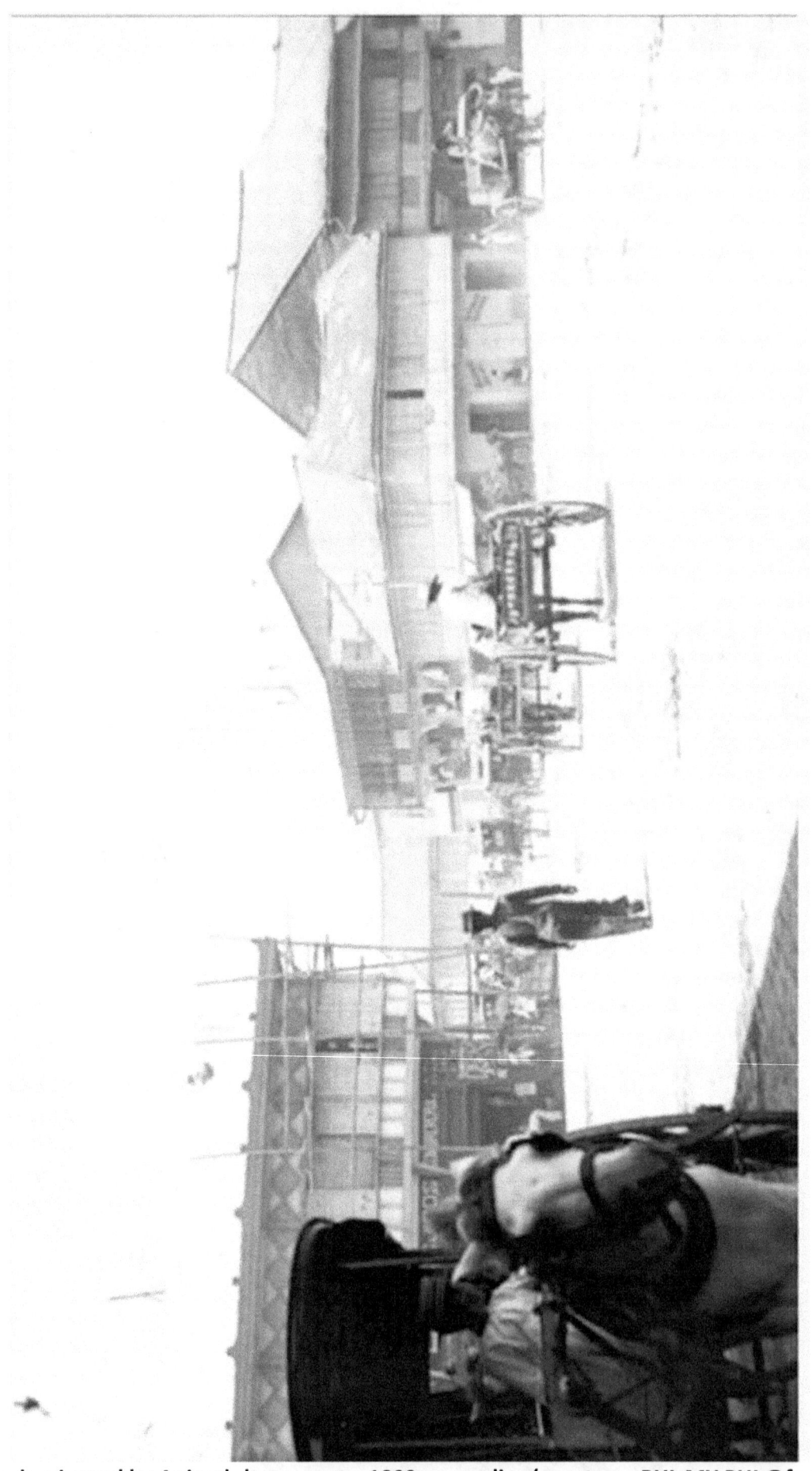

Manila dominated by Animal-drawn carts, 1900s or earlier (courtesy: PHL MY PHL@facebook)

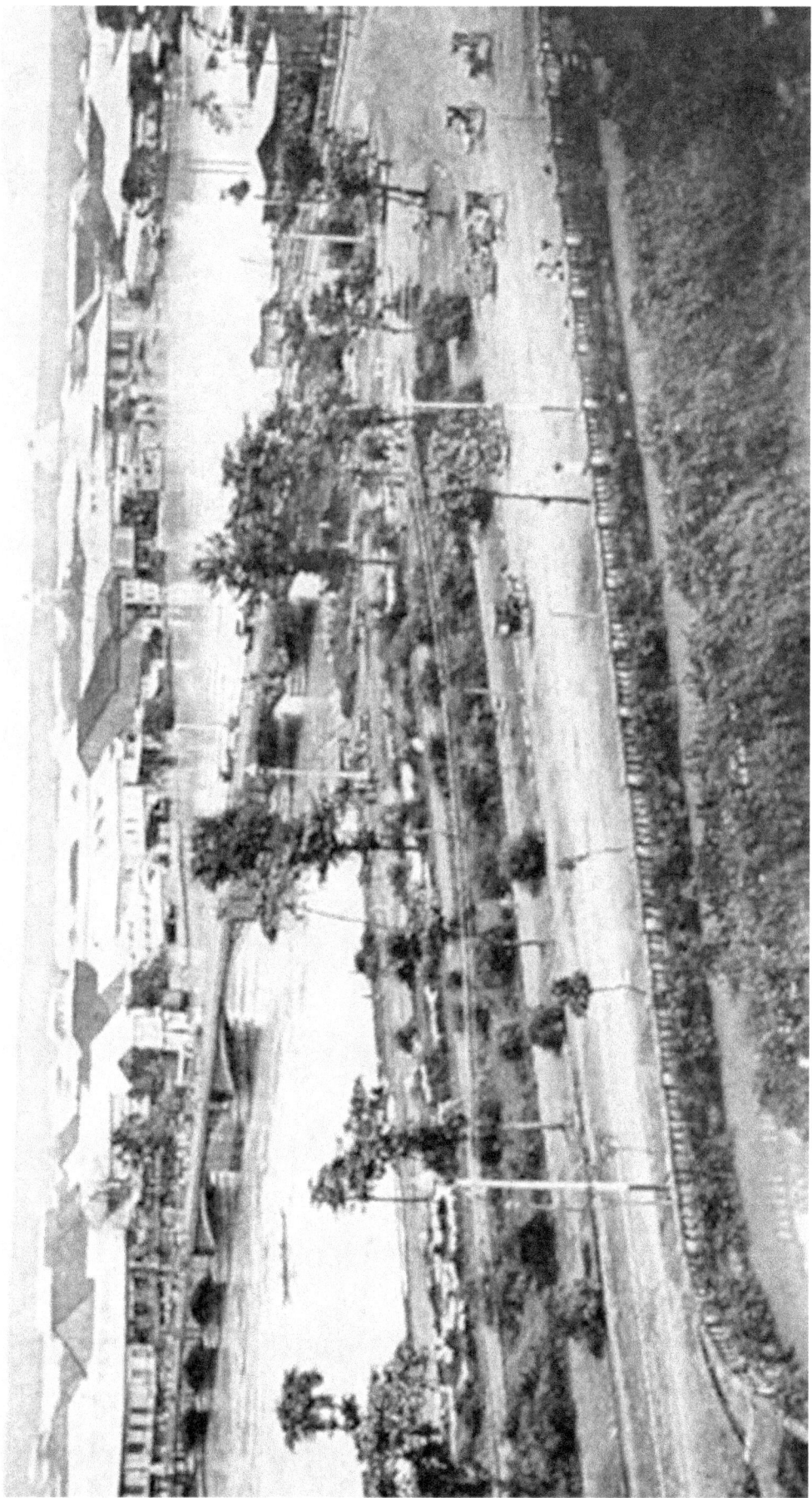

Pasig River, showing old Colgante Bridge in the 1900s (courtesy: PHL MY PHL@facebook)

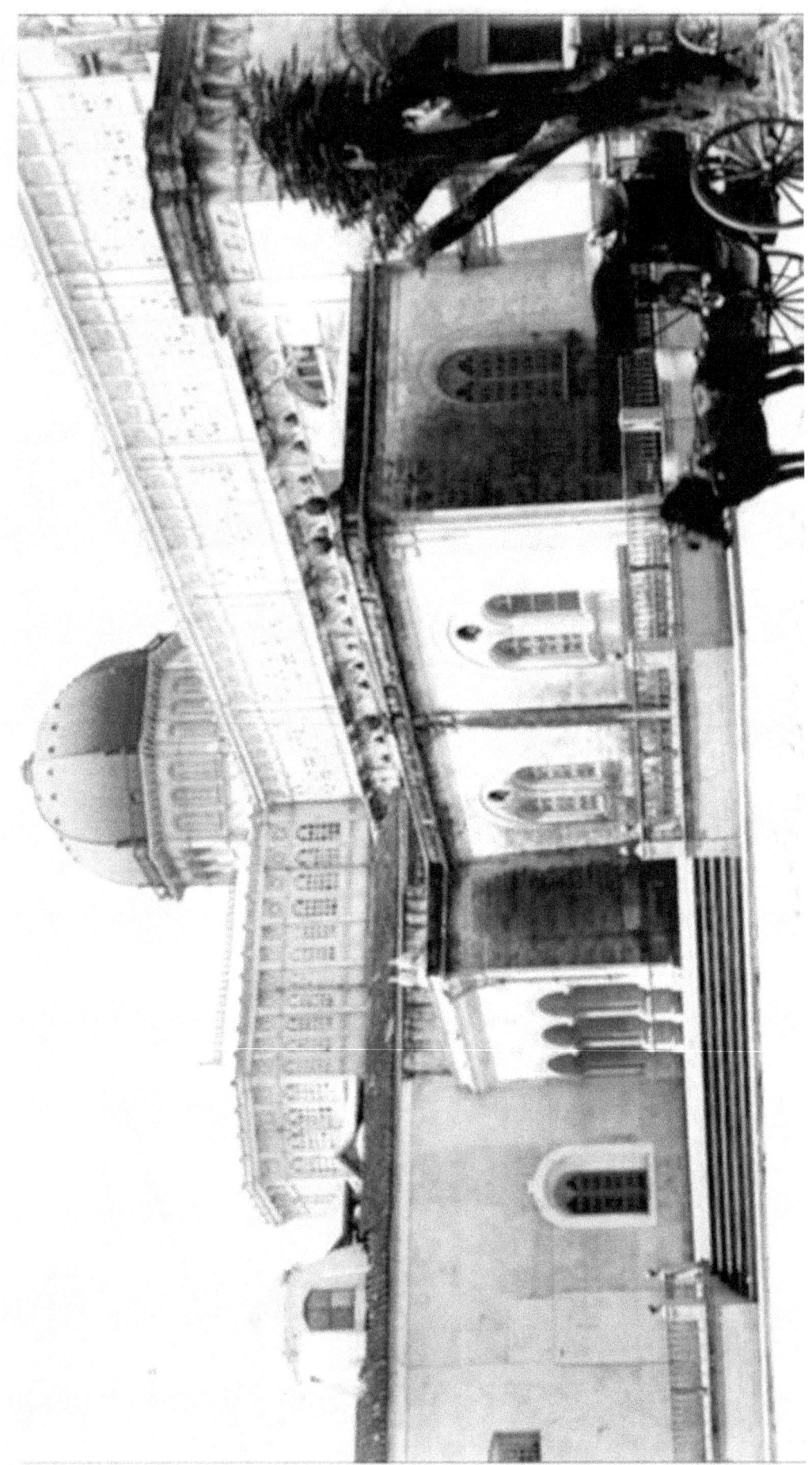

Manila Cathedral, shown in the 1900s, back of the bldg.. (courtesy: PHL MY PHL@facebook)

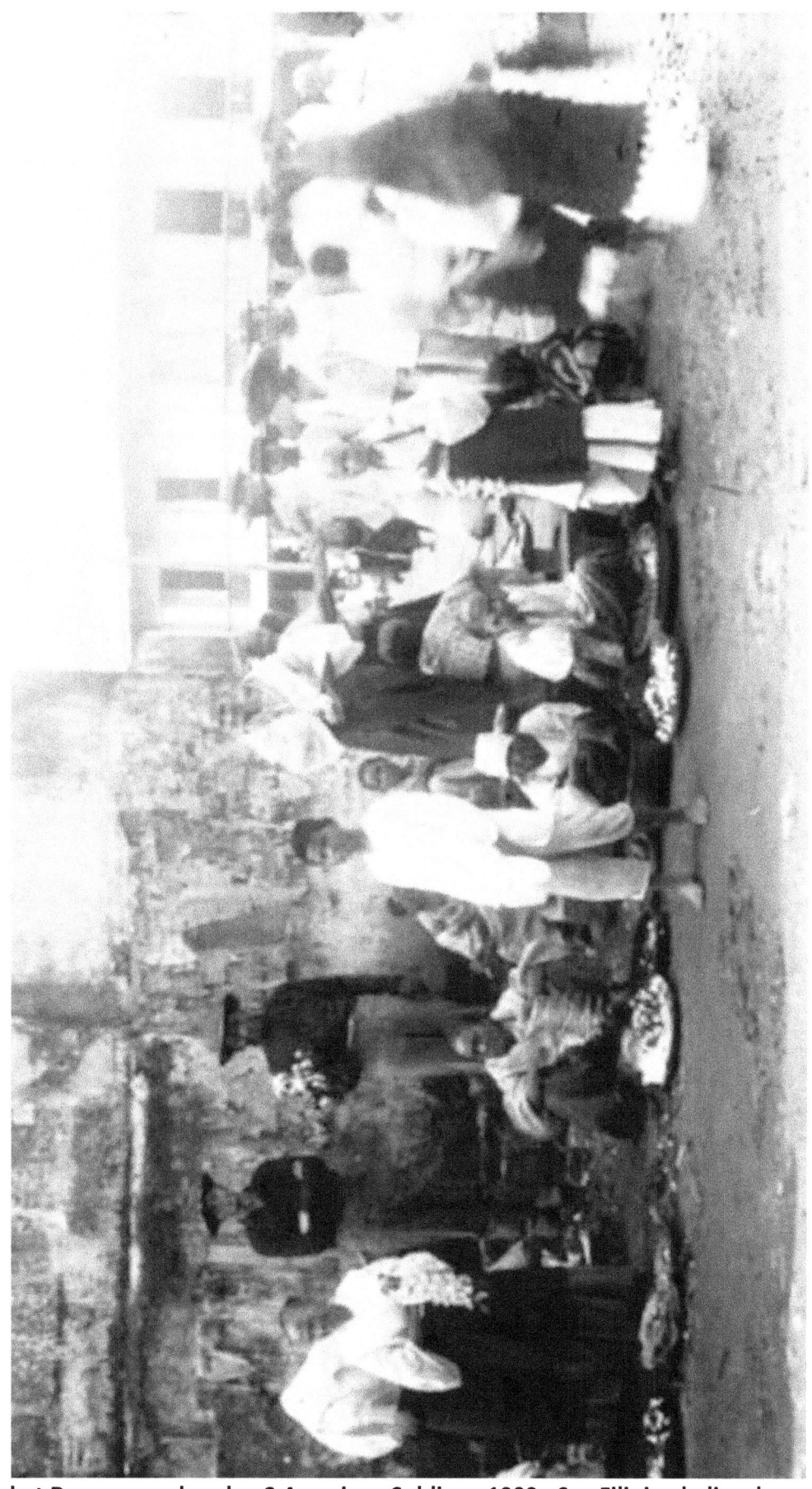

Typical Market Day near a church + 2 American Soldiers, 1900 - See Filipina ladies dressed formally.
(courtesy: PHL MY PHL@facebook)

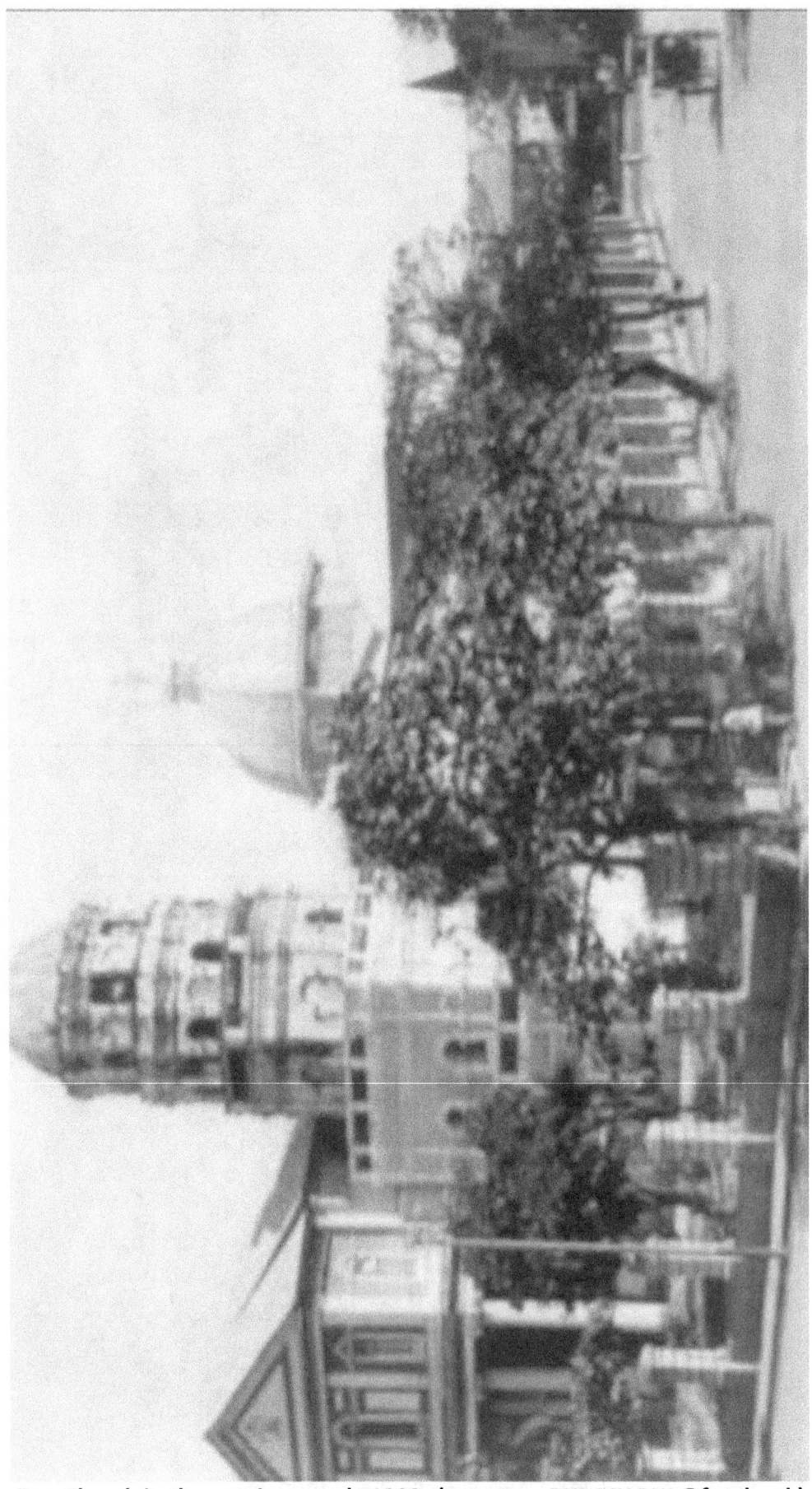

One Church in the province, early 1900s (courtesy: PHL MY PHL@facebook)

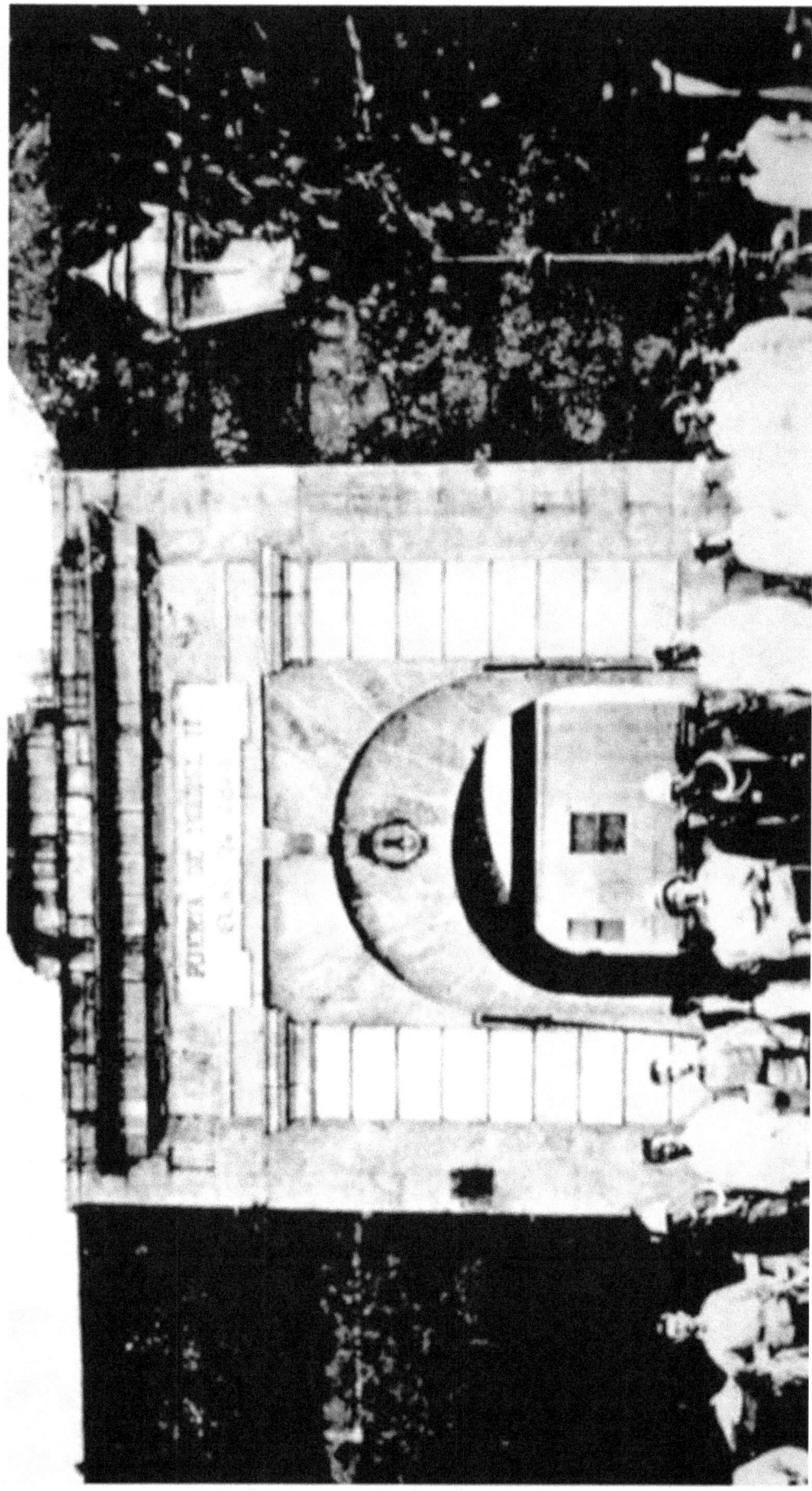

One Gate to Intramuros or Walled City, Spanish times, 1900s (courtesy: PHL MY PHL@facebook)

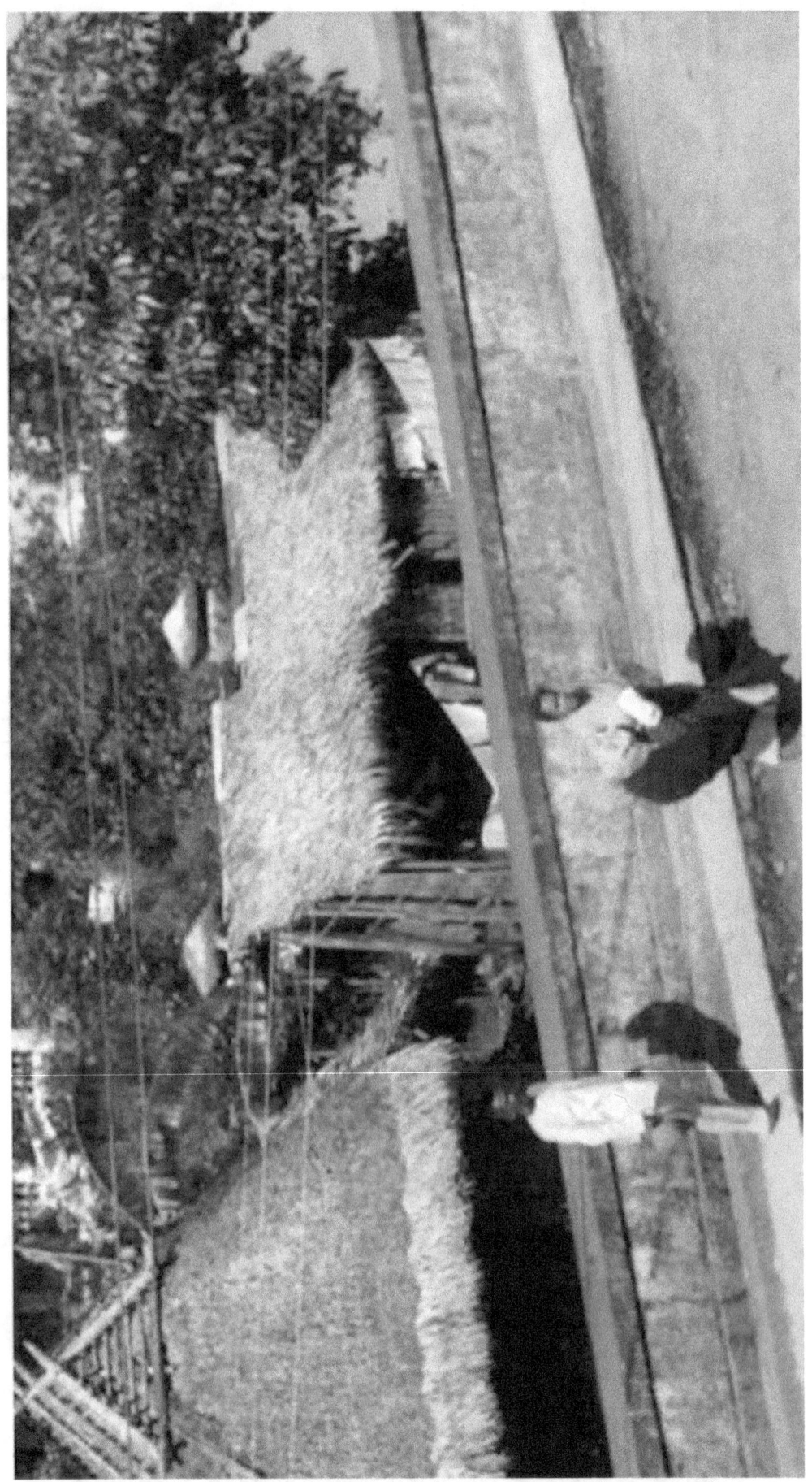

Typical urban houses and dress costumes of Filipino and Filipina, 1900s (courtesy: PHL MY PHL@facebook)

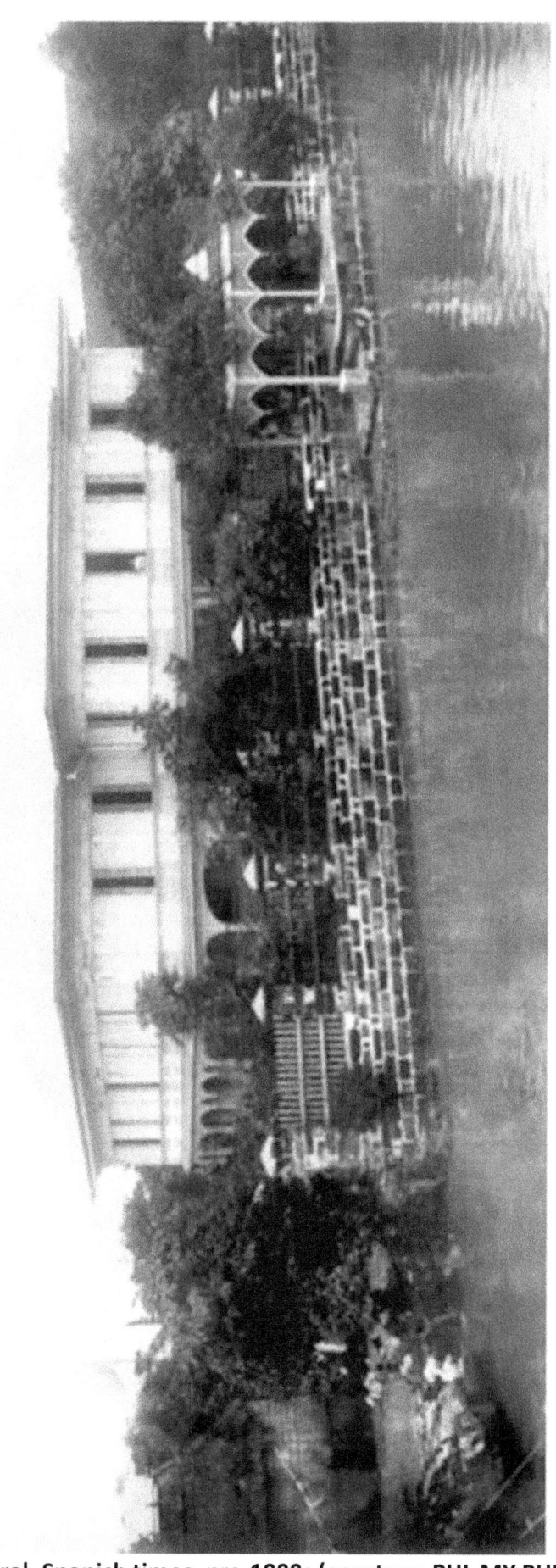

Malacanang Palace of Spanish Gov. General, Spanish times, pre-1900s (courtesy: PHL MY PHL@facebook)

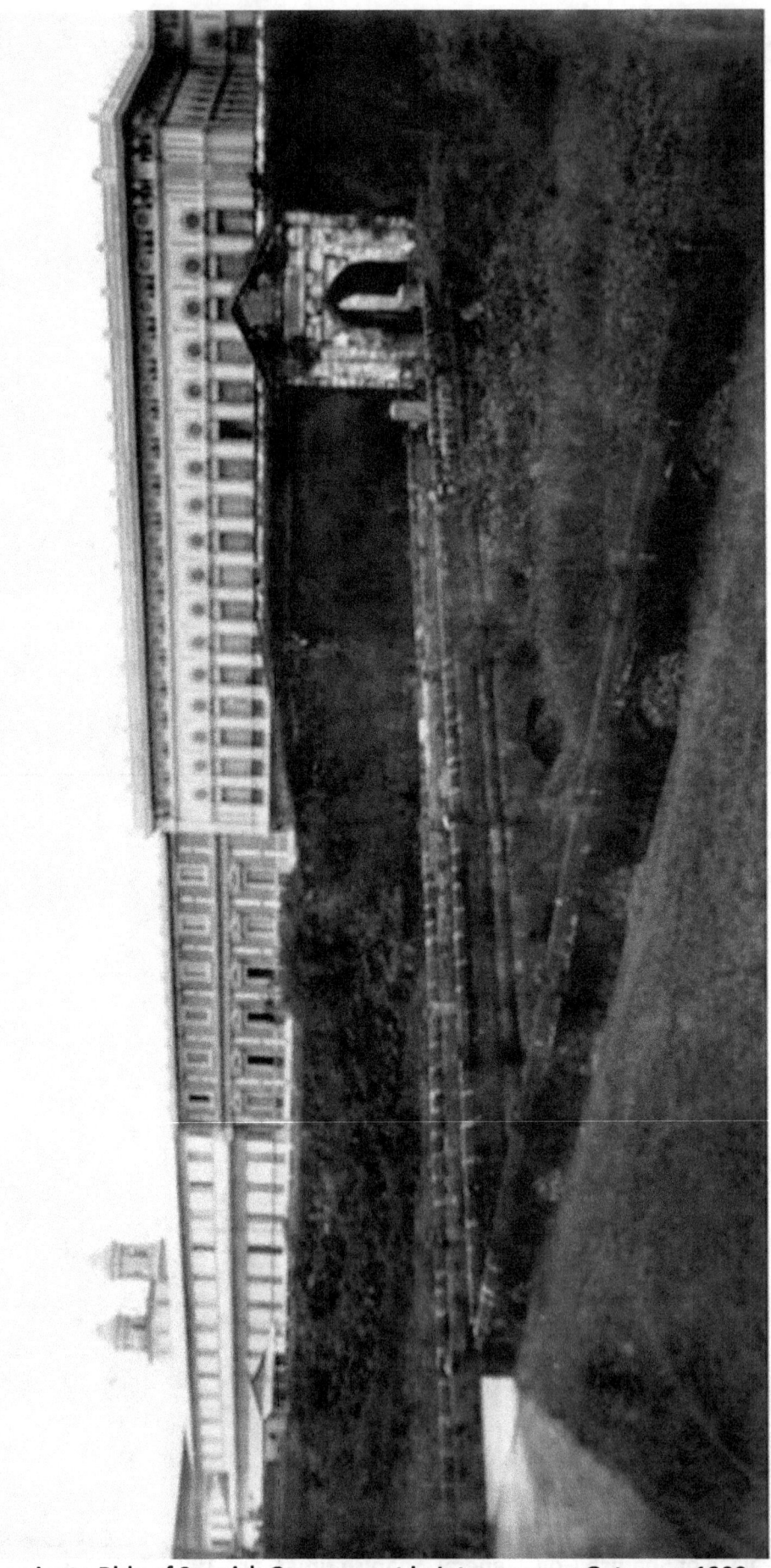

Ayuntamiento Bldg of Spanish Government in Intramuros + Gate, pre-1900s

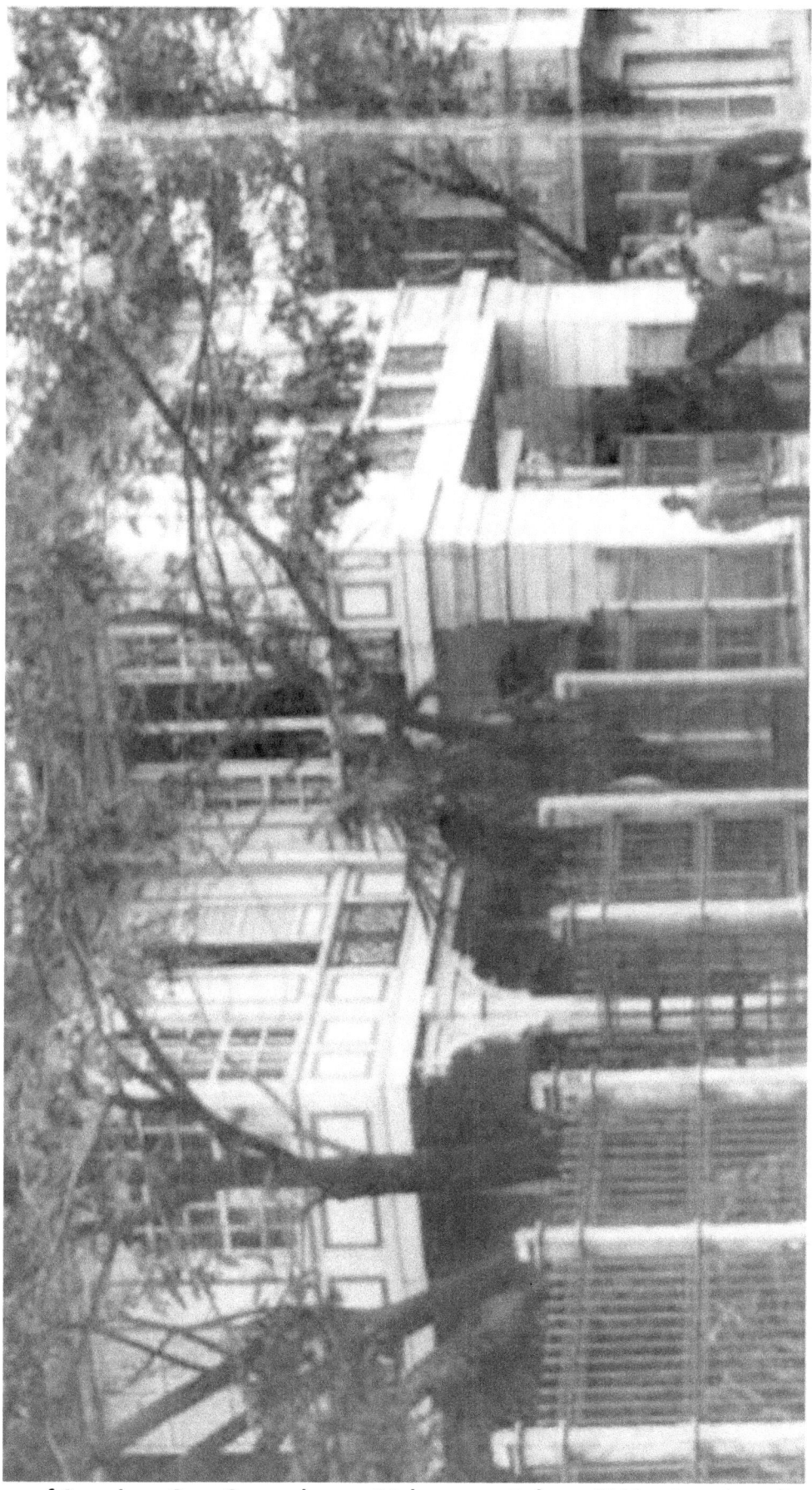

**Home of American Gov. General, near Malacanang Palace, 1900 + American Guards
(courtesy: PHL MY PHL@facebook)**

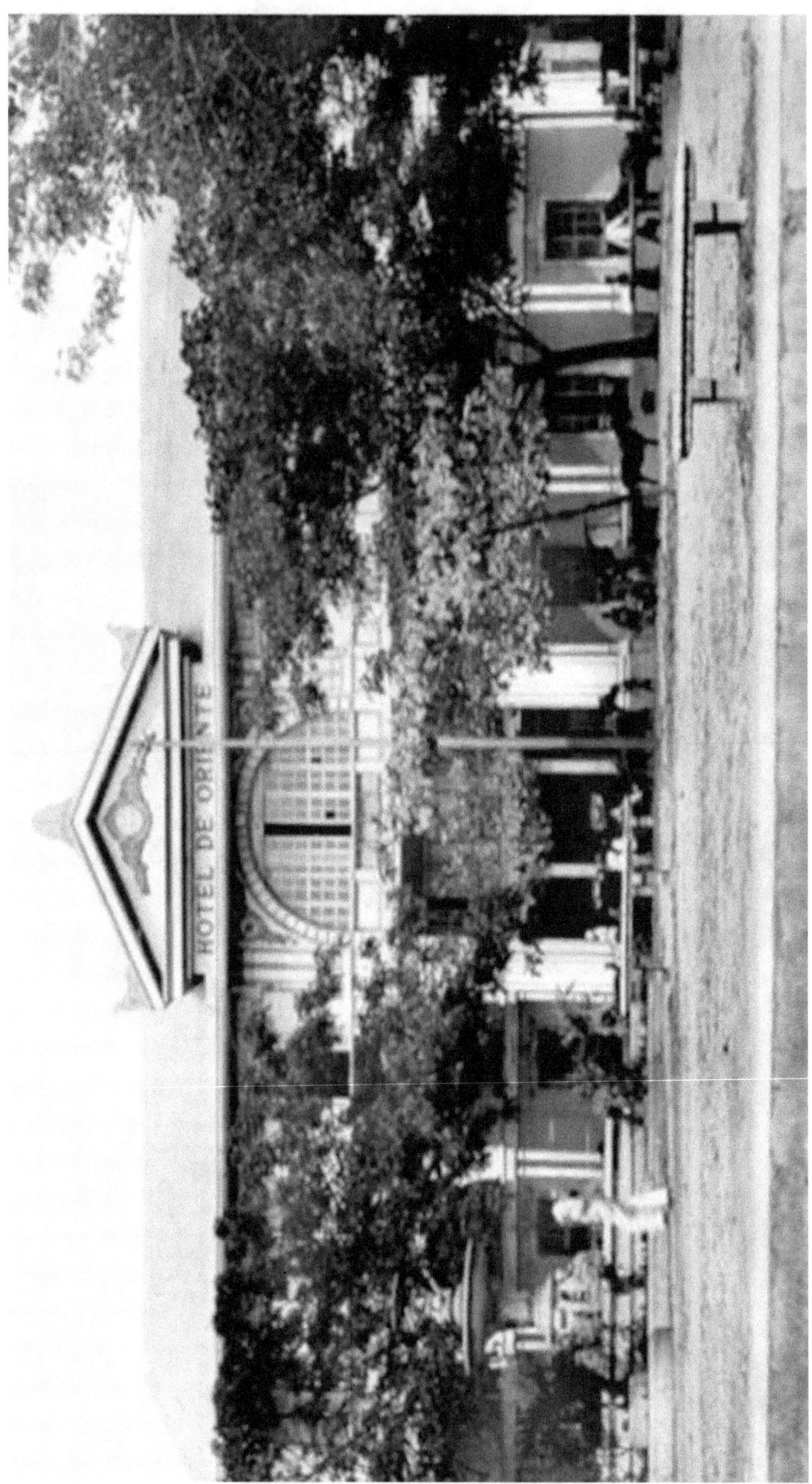

Hotel de Oriente, near Malacanang Palace, favorite of American Forces, 1900s
(courtesy: PHL MY PHL@facebook)

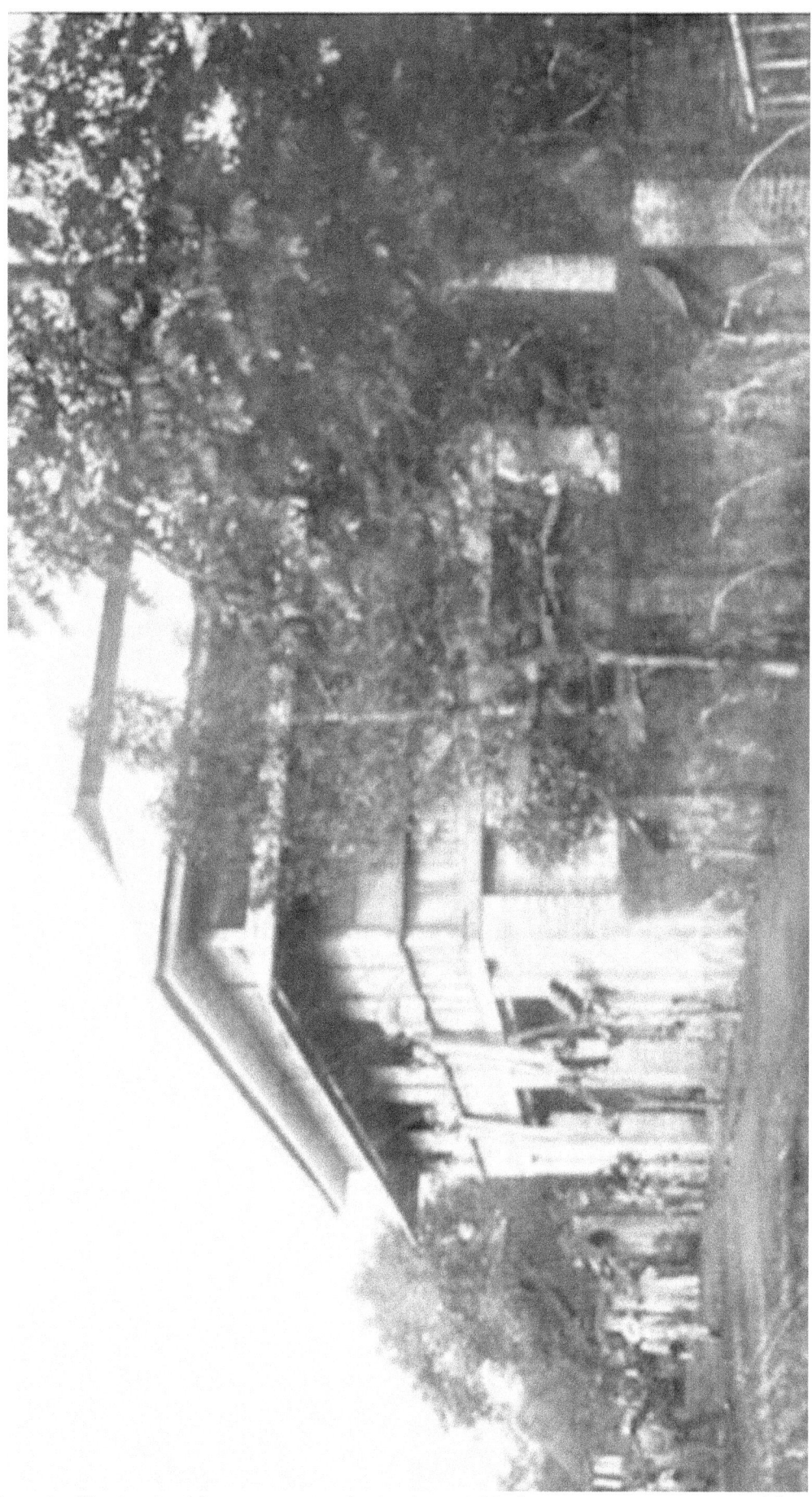

President Emilio Aguinaldo Home, Kawit, Cavite, 1900s (courtesy: PHL MY PHL@facebook)

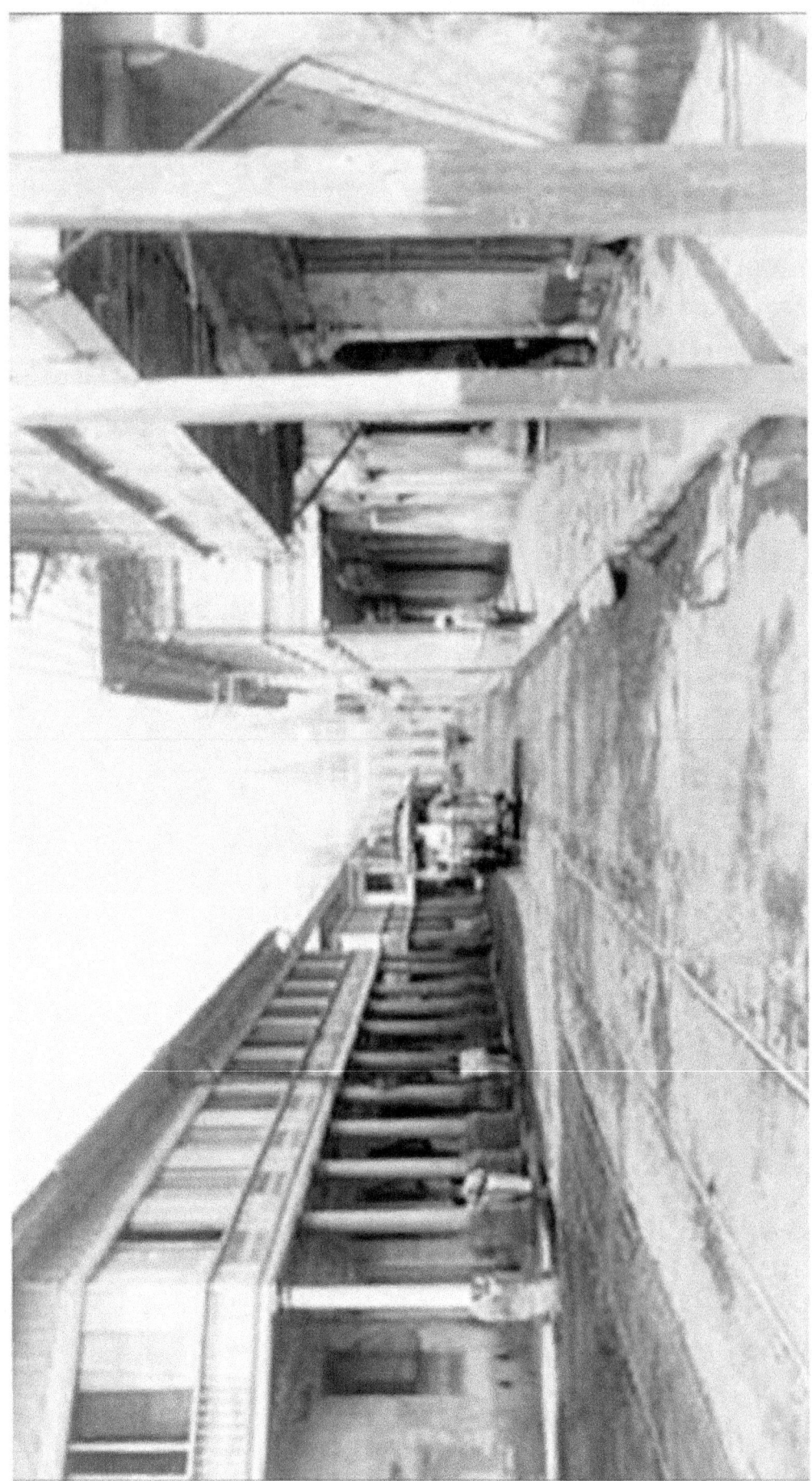

Inside Intramuros or Walled City of Manila, 1900s (courtesy: PHL MY PHL@facebook)

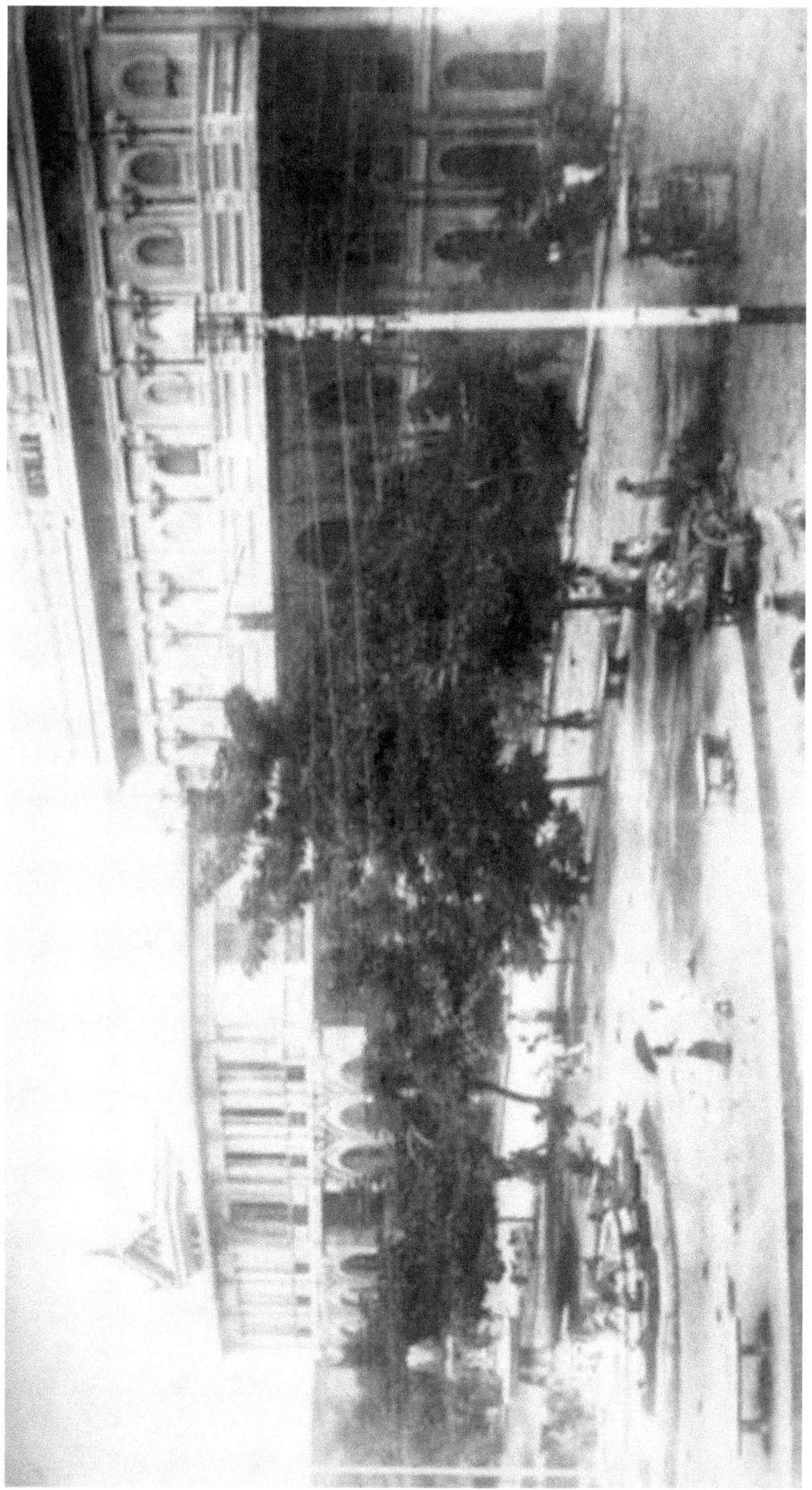

Intramuros, Spanish Government Plaza, 1900s (courtesy: PHL MY PHL@facebook)

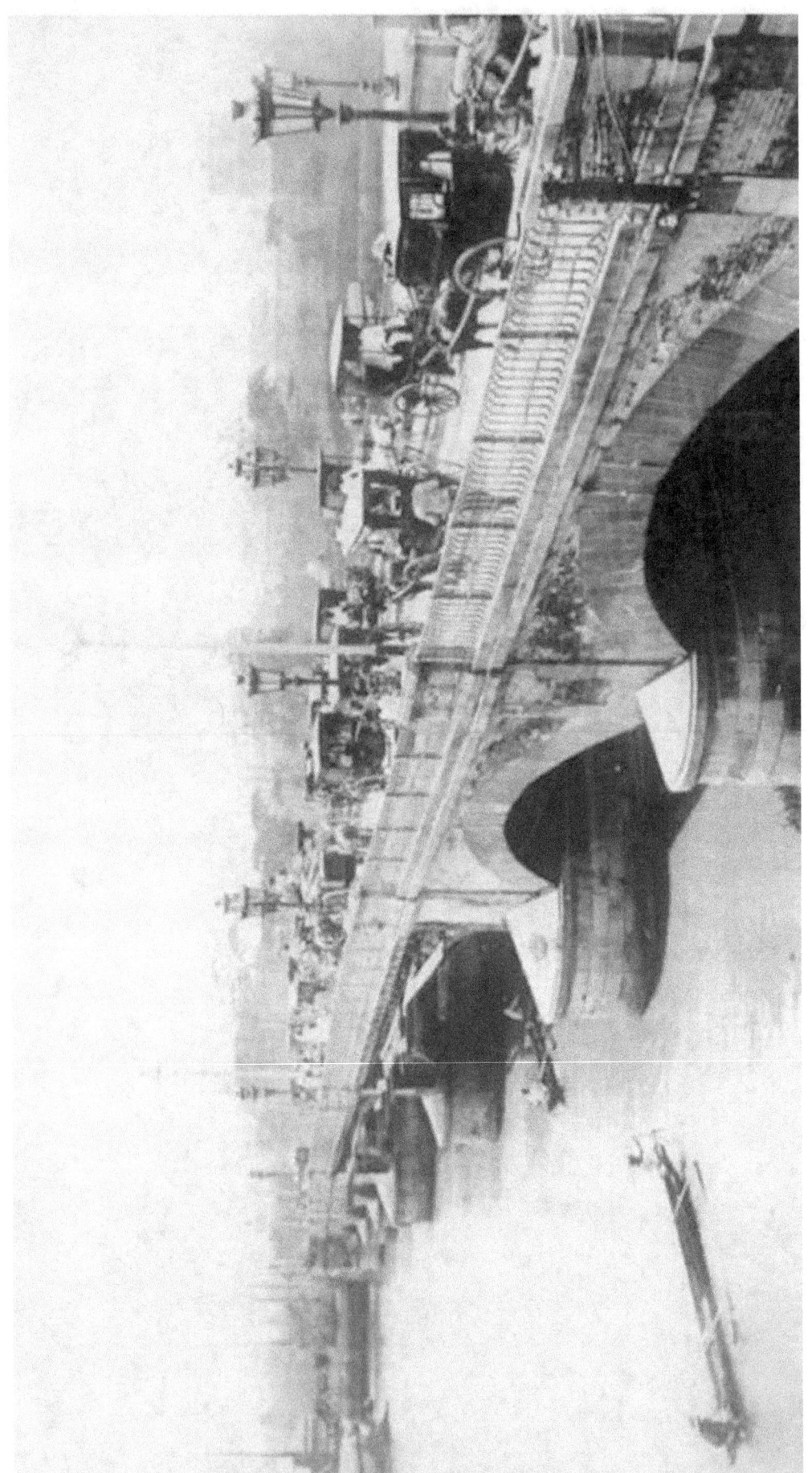

Pasig River Old Bridge Horse Drawn Carts, circa 1900s (courtesy: PHL MY PHL@facebook)

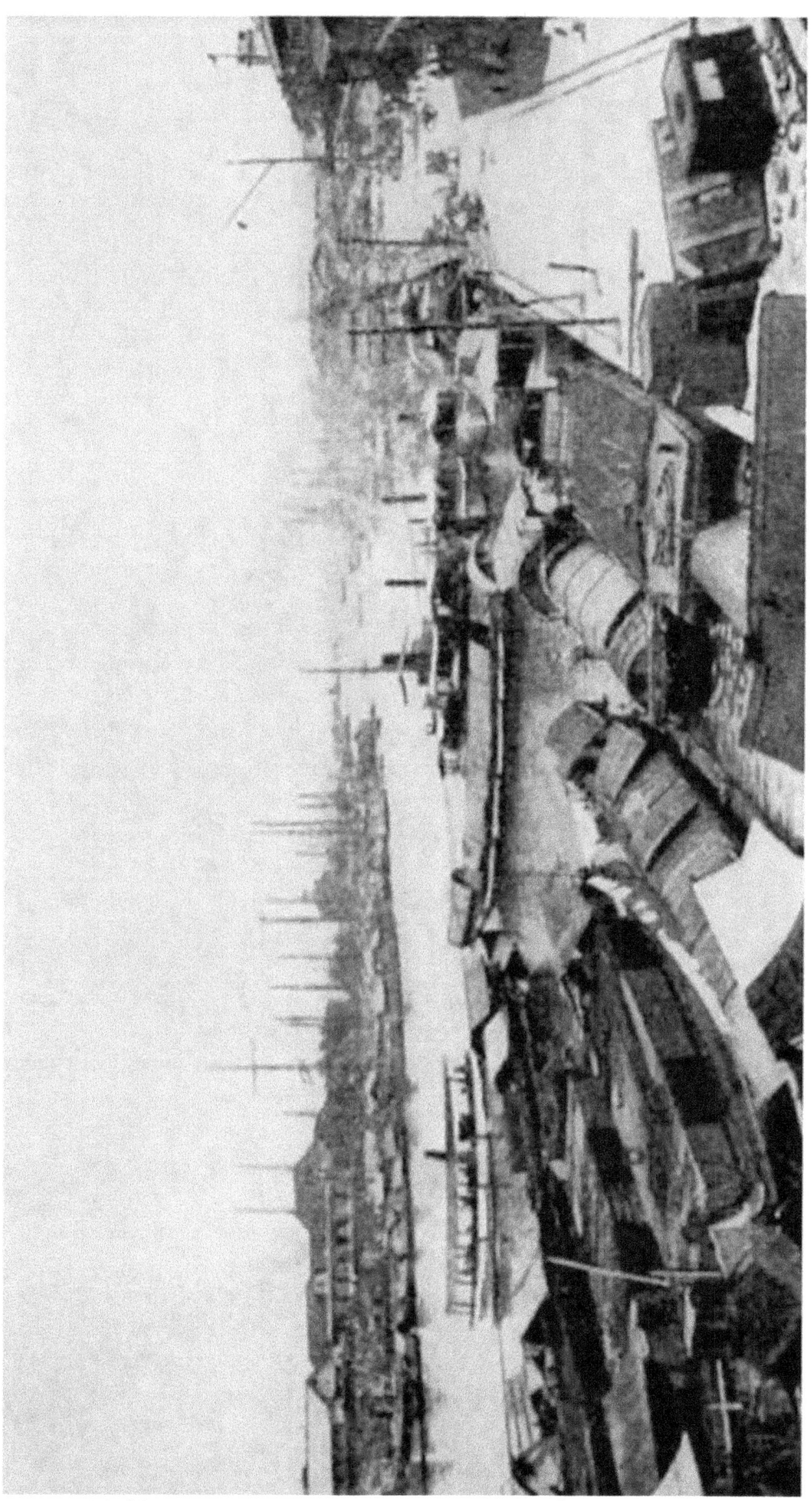

Old type commercial shipping piers at Pasig river mouth, 1900s (courtesy: PHL MY PHL@facebook)

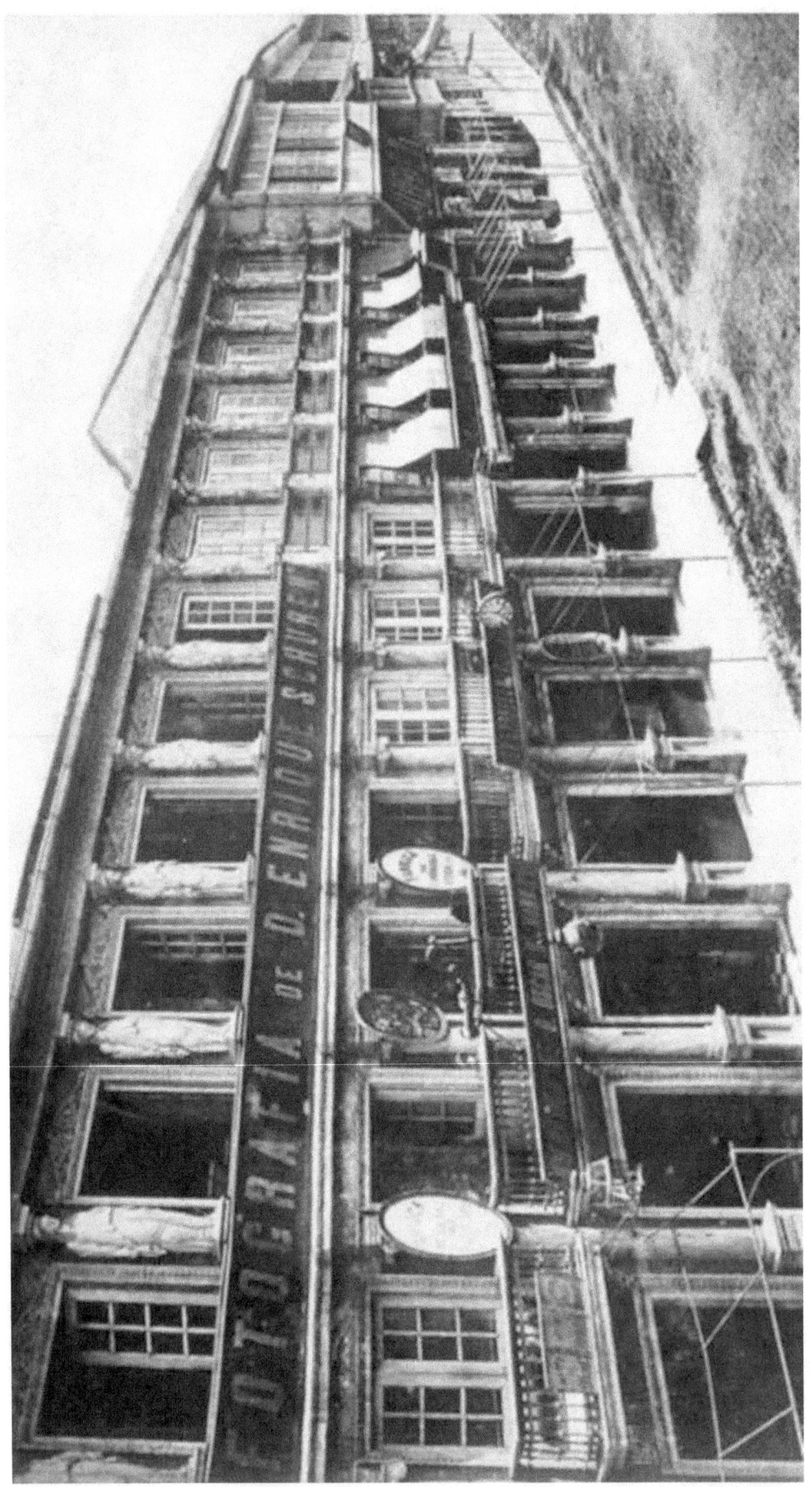

Escolta Street & Commercial Buildings, 1900s (courtesy: PHL MY PHL@facebook)

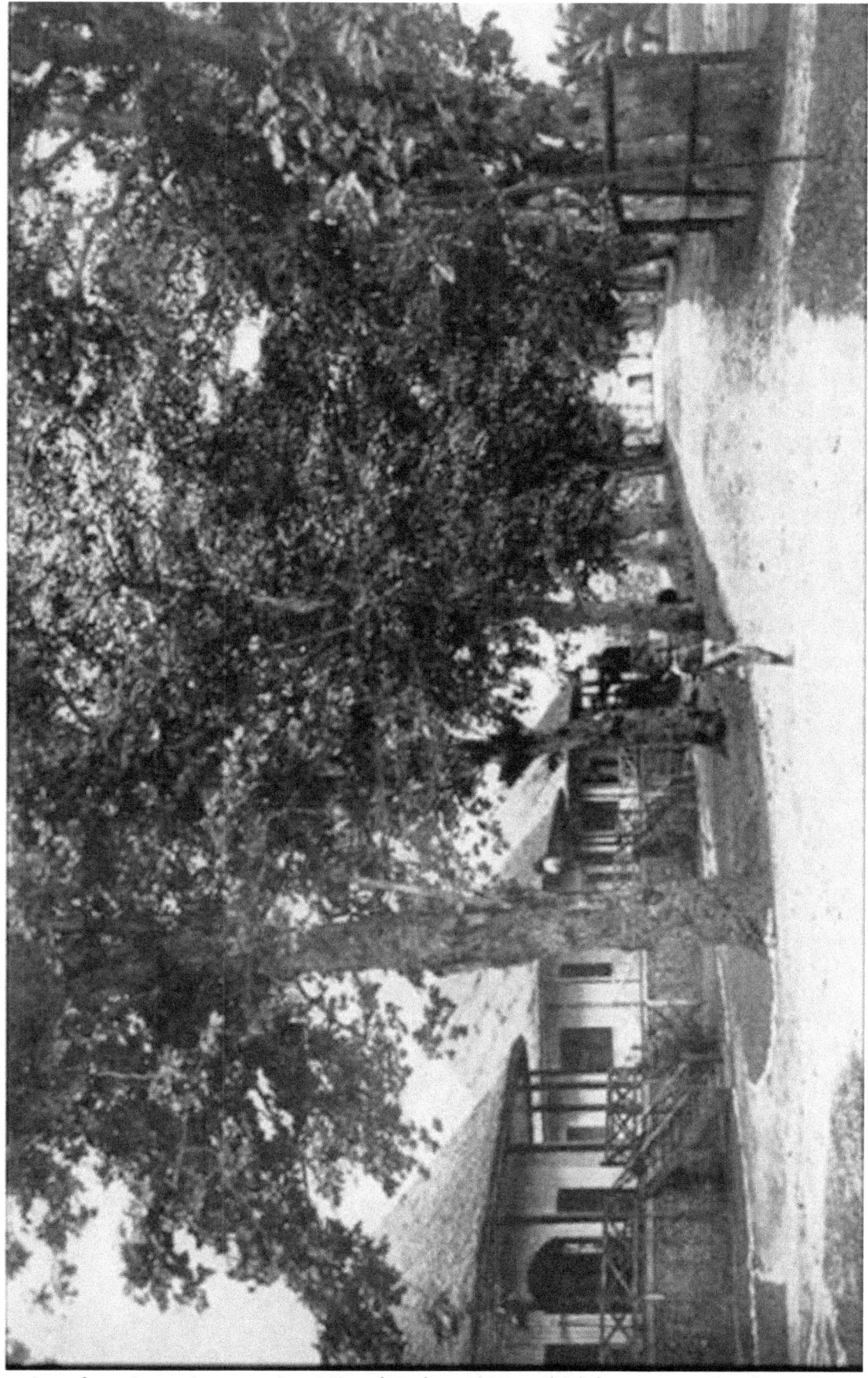

**American Army Camp at San Miguel Tarlac, 1900s, which became Hacienda Luisita
(courtesy: PHL MY PHL@facebook)**

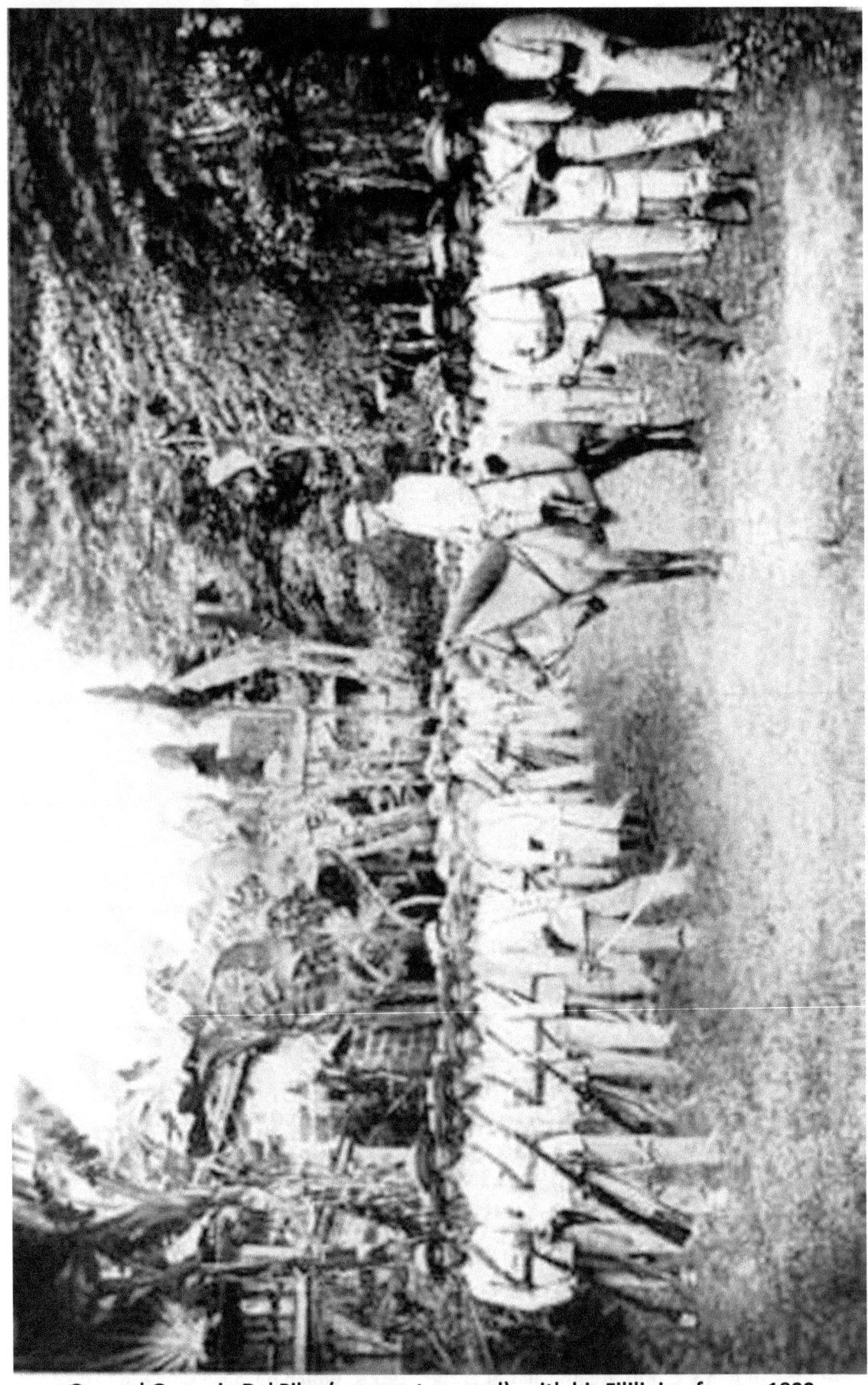

General Gregorio Del Pilar (youngest general), with his Fililipino forces, 1899
(courtesy: PHL MY PHL@facebook)

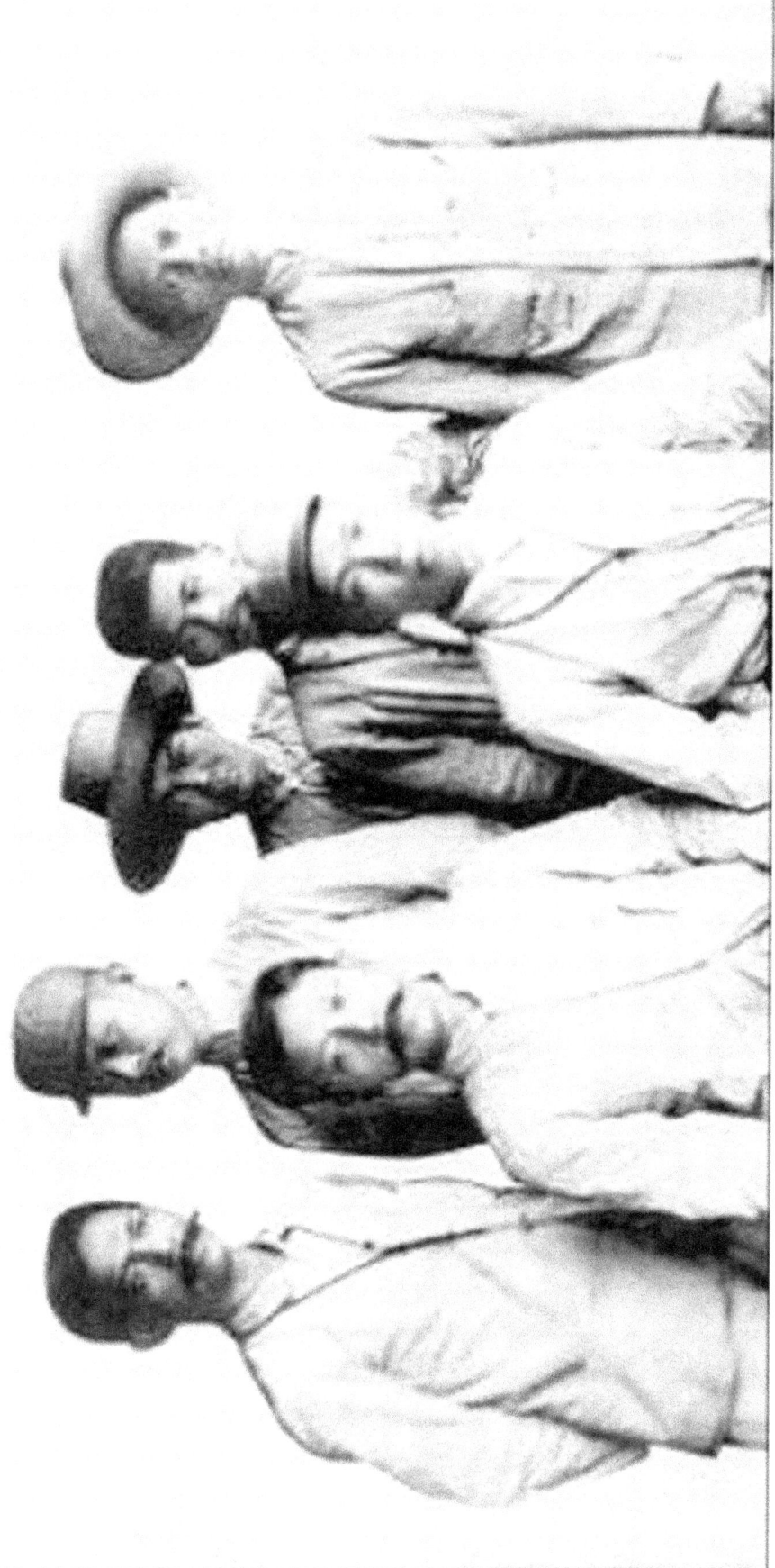

**Pedro Paterno and Gen. Emilio Aguinaldo with team of "Pact of Biak Na Bato" Treaty with Spain –
Standing, left to right: Isabelo Artacho, Baldomero Aguinaldo, Severino de las
Alas, Antonio Montenegro, and Vito Belarmino. (courtesy: PHL MY PHL@facebook)**

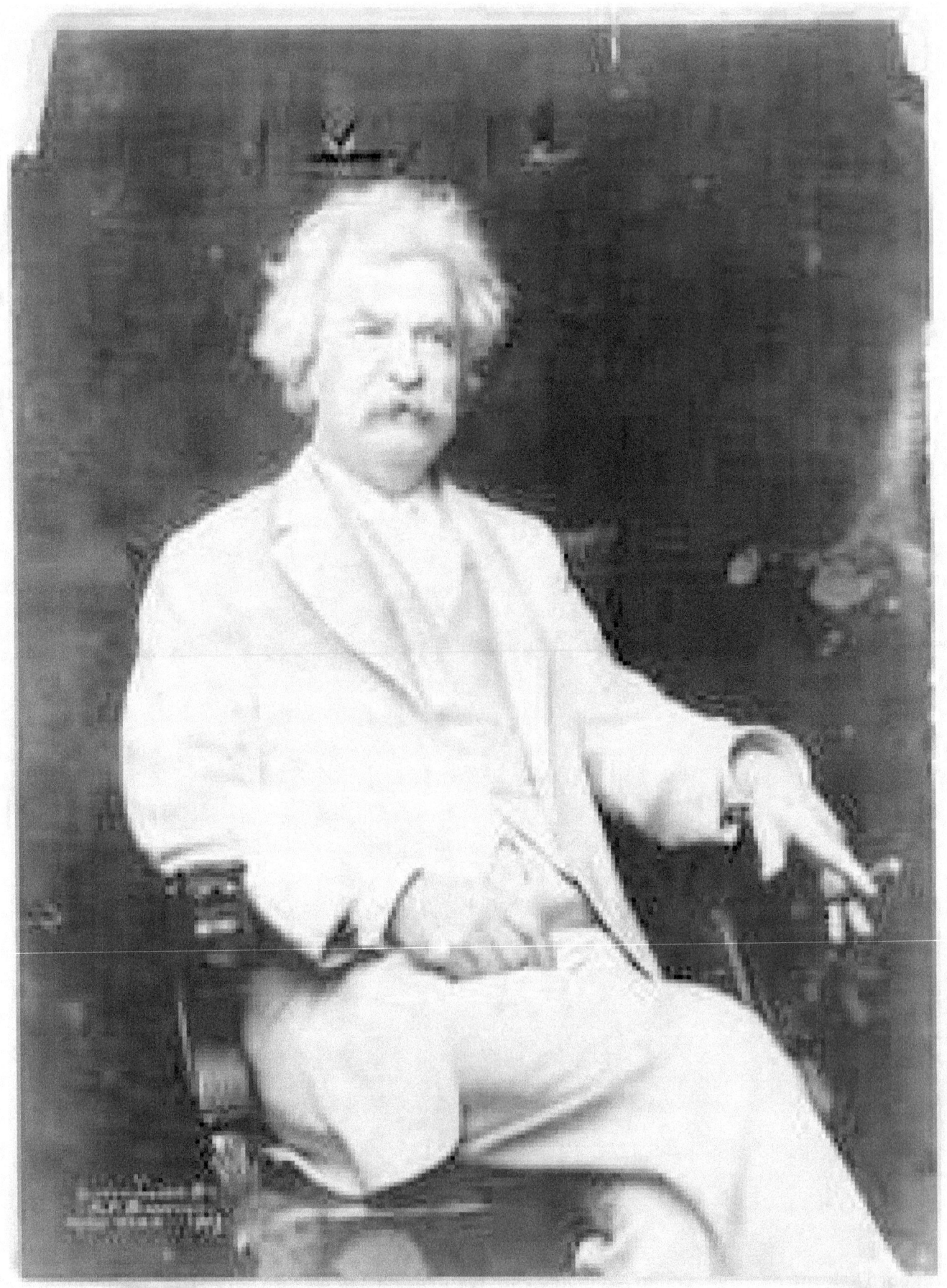

Mark Twain, Famous American Writer & Philosopher – Champion of Anti-colonialism, protecting the rights of Philippines, not subject to American colonization, 1900s (courtesy: PHL MY PHL@facebook)

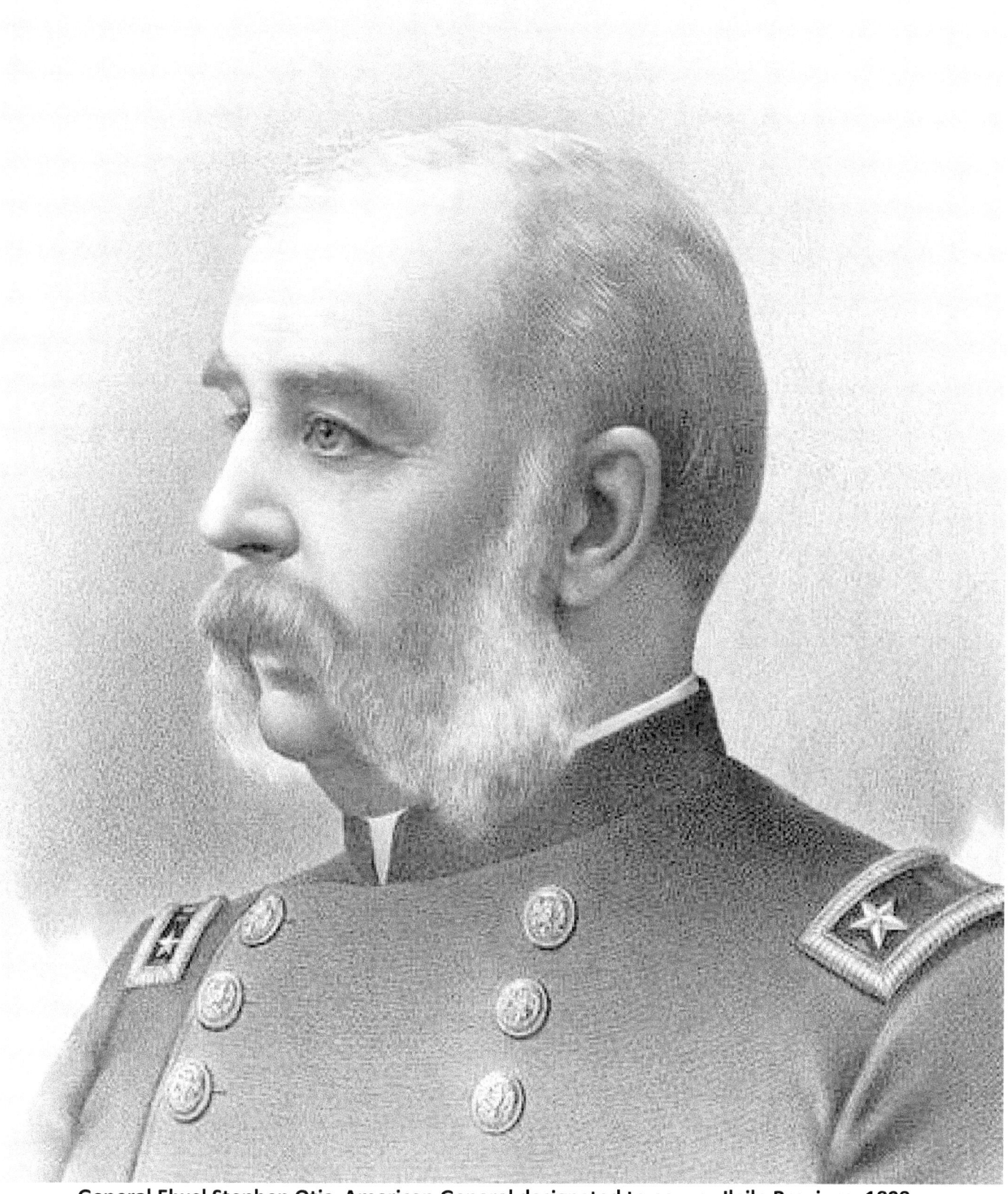

General Elwel Stephen Otis, American General designated to occupy Iloilo Province, 1898, and played a key role in battling Filipino Revolutionary forces. (courtesy: PHL MY PHL@facebook)

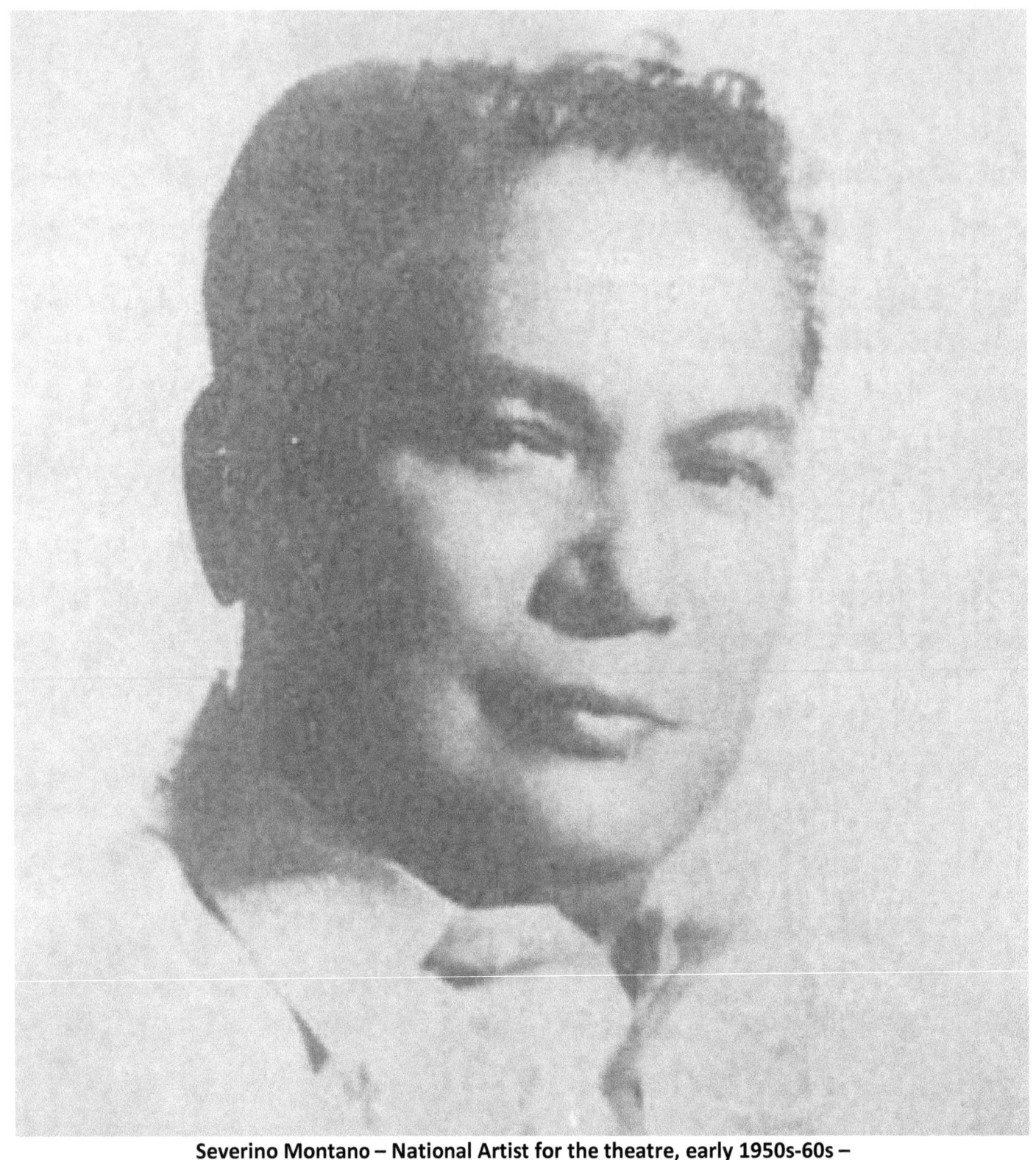

**Severino Montano – National Artist for the theatre, early 1950s-60s –
Also famous playright. (from National Museum)**

Charito Solis – famous movie star of yesteryears (movie stars magazines)

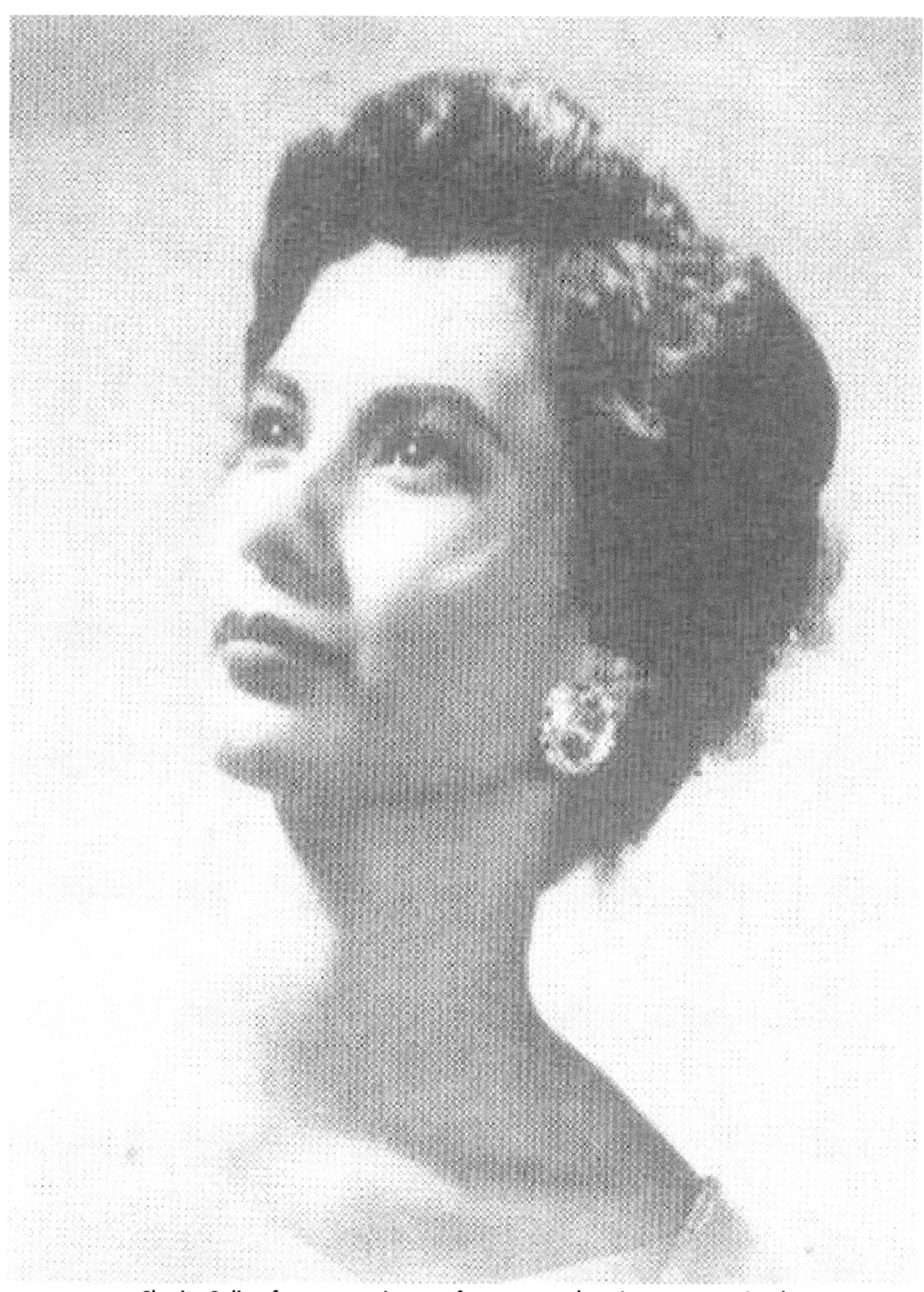

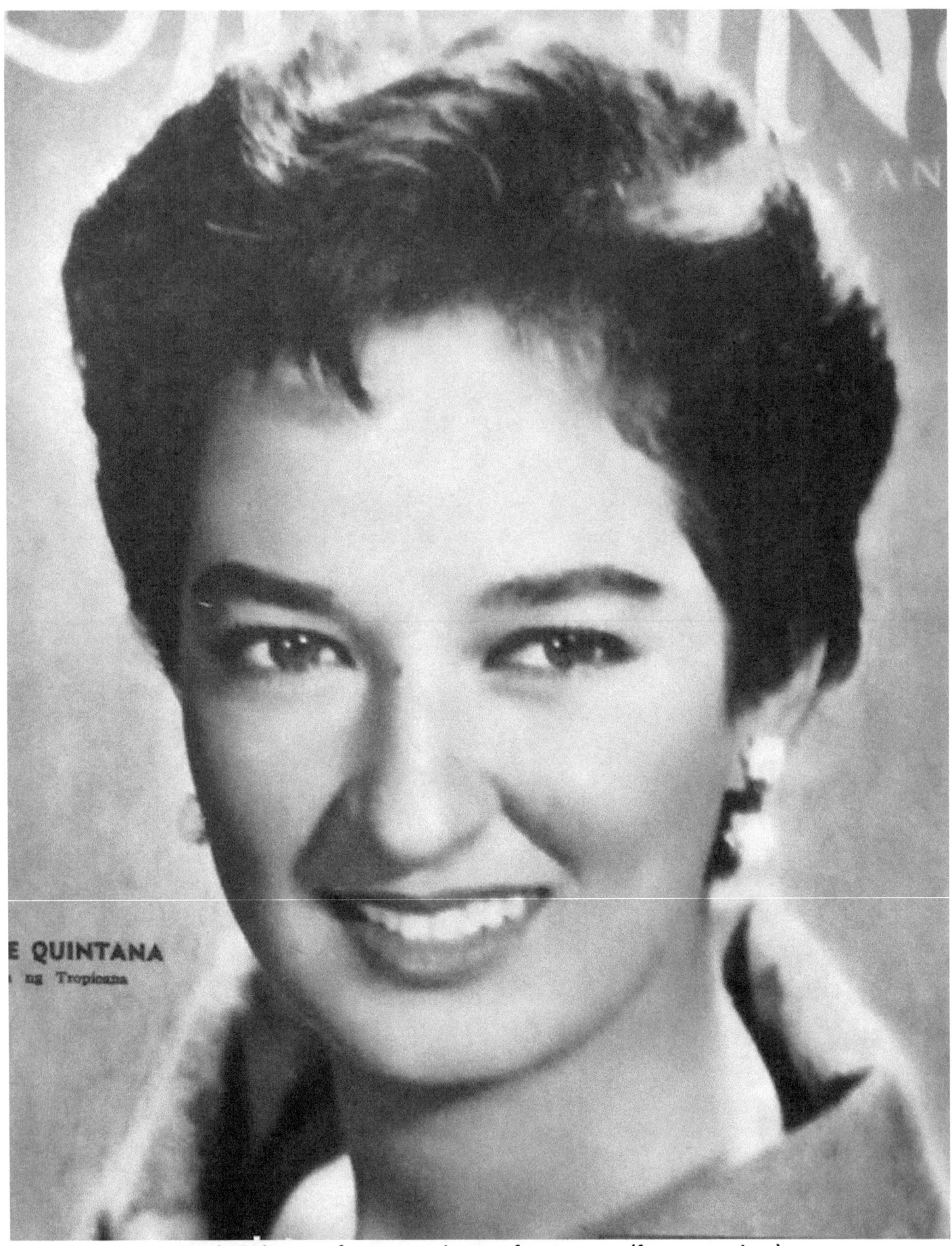

Tessie Quintana – famous movie star of yesteryears (from magazines)

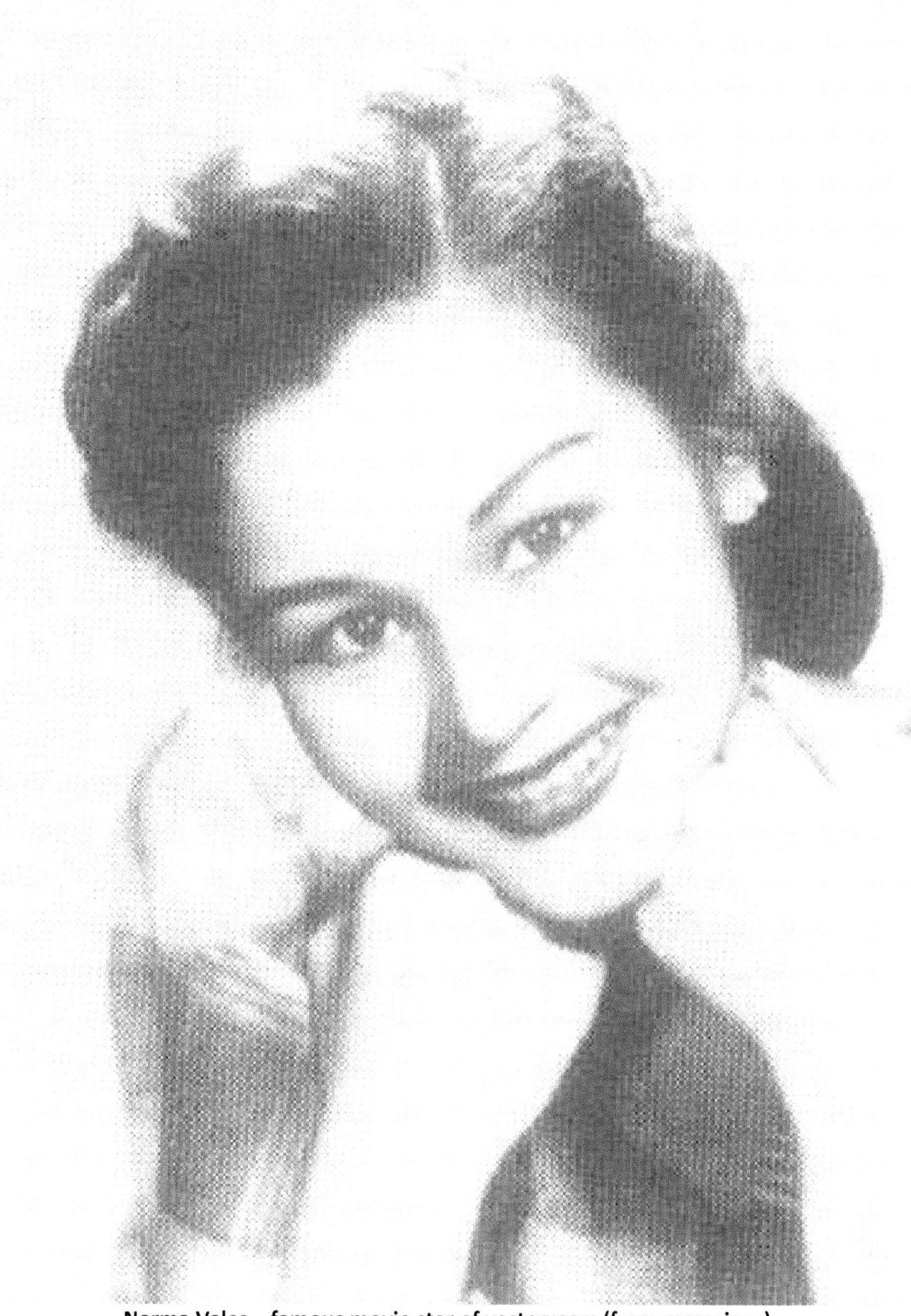

Norma Vales – famous movie star of yesteryears (from magazines)

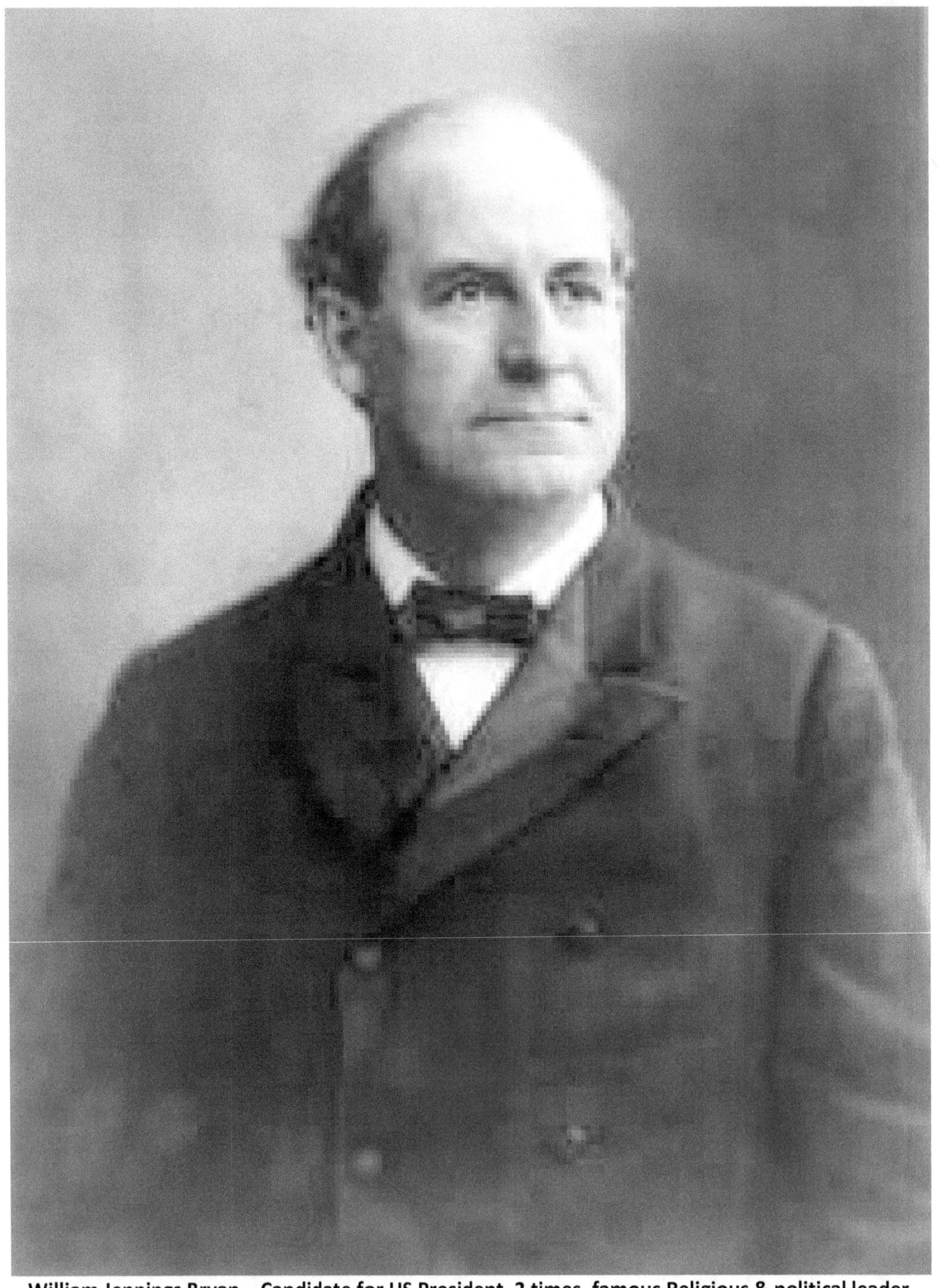

William Jennings Bryan – Candidate for US President, 2 times, famous Religious & political leader. Champion for anti-colonialism of the Philippines. (courtesy: PHL MY PHL@facebook)

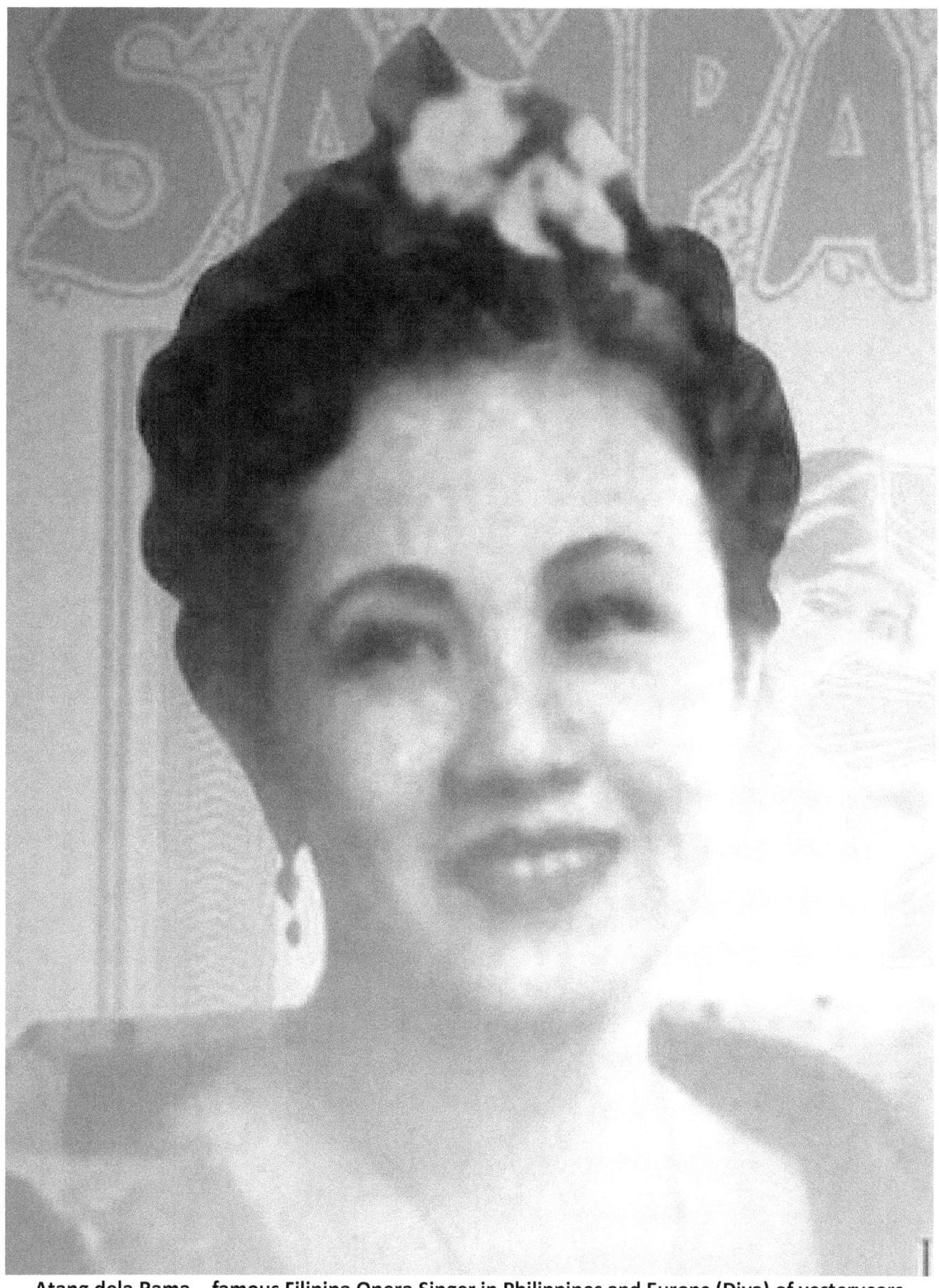

Atang dela Rama – famous Filipina Opera Singer in Philippines and Europe (Diva) of yesteryears (from National Museum)

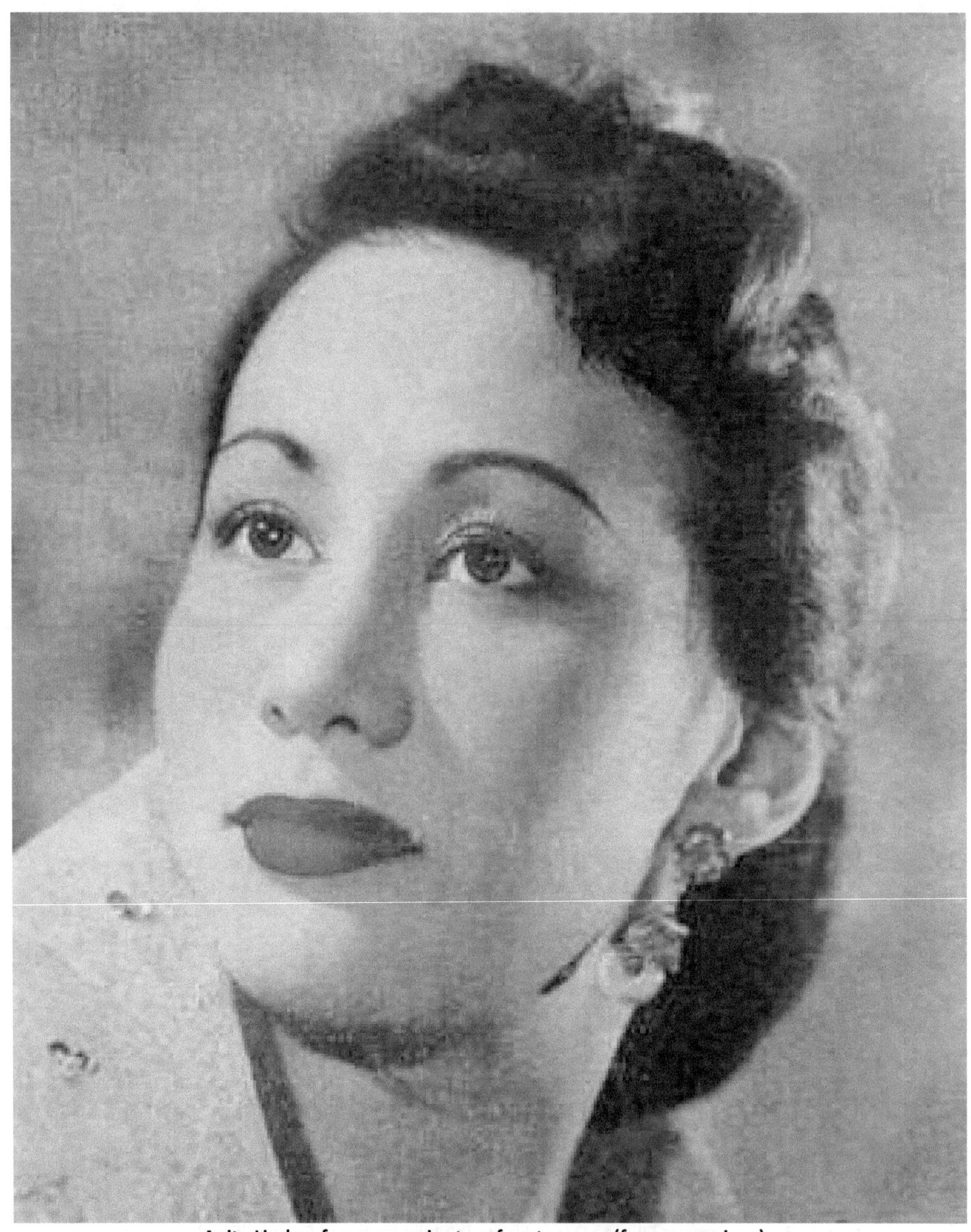

Anita Linda – famous movie star of yesteryears (from magazines)

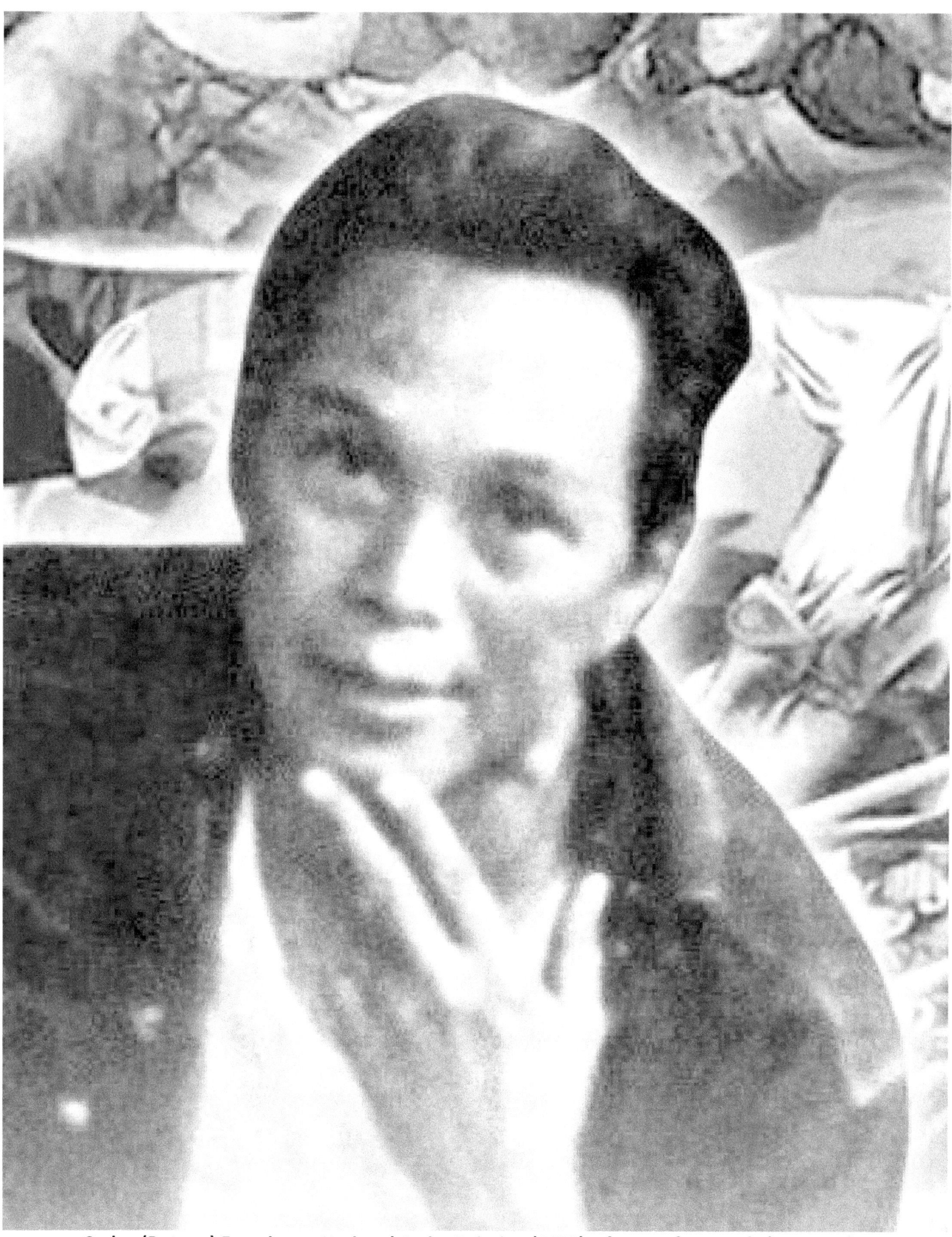

Carlos (Botong) Francisco – National Artist-Painting (1973) – famous for murals (Museum)

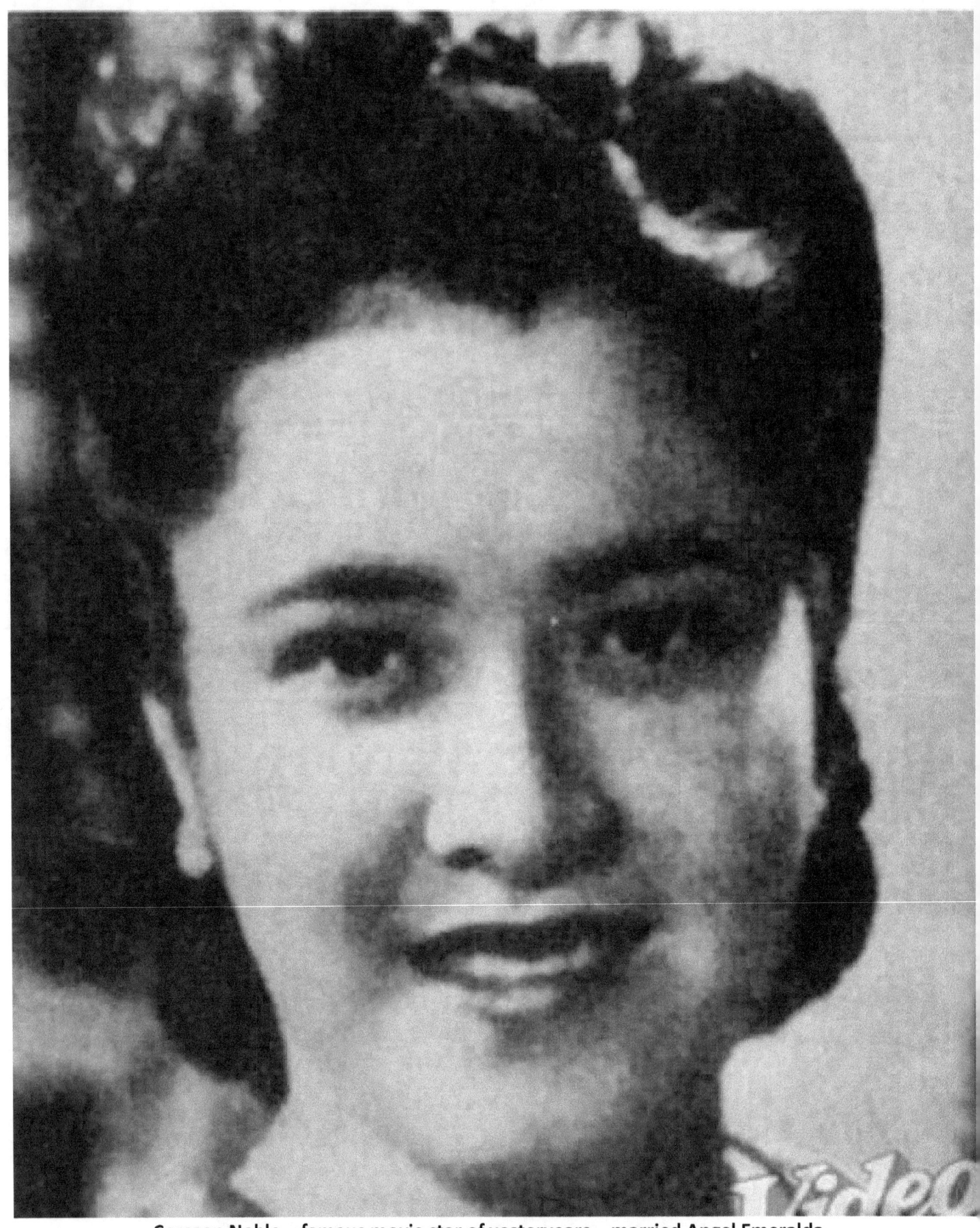

Corazon Noble – famous movie star of yesteryears – married Angel Emeralda
And became parents of Jay Ilagan (Angel Esmeralda's real last name is Ilagan) (from magazines)

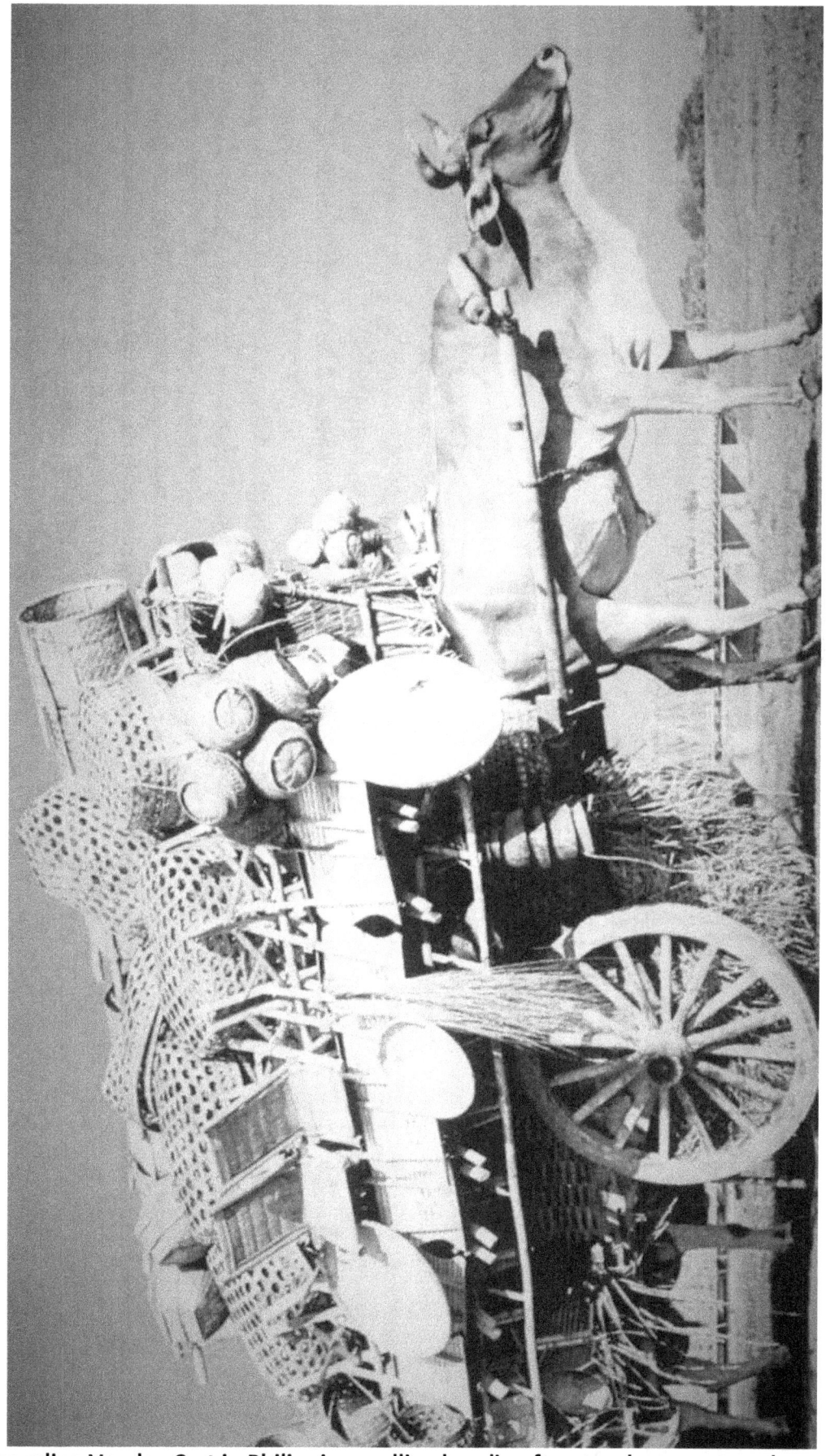

**Traveling Vendor-Cart in Philippines selling handicrafts, etc, ala-gypsy travelers
(courtesy: PHL MY PHL@facebook)**

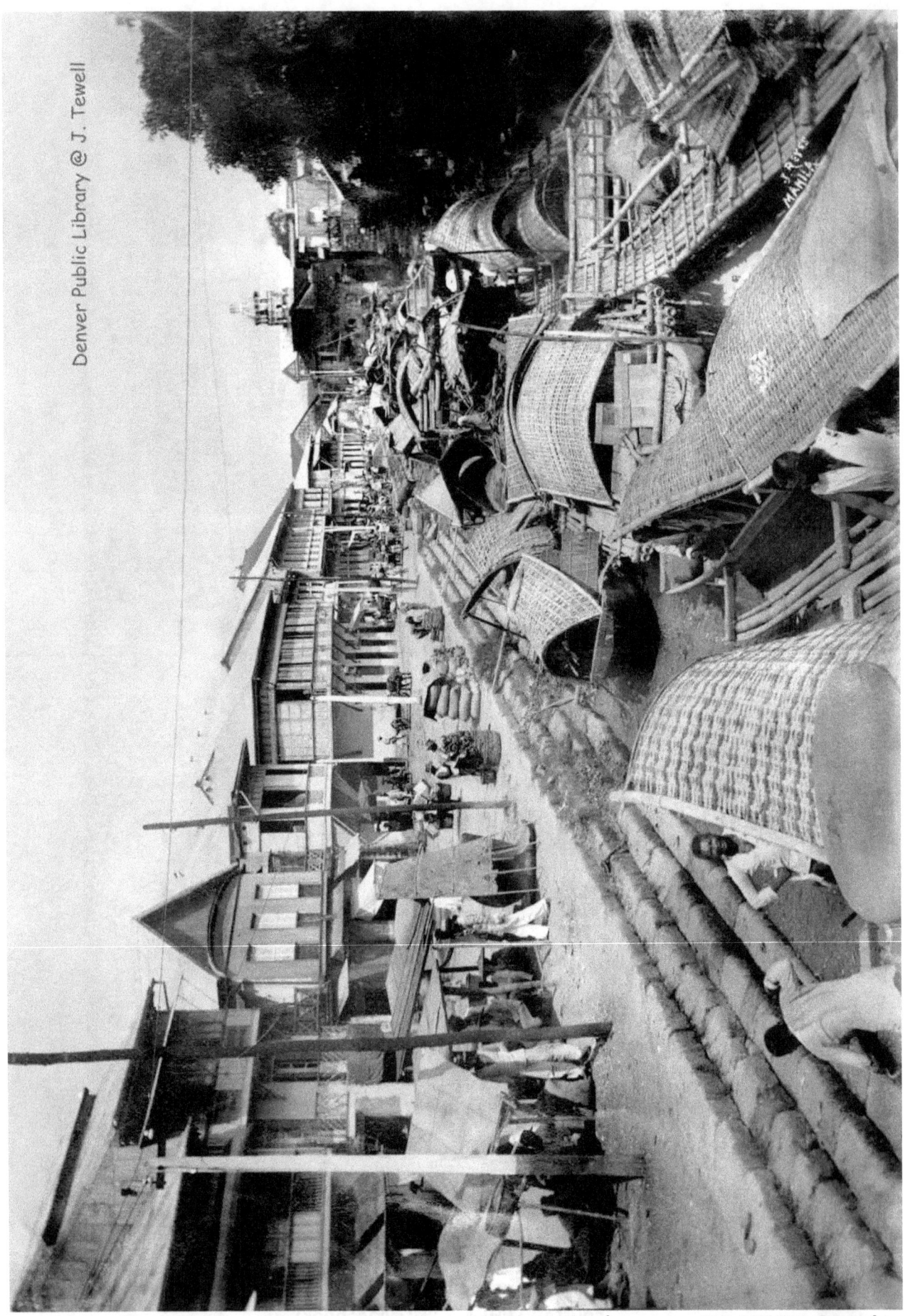

Casco river traffic, Santa Cruz river bank, Pasig River, Manila, 1890s (courtesy: PHL MY PHL@Facebook)

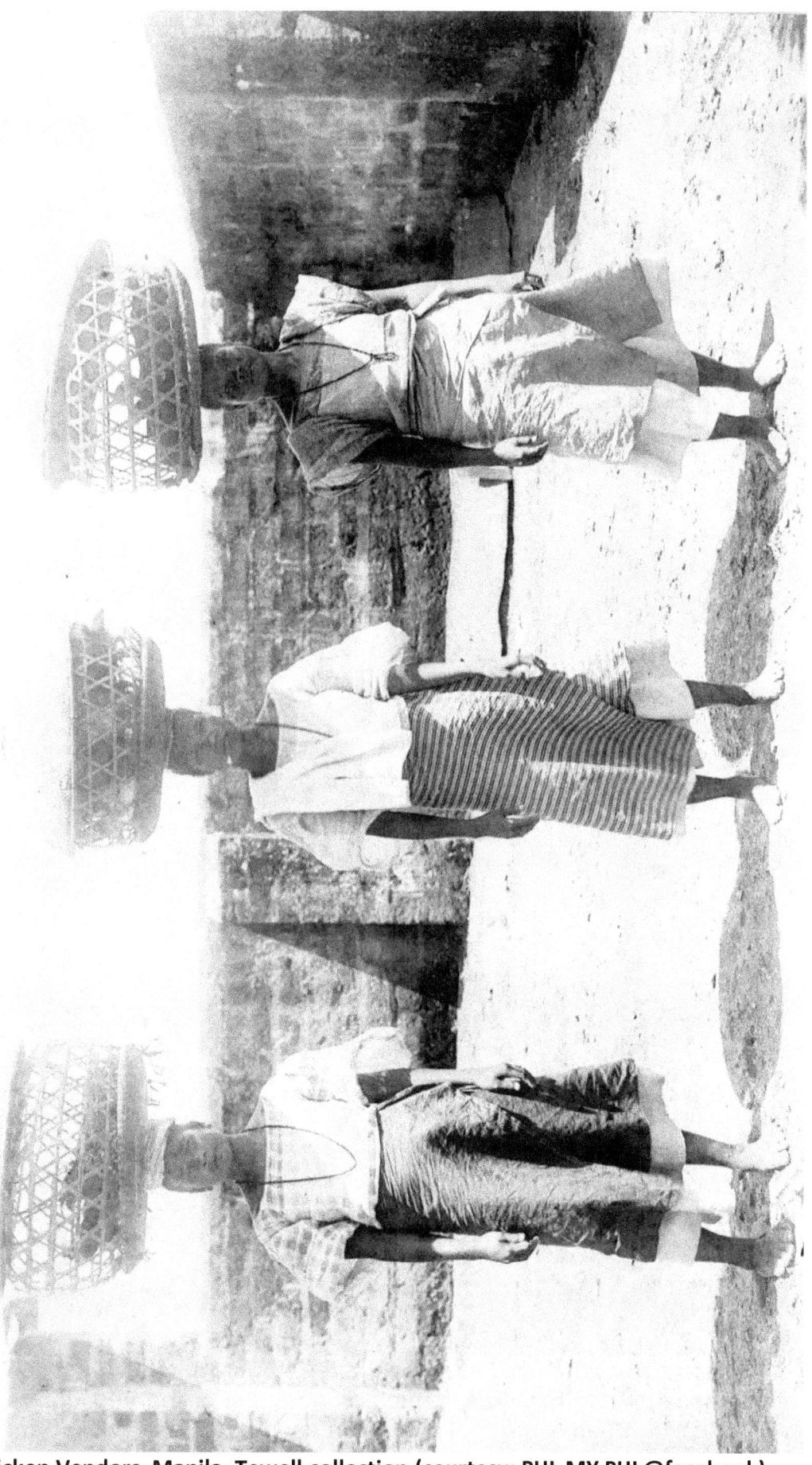

1900 Chicken Vendors, Manila, Tewell collection (courtesy: PHL MY PHL@facebook)

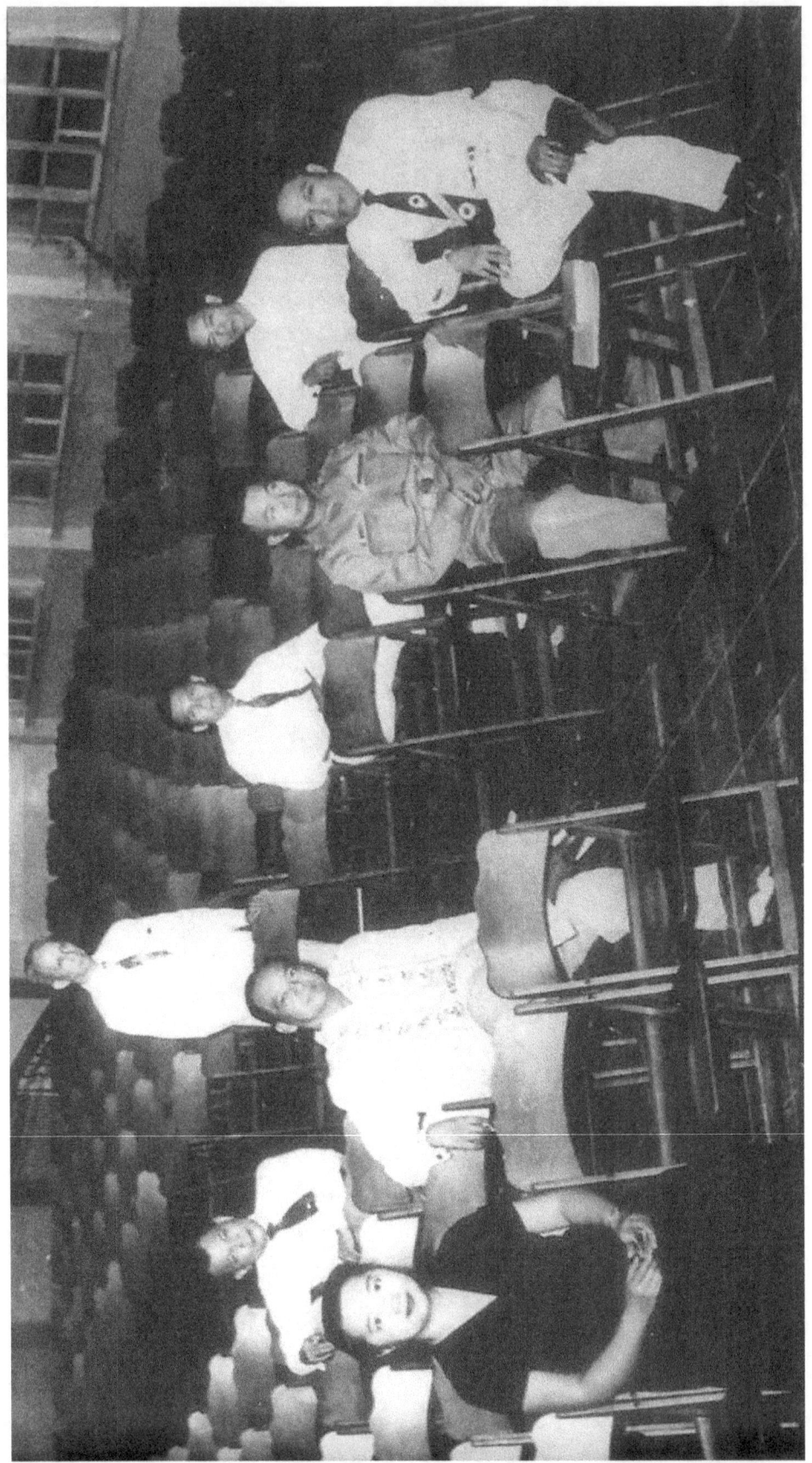

Some of the country's renowned composers, here photographed in 1956, include from left, Lucrecia Kasilag, Rodolfo Cornejo, Lucino Sacramento, Antonio Molina, Eliseo Pajaro, Antonino Buenaventura, Felipe Padilla de Leon, and Lucio San Pedro.
(courtesy: PHL MY PHL@facebook)

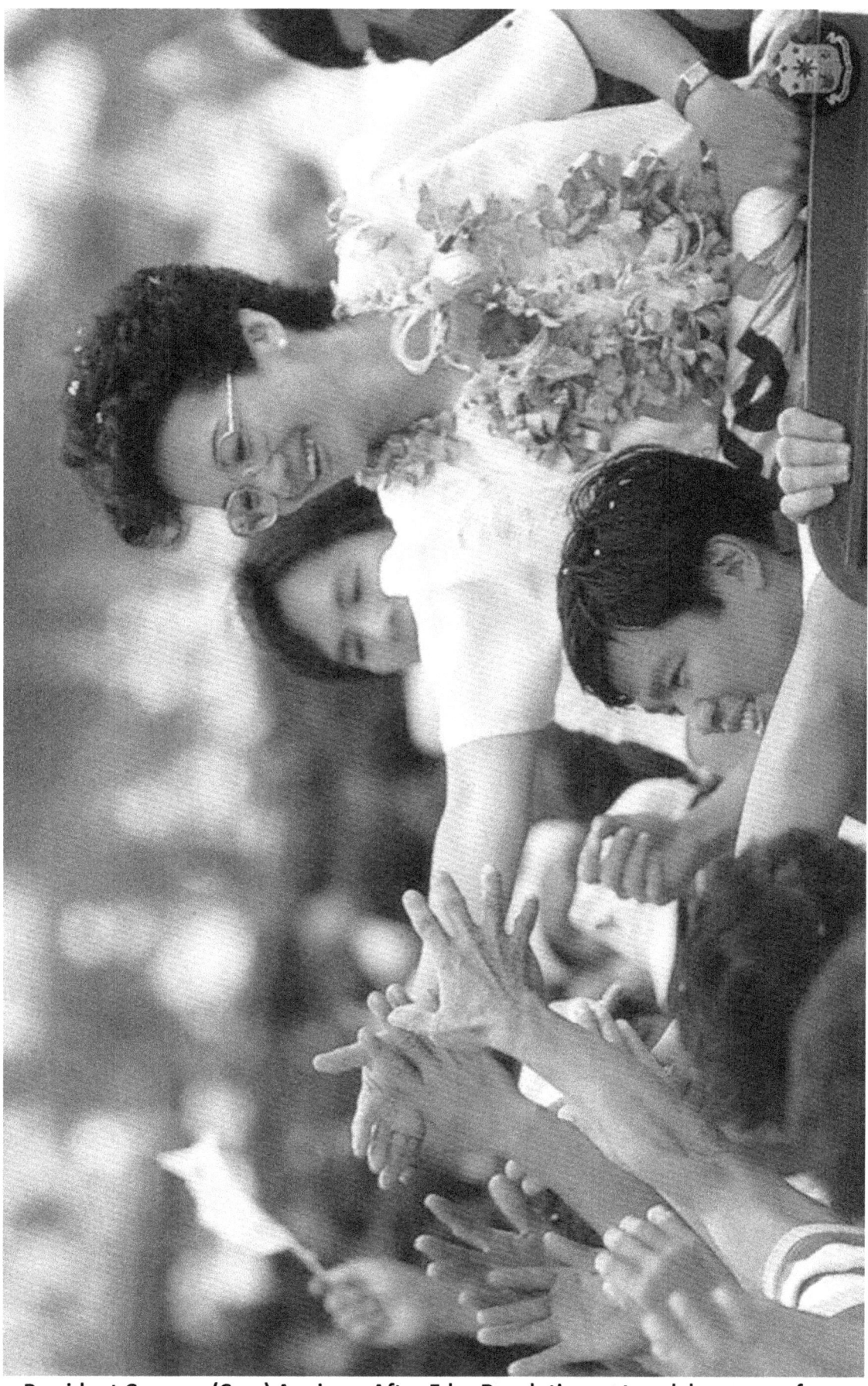

President Corazon (Cory) Aquino – After Edsa Revolution restored democracy from Marcos dictatorship, 1986 (courtesy: PHL MY PHL@facebook)

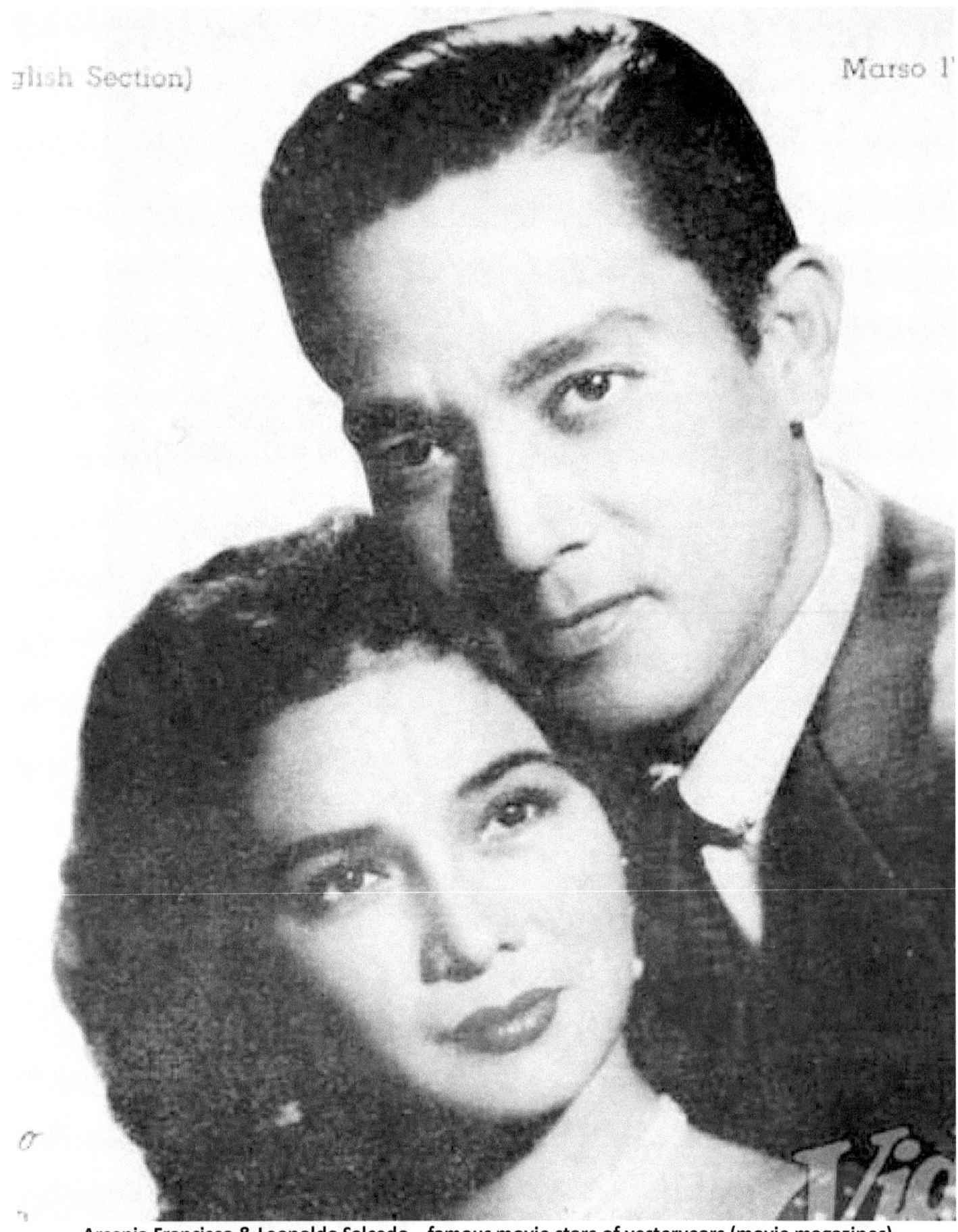

Arsenia Francisco & Leopoldo Salcedo – famous movie stars of yesteryears (movie magazines)

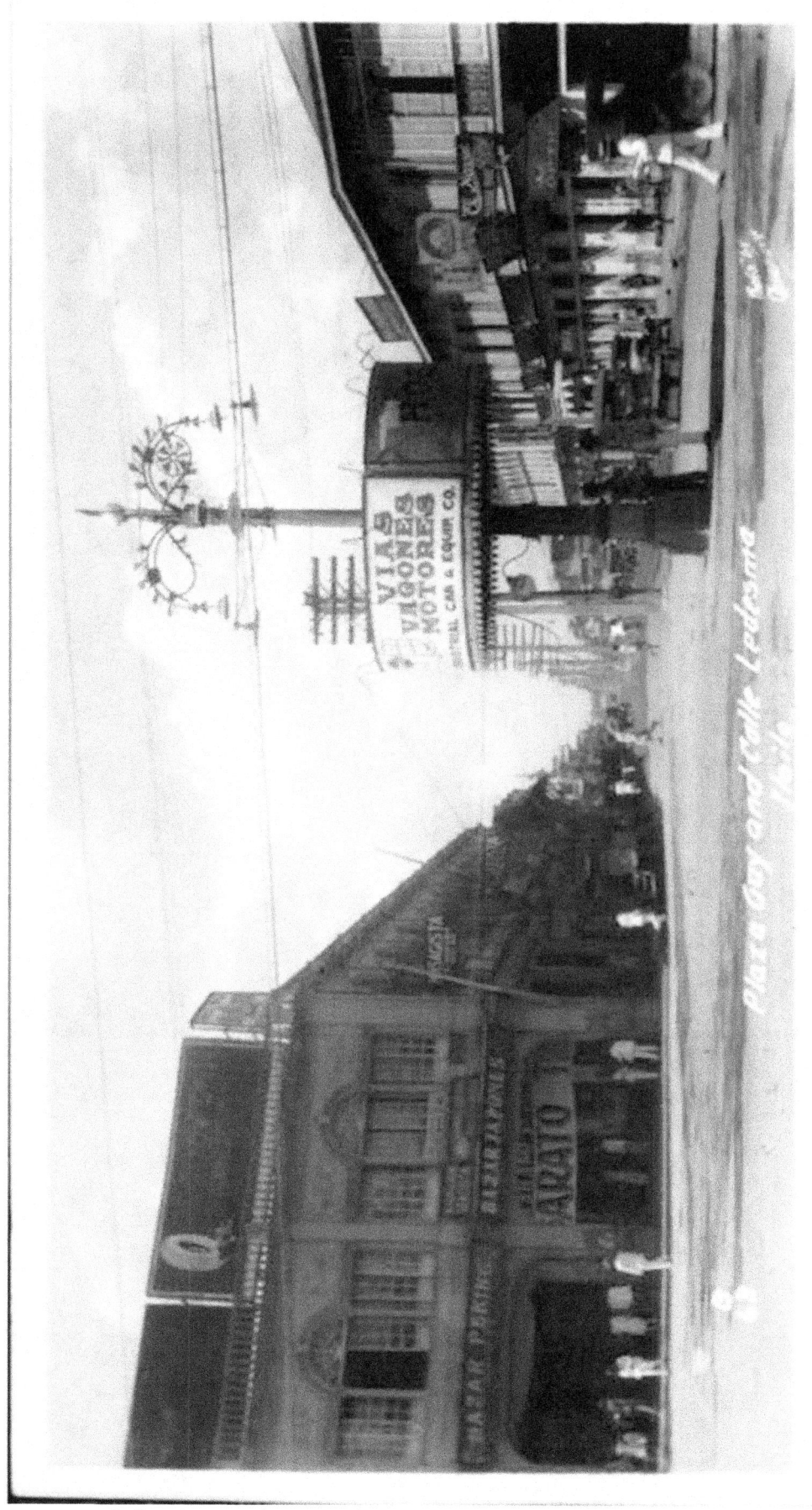

Iloilo City - Early 1900s (courtesy: PHL MY PHL@facebook)

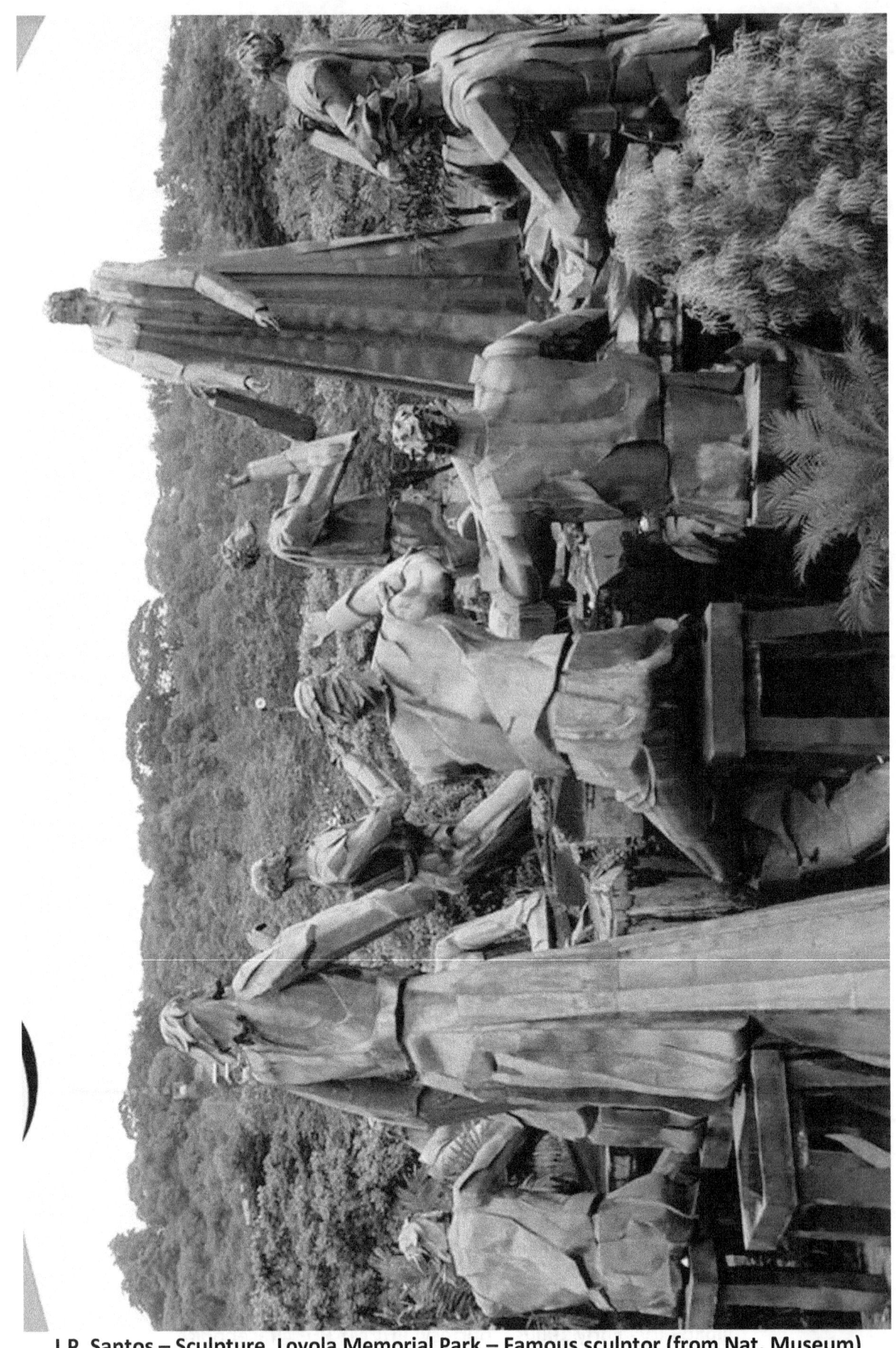

I.P. Santos – Sculpture, Loyola Memorial Park – Famous sculptor (from Nat. Museum)

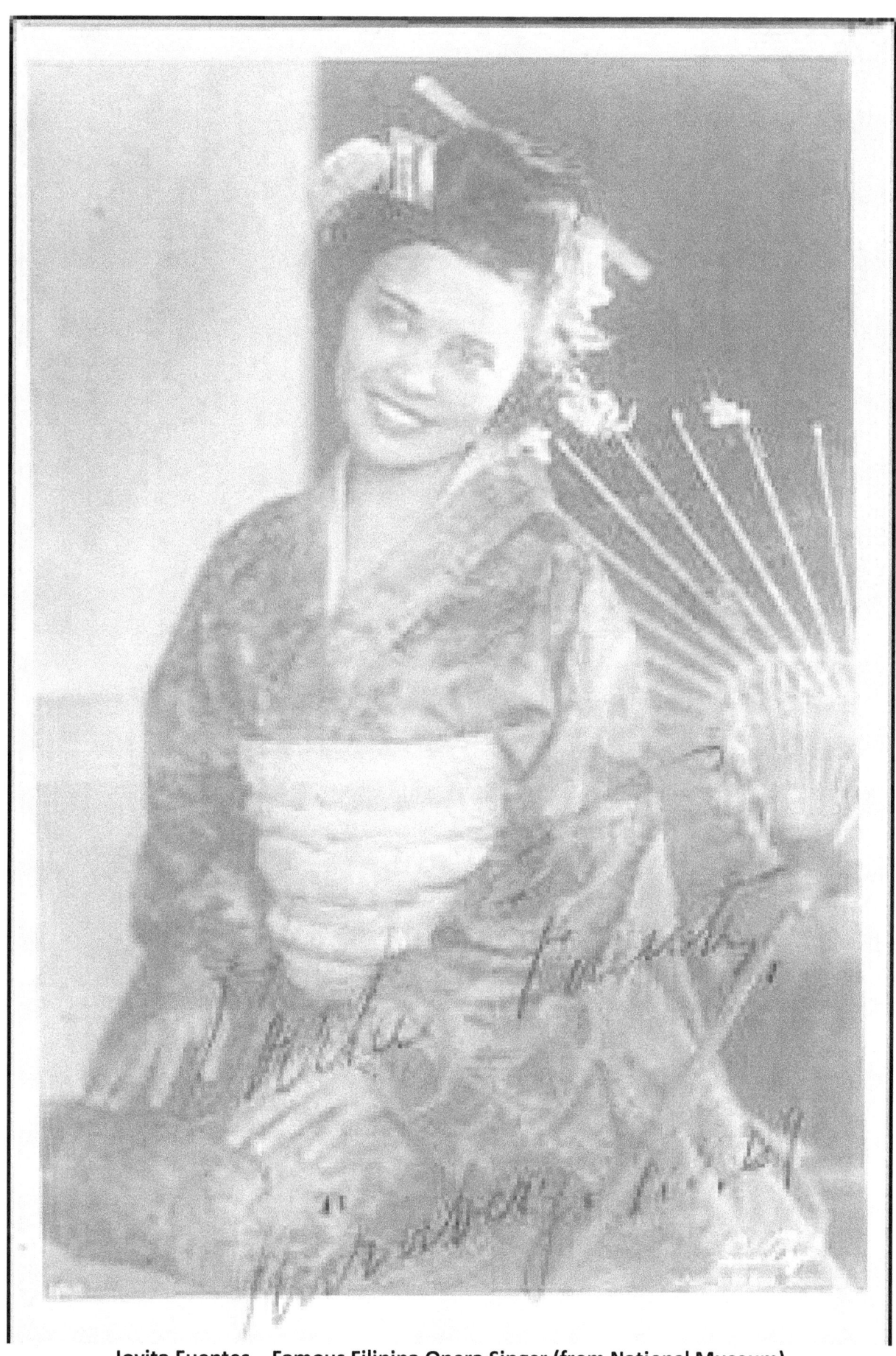

Jovita Fuentes – Famous Filipina Opera Singer (from National Museum)

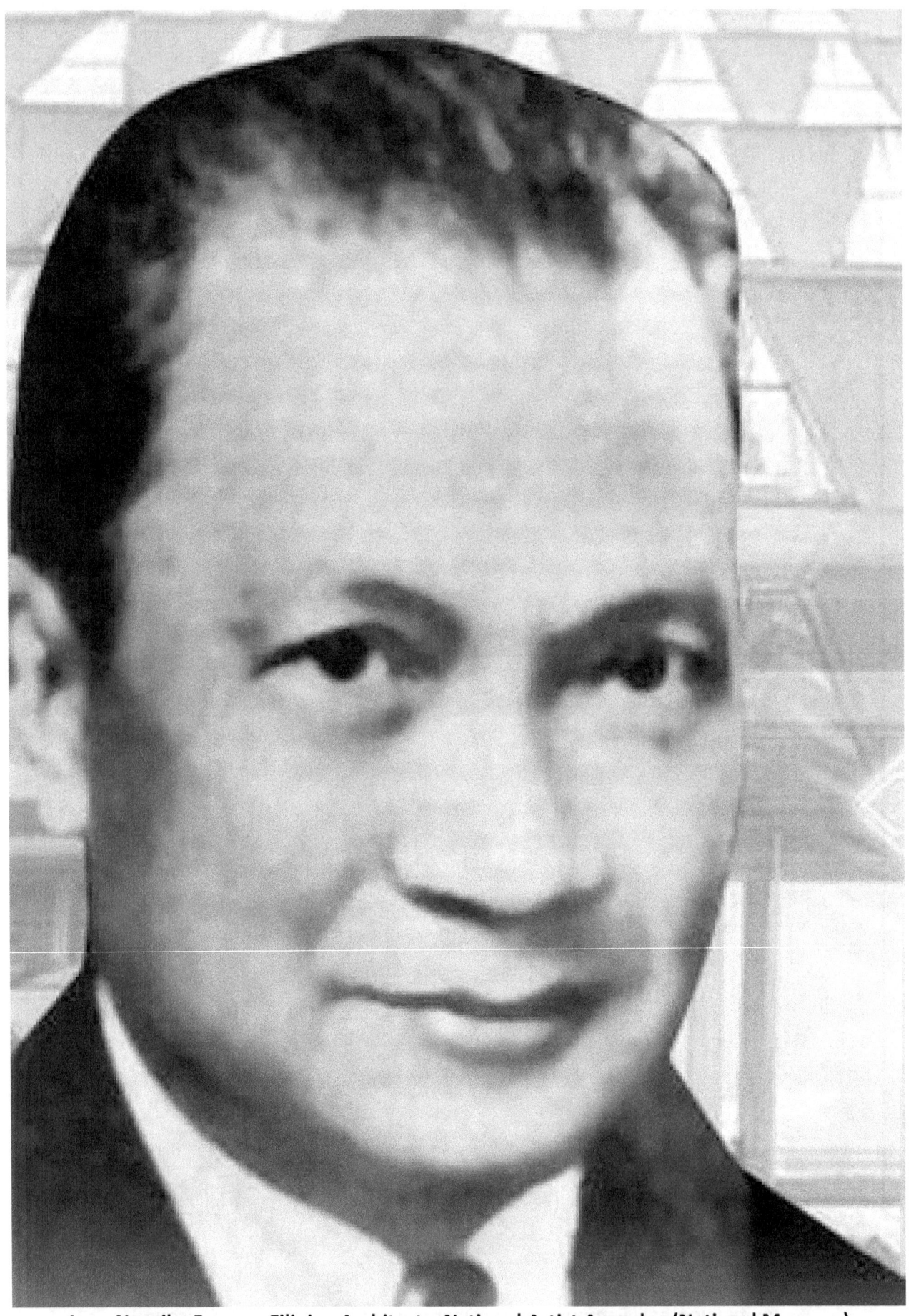

Juan Nacpil – Famous Filipino Architect – National Artist Awardee (National Museum)

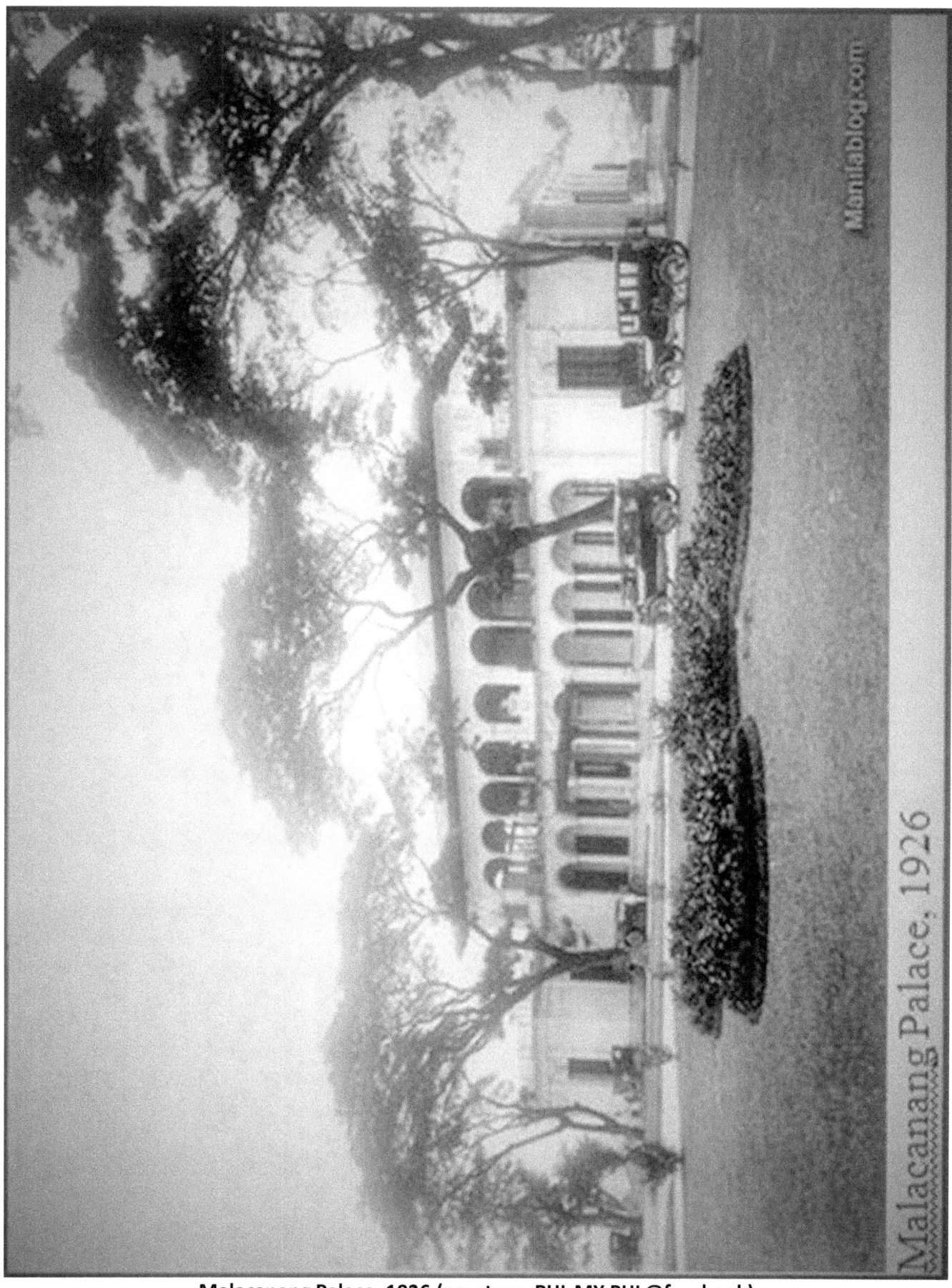

Malacanang Palace, 1926 (courtesy: PHL MY PHL@facebook)

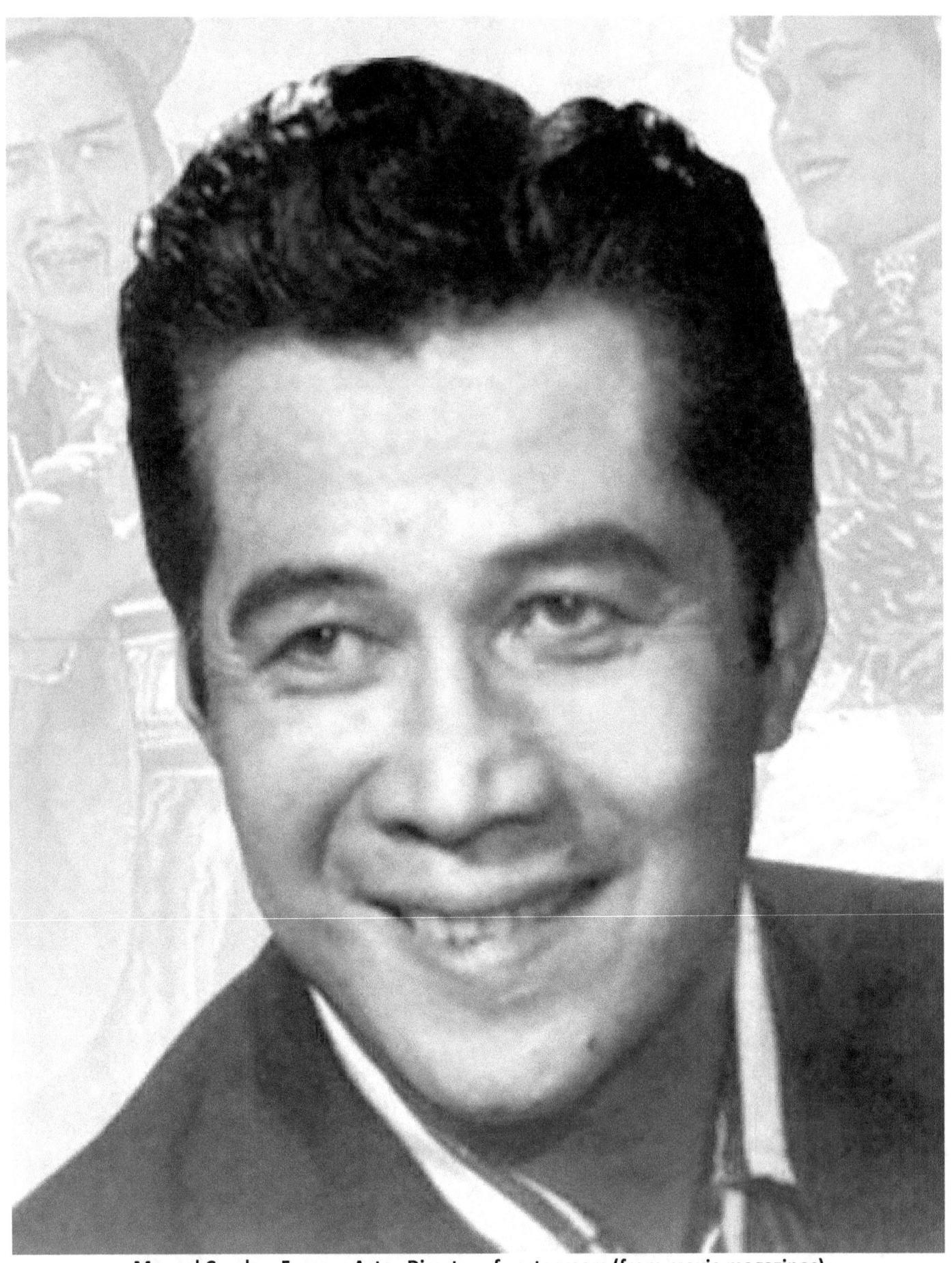

Manuel Conde – Famous Actor-Director of yesteryears (from movie magazines)

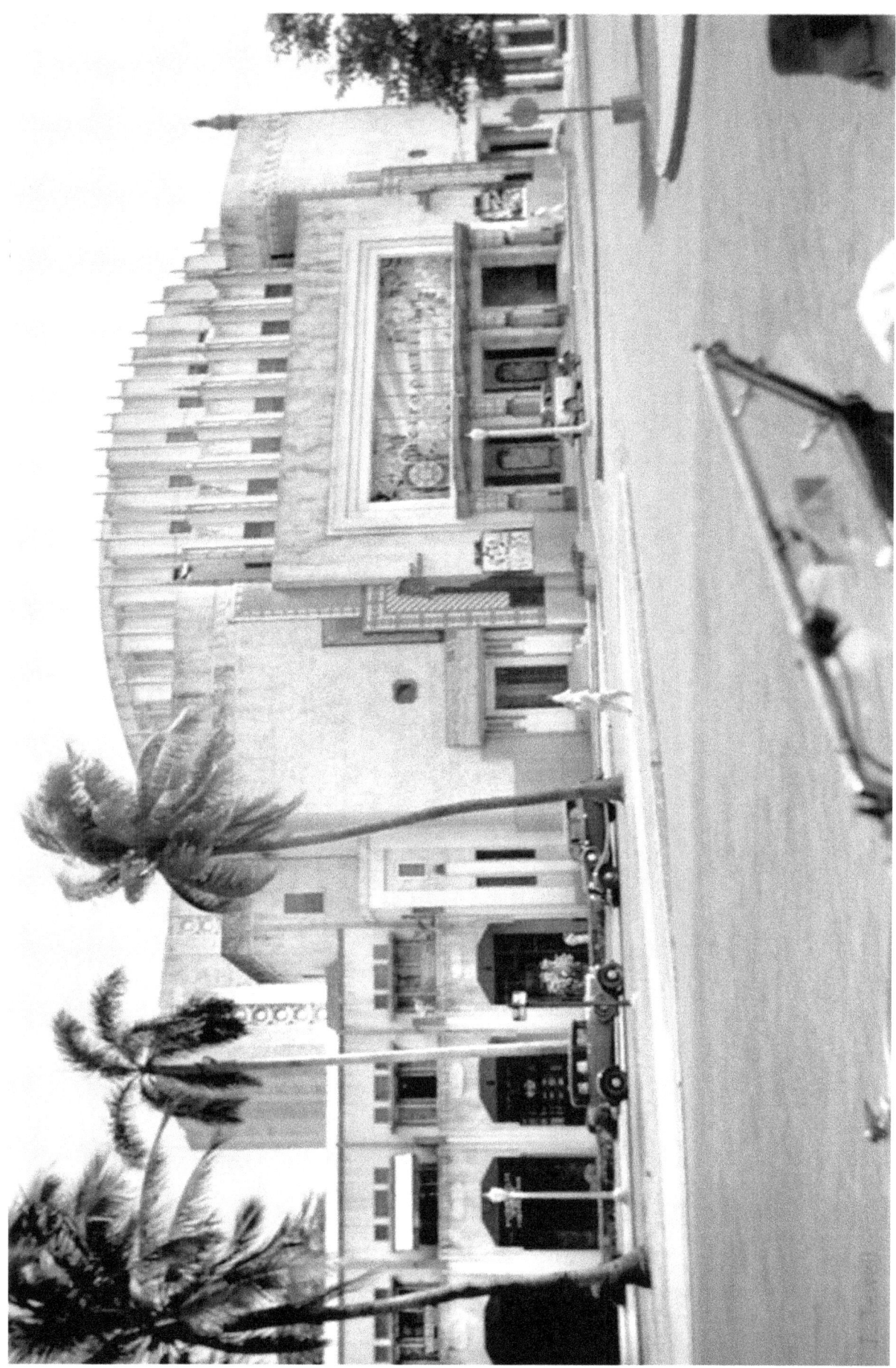

Metropolitan Theatre, Plaza Post Office Front, 1930s (courtesy: PHL MY PHL@facebook)

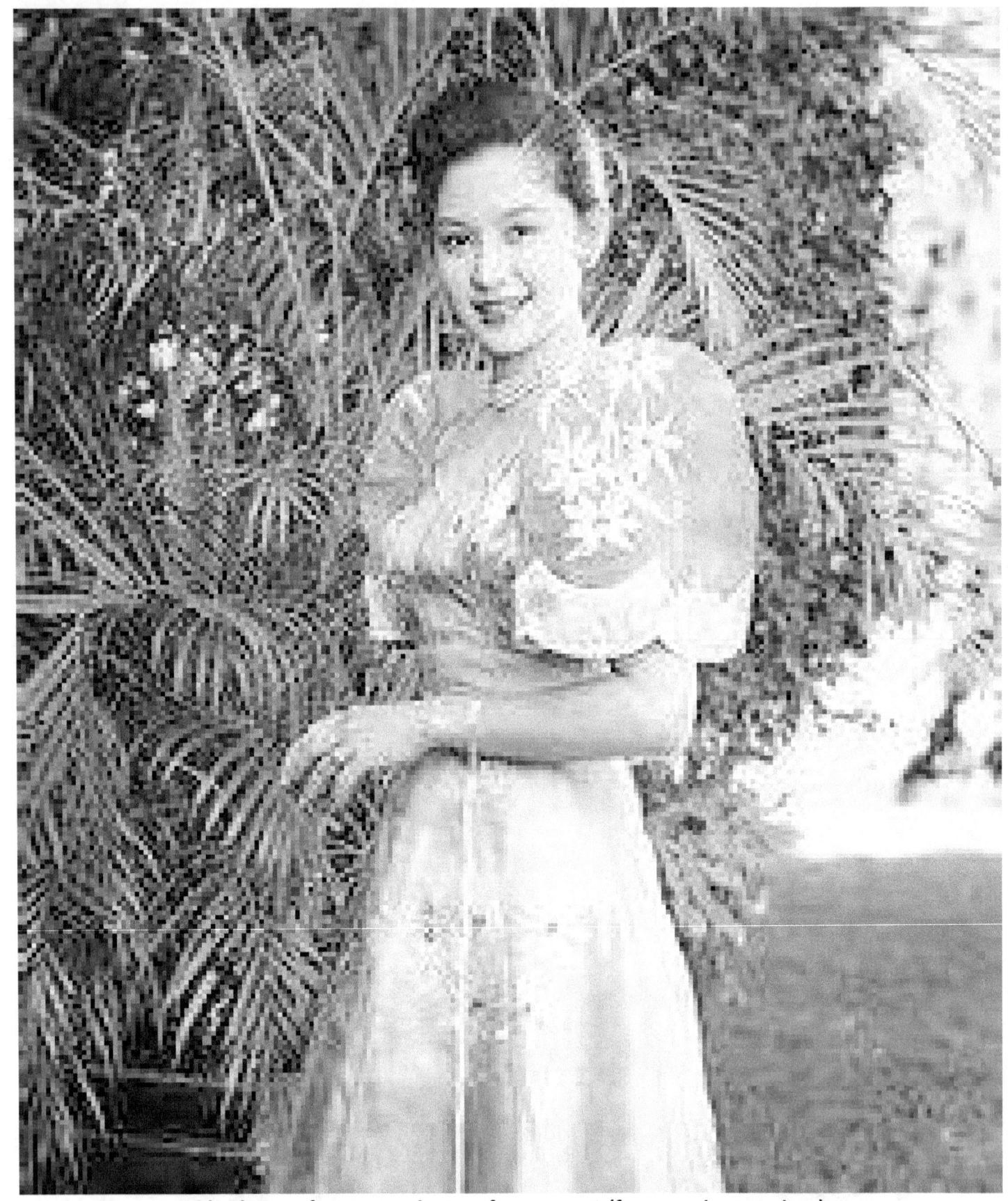

Nida Blanca – famous movie star of yesteryears (from movie magazines)

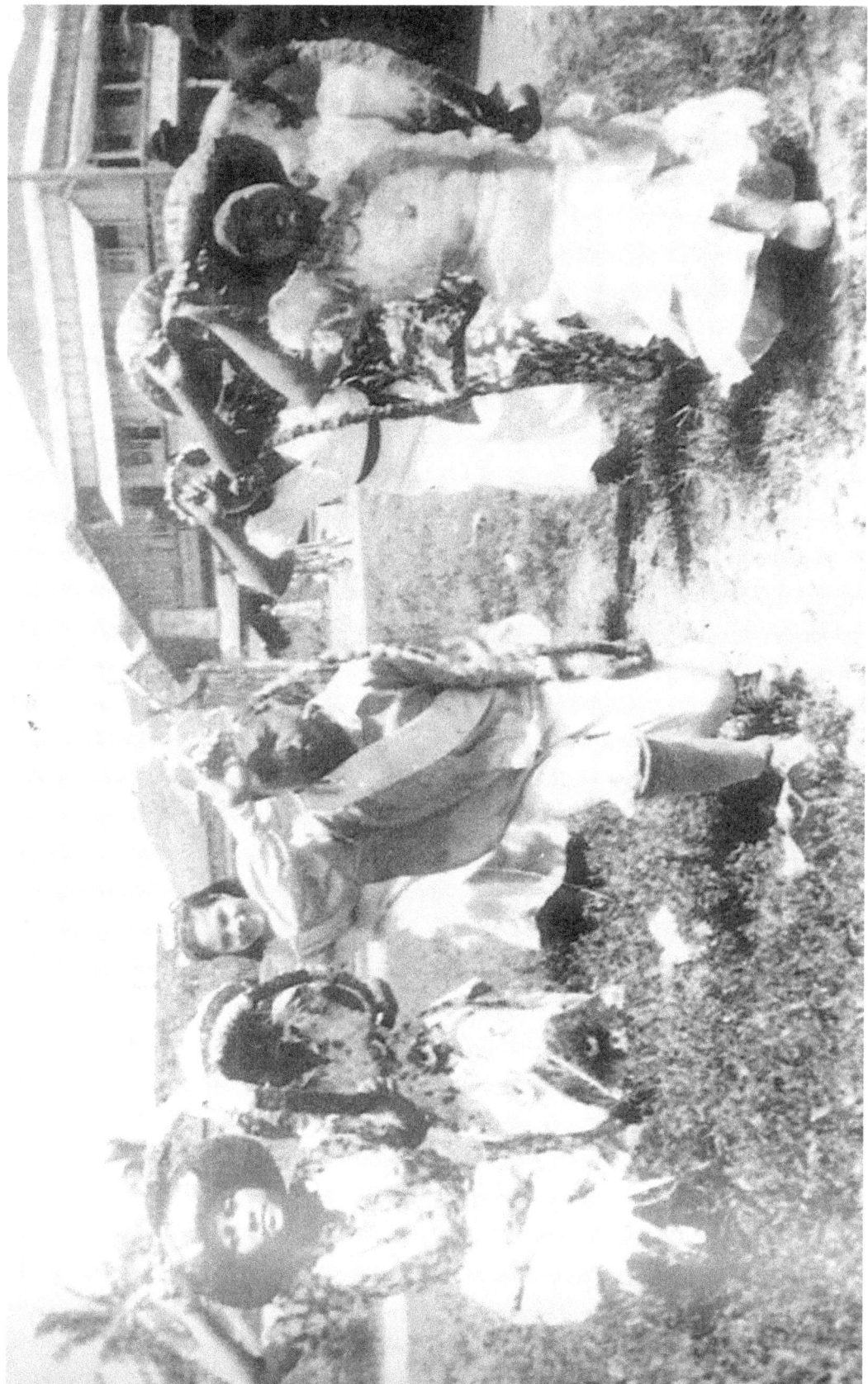

Christmas "pastores" in Bicol, 1900s - The Pastores dance, a unique Bicolano Christmas tradition, represents shepherds visiting the manger. They dance with castanets and tambourines and sing carols. Legazpi, Albay, 1938. (Photo credit: Francesca Reyes-Aquino Collection)

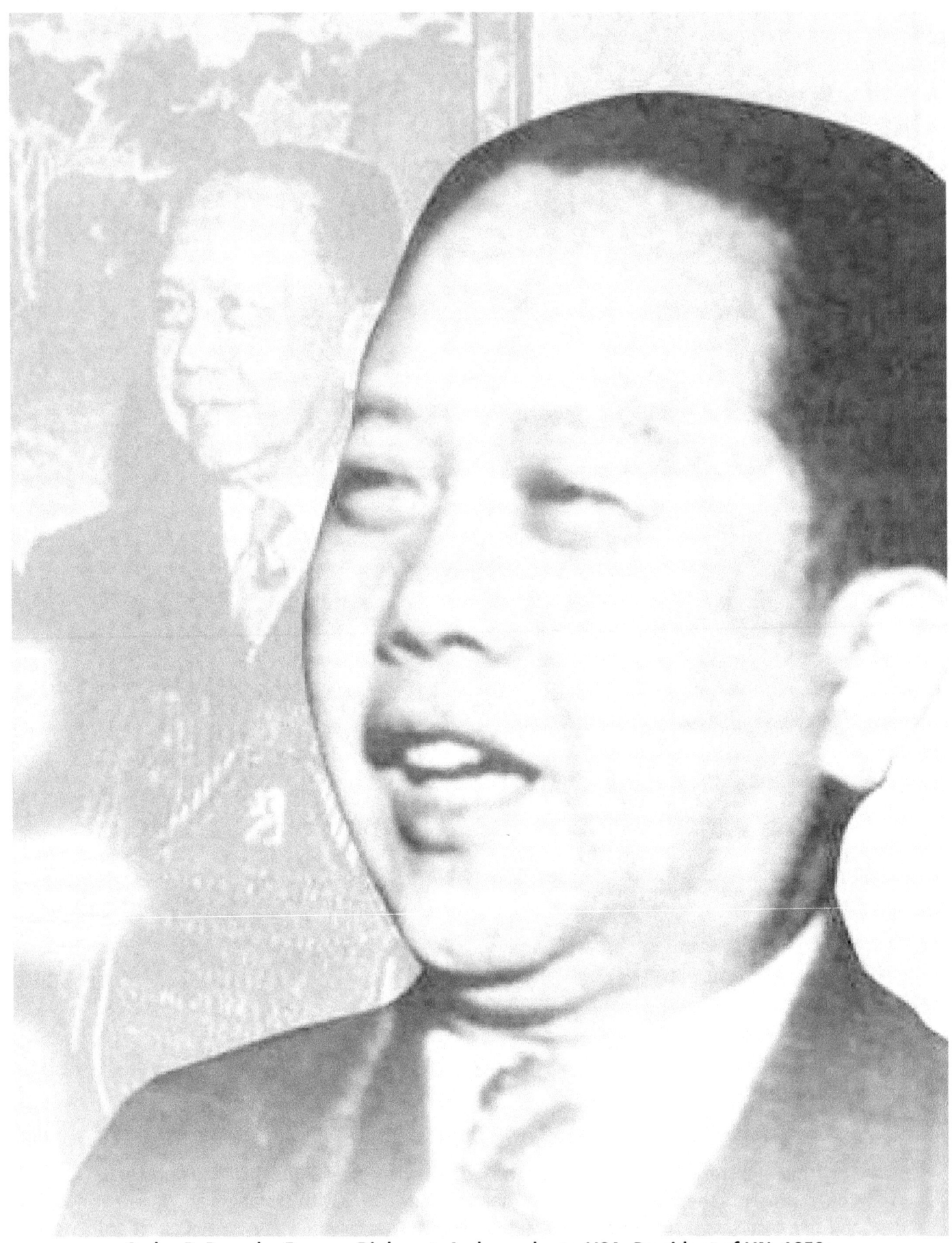

Carlos P. Romulo- Famous Diplomat, Ambassador to USA, President of UN, 1950s, Journalist and Pulitzer Prize Winner (from National Museum)

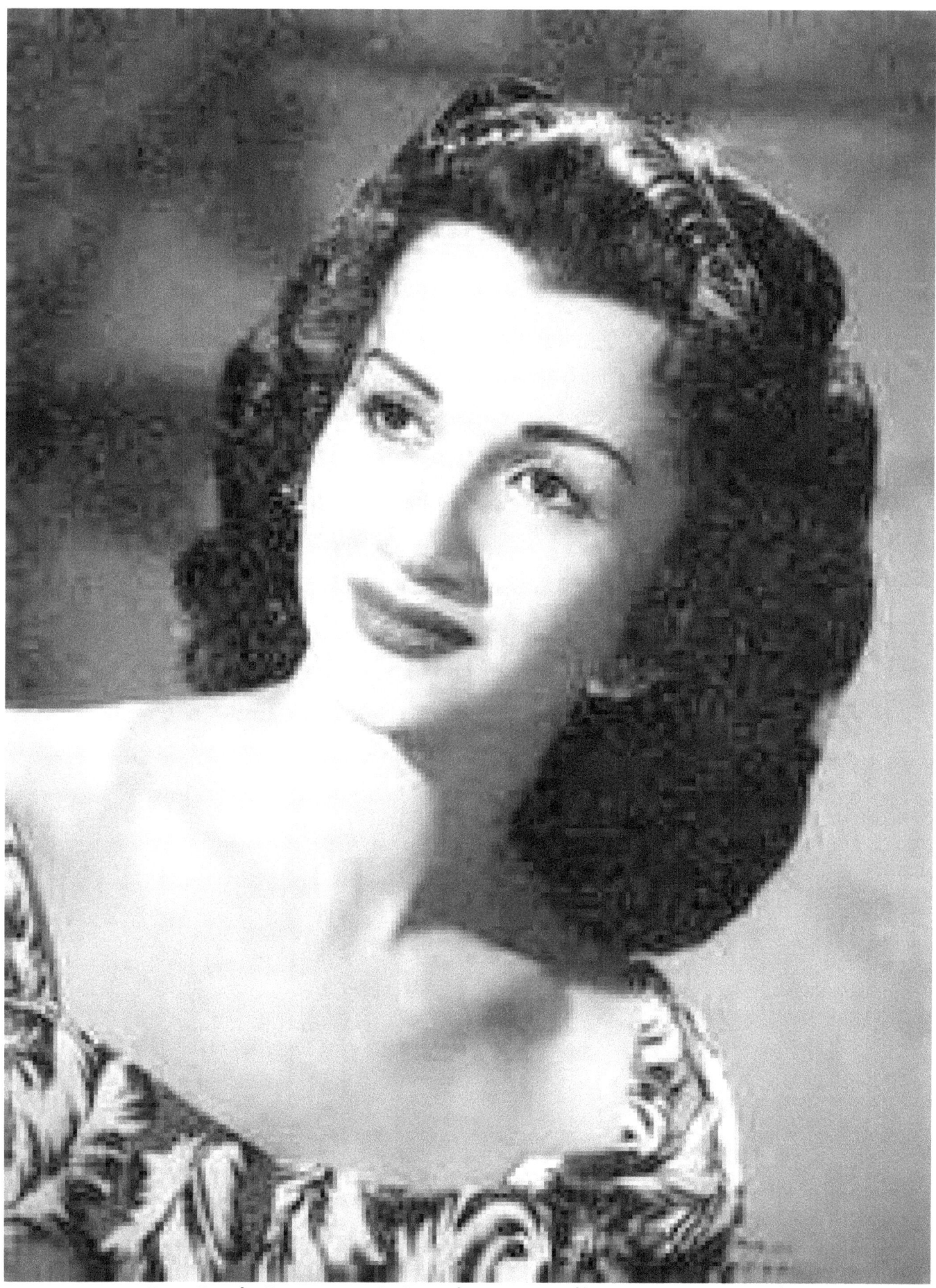

Rosa Rosal – Famous movie Star of yesteryears (from movie magazines)

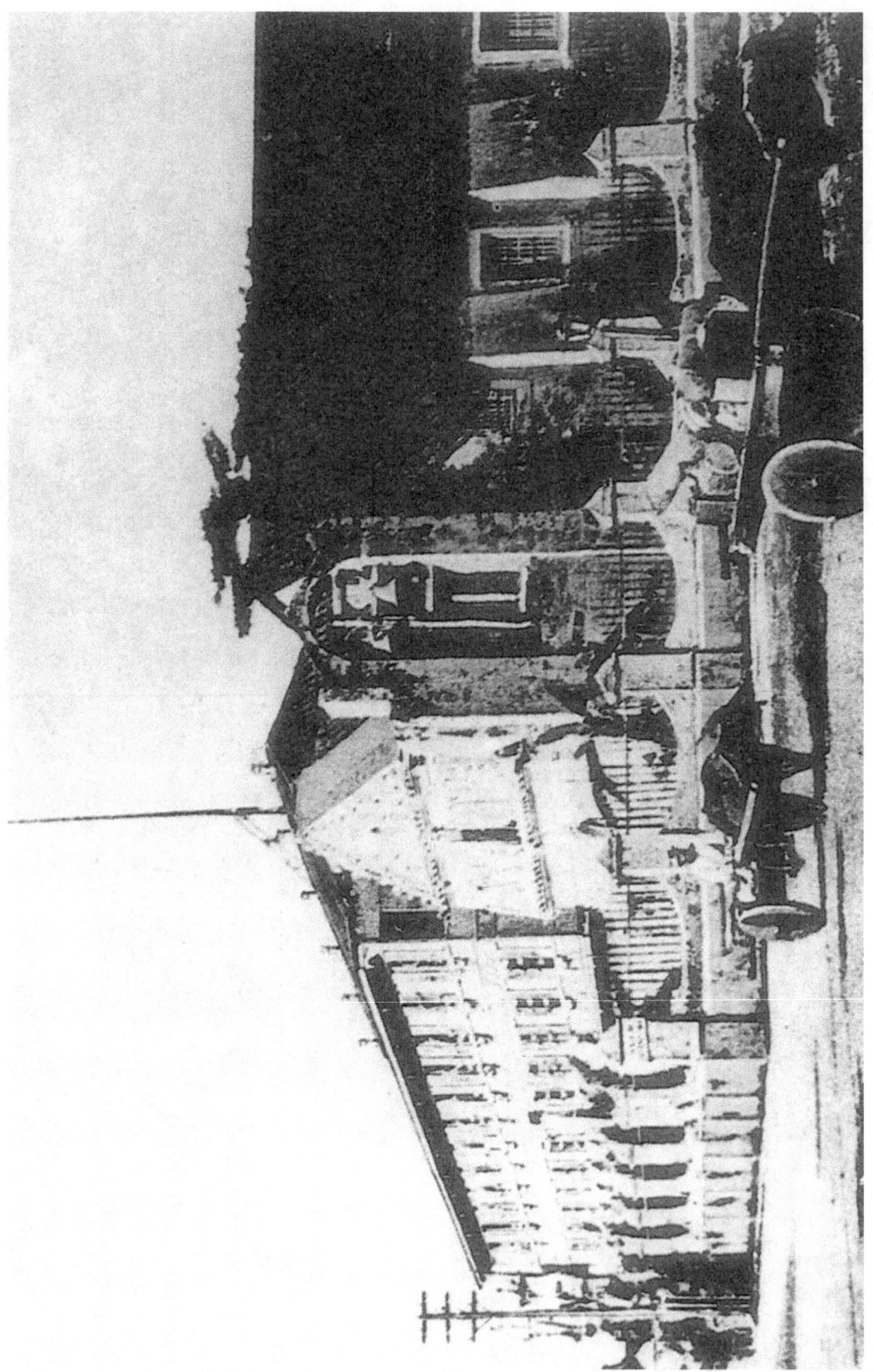

San Carlos University, Cebu City, circa 1910 – an old university (courtesy: PHL MY PHL@facebook)

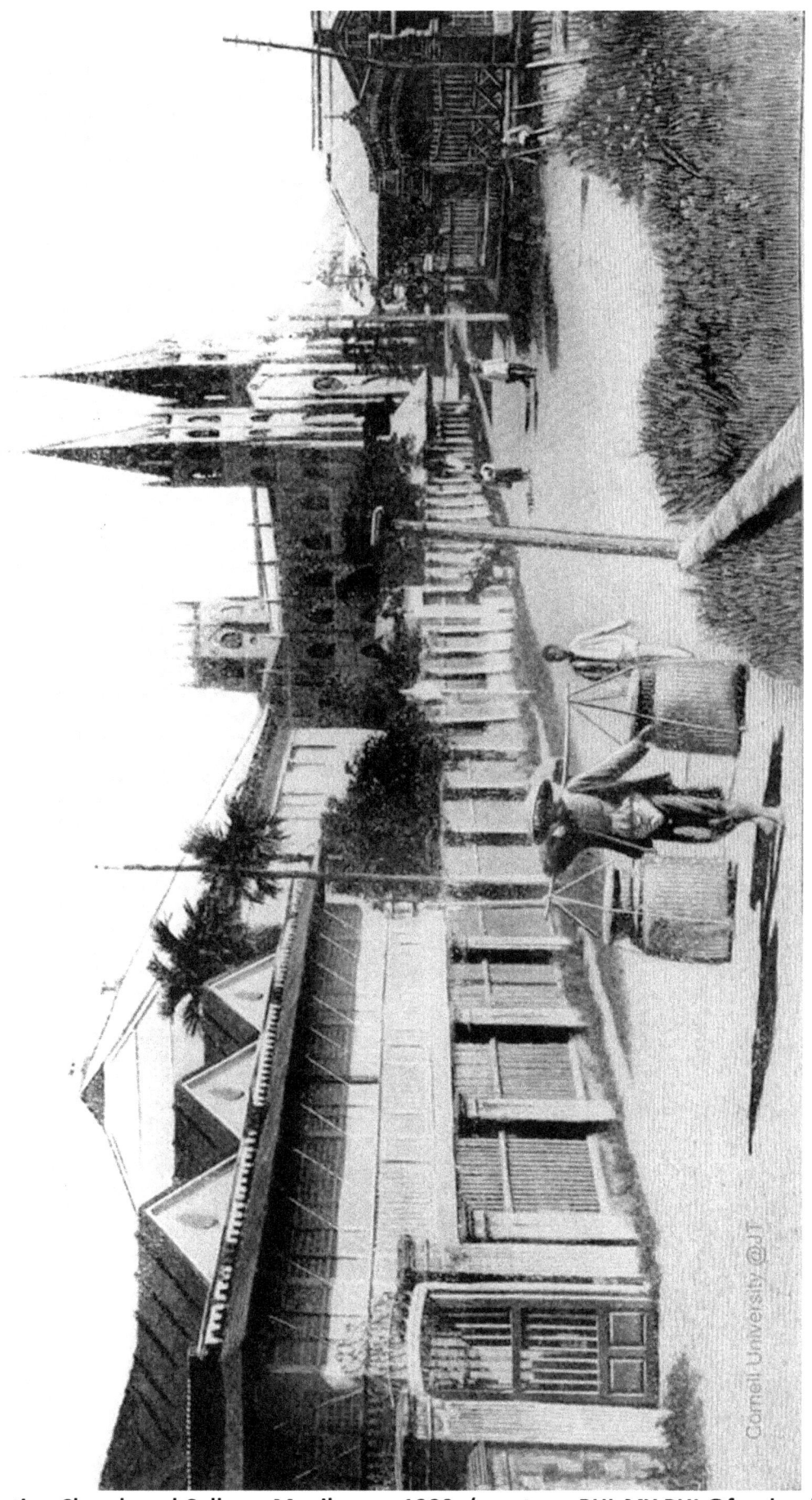

San Sebastian Church and College, Manila, pre-1900s (courtesy: PHL MY PHL@facebook)

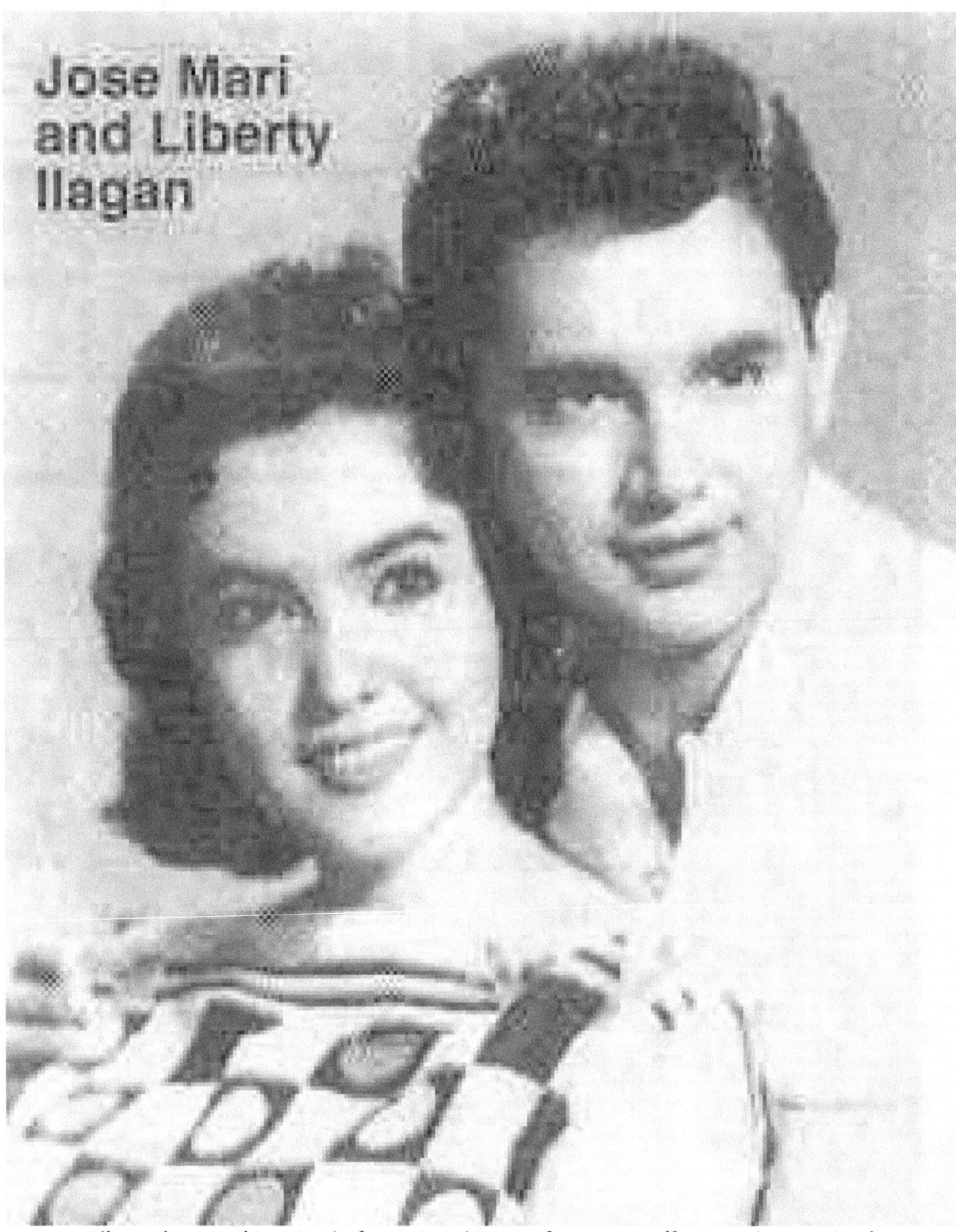

Jose Mari and Liberty Ilagan

Liberty Ilagan and Jose Mari – famous movie stars of yesteryears (from movie magazines)

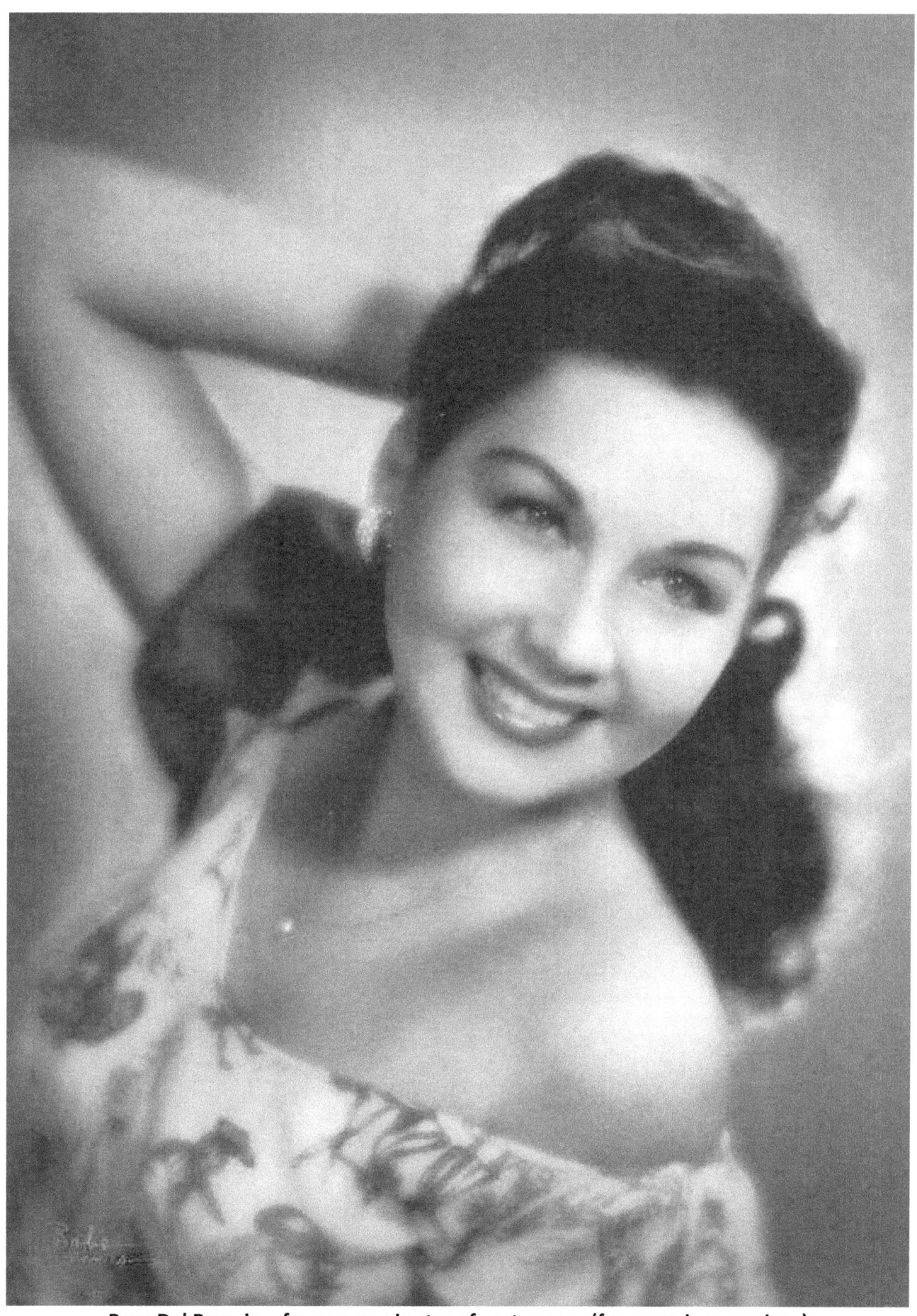

Rosa Del Rosario – famous movie star of yesteryears (from movie magazines)

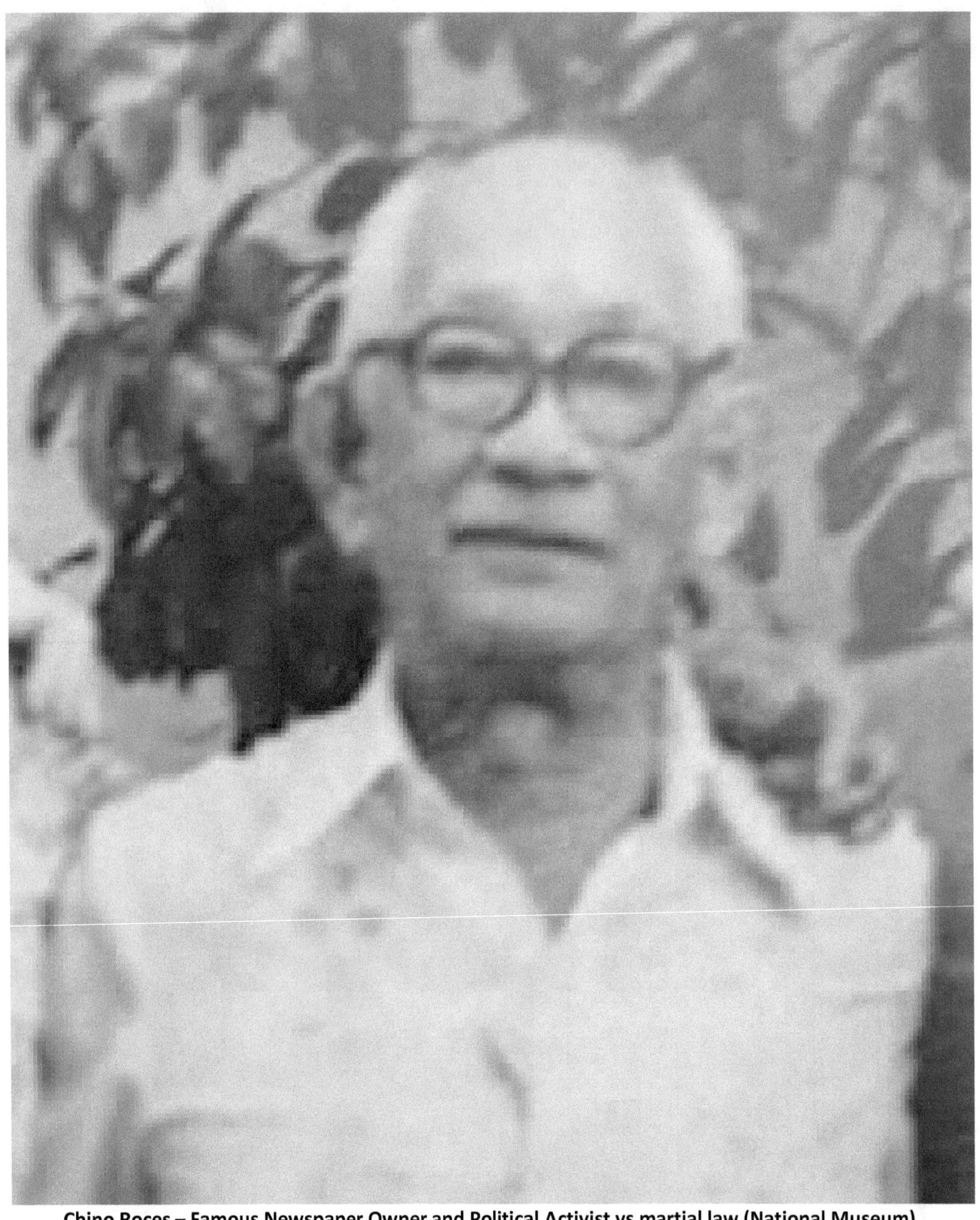

Chino Roces – Famous Newspaper Owner and Political Activist vs martial law (National Museum)

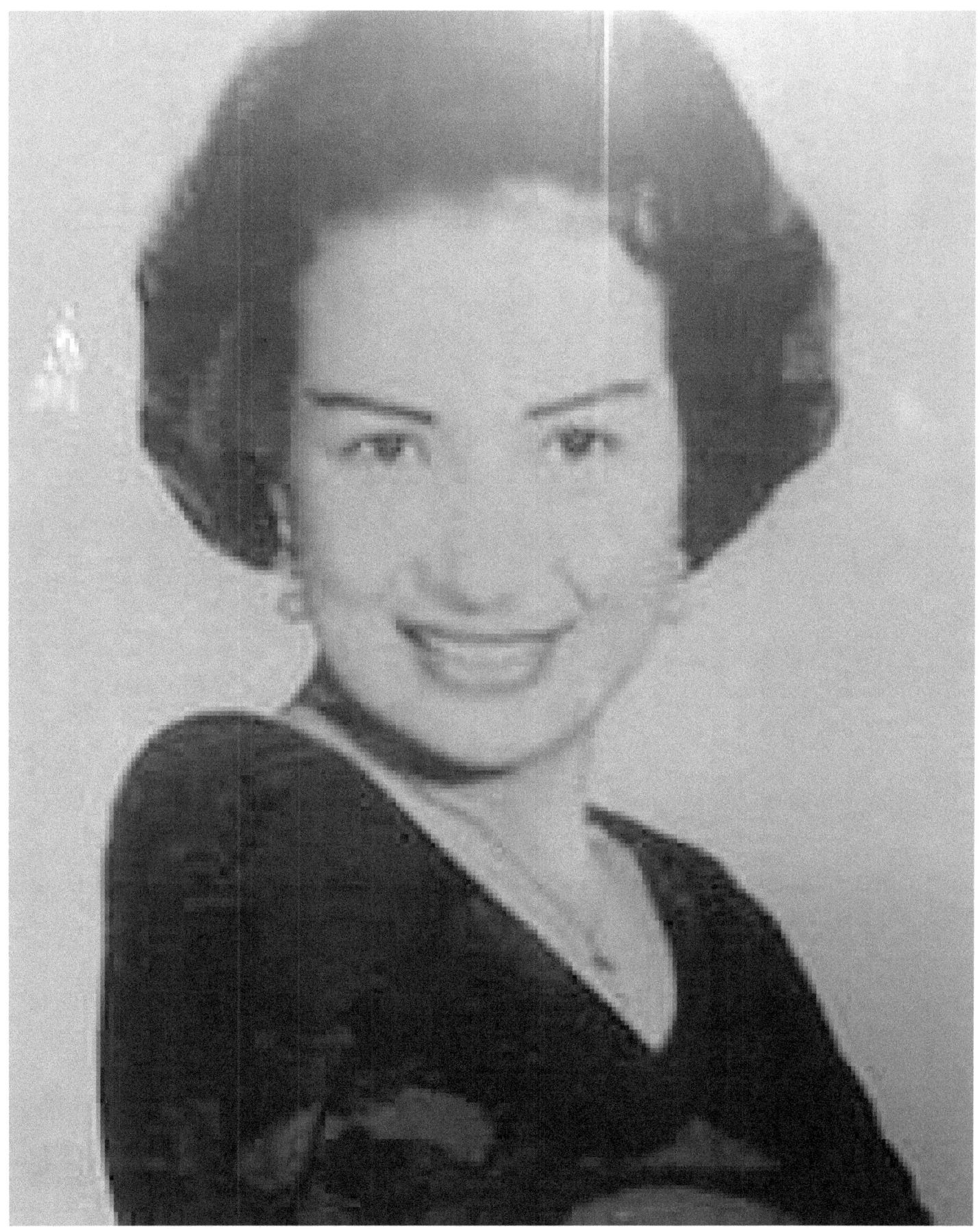

Mila Del Sol – famous movie star of yesteryears (from movie magazines)

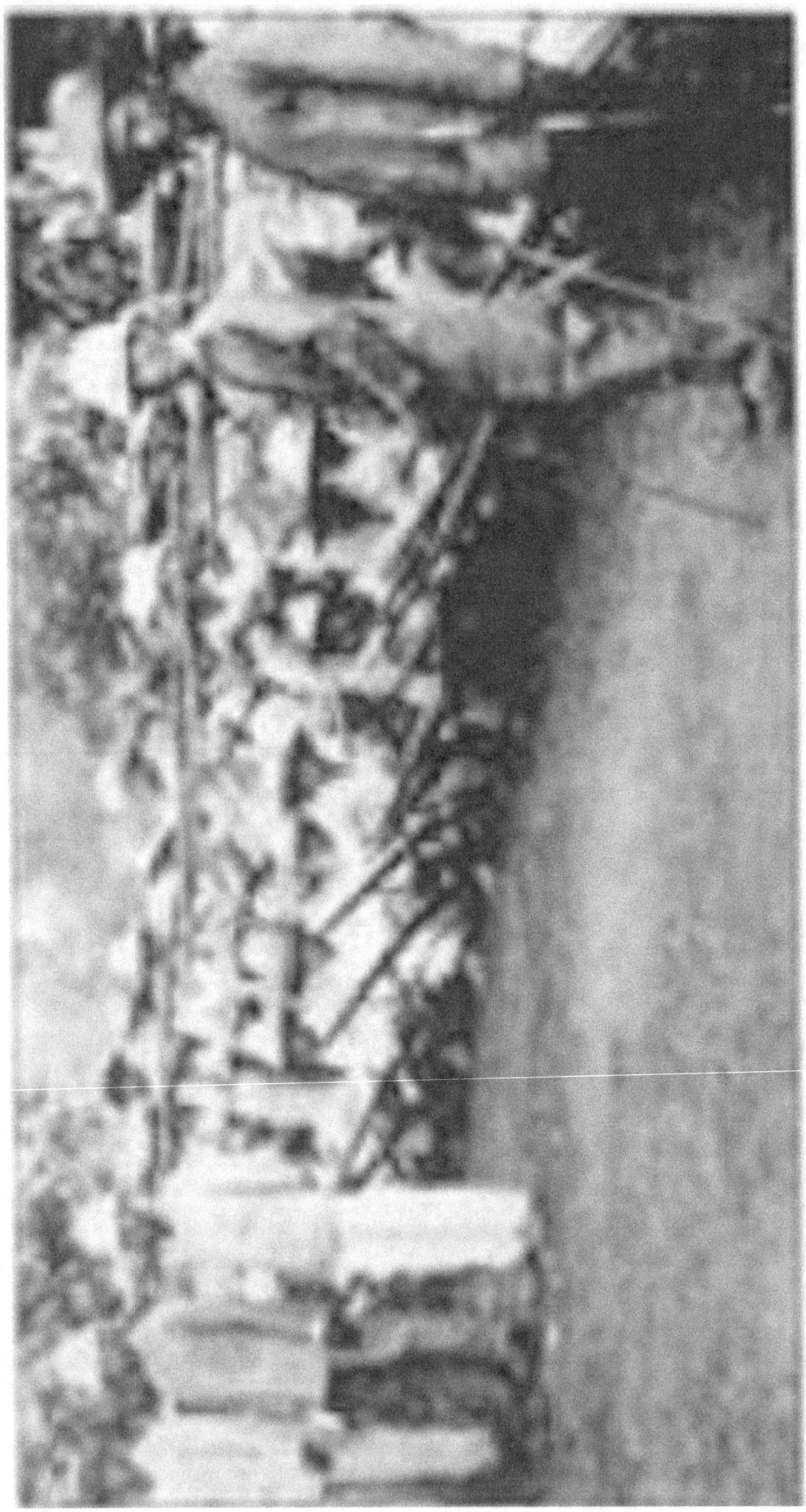

Philippine Revolutionary Soldiers, 1897 (courtesy: PHL MY PHL@facebook)

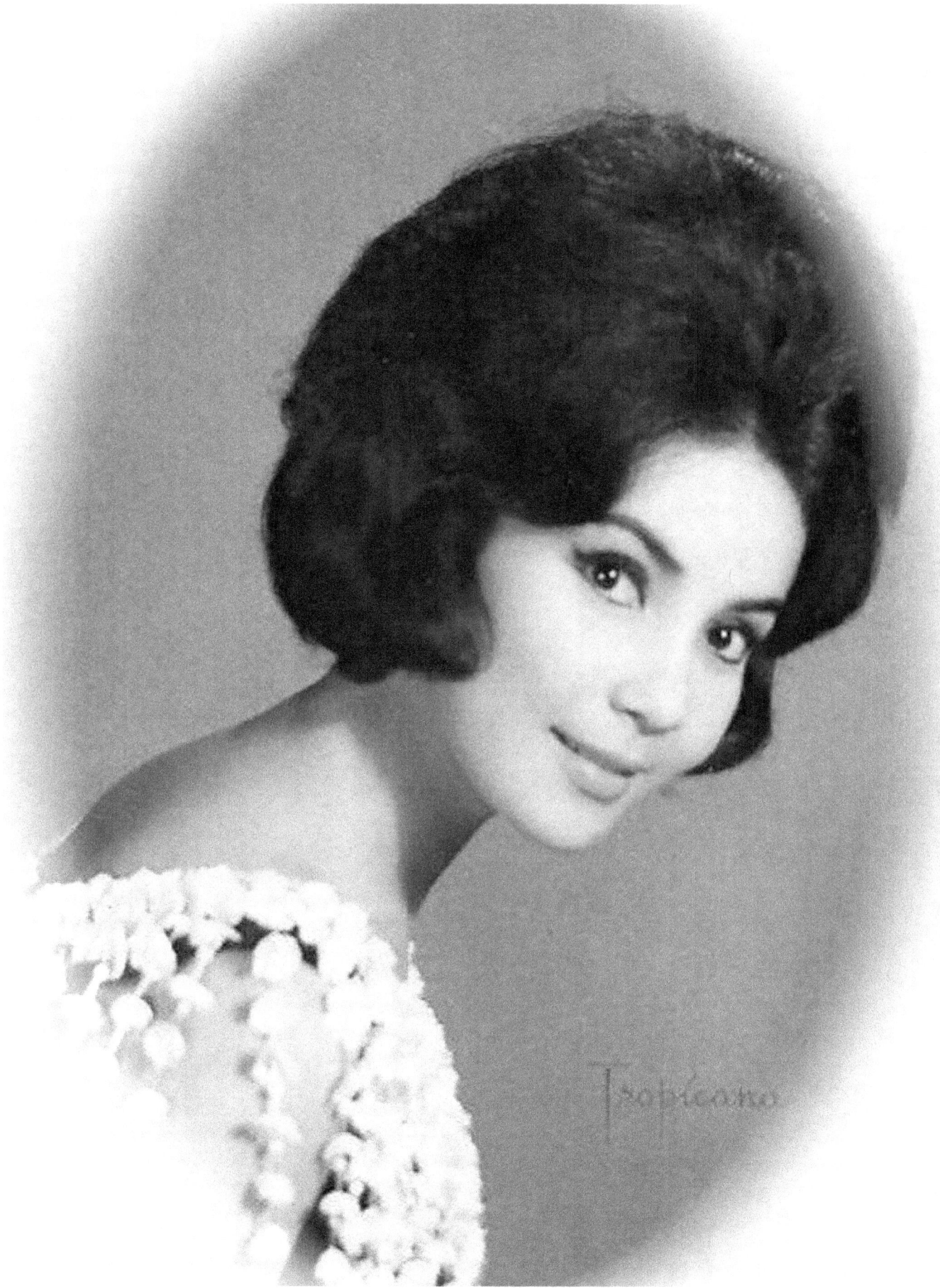

Amalia Fuentes – famous movie star of yesteryears (from movie magazines)

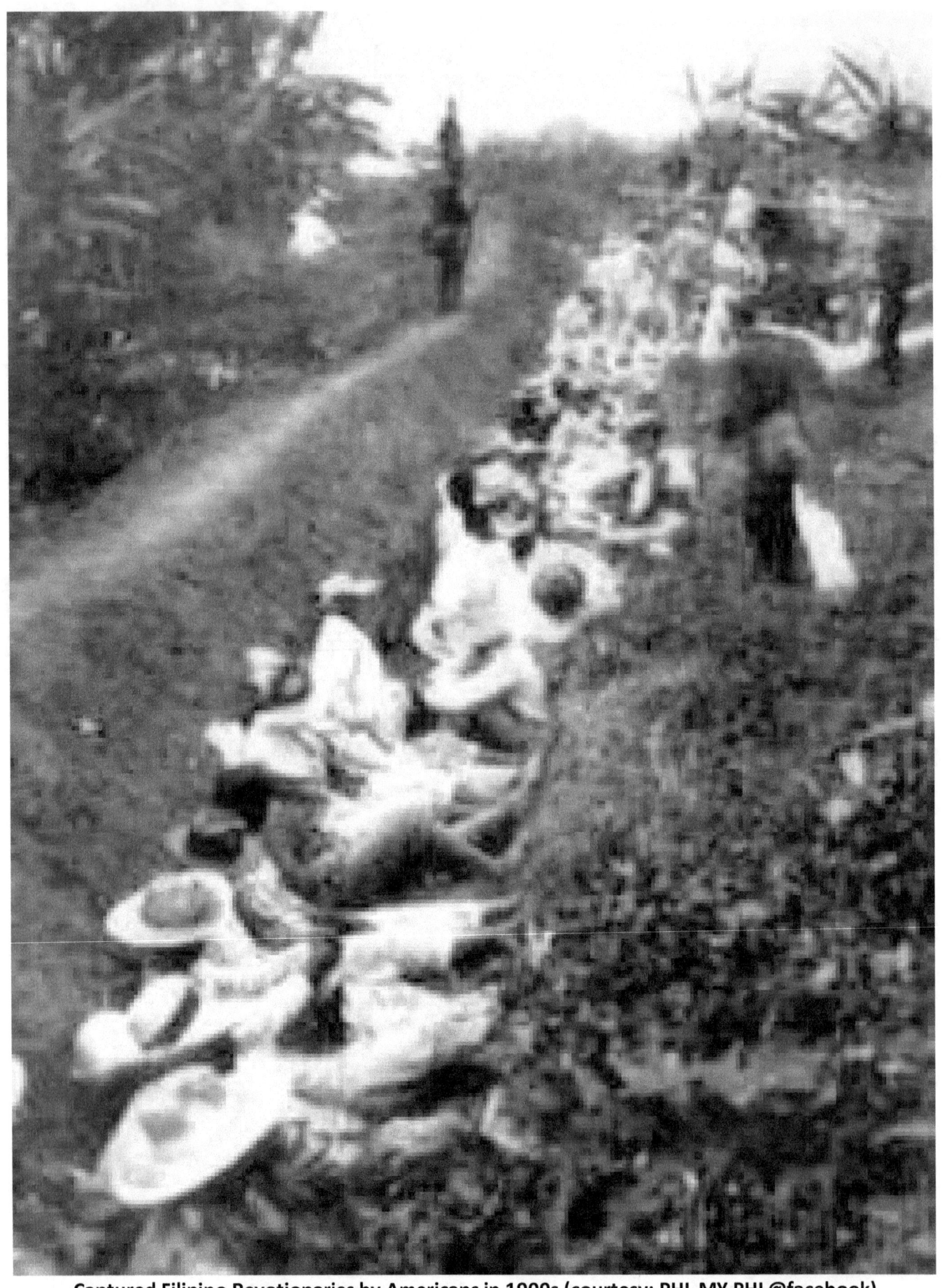

Captured Filipino Revotionaries by Americans in 1900s (courtesy: PHL MY PHL@facebook)

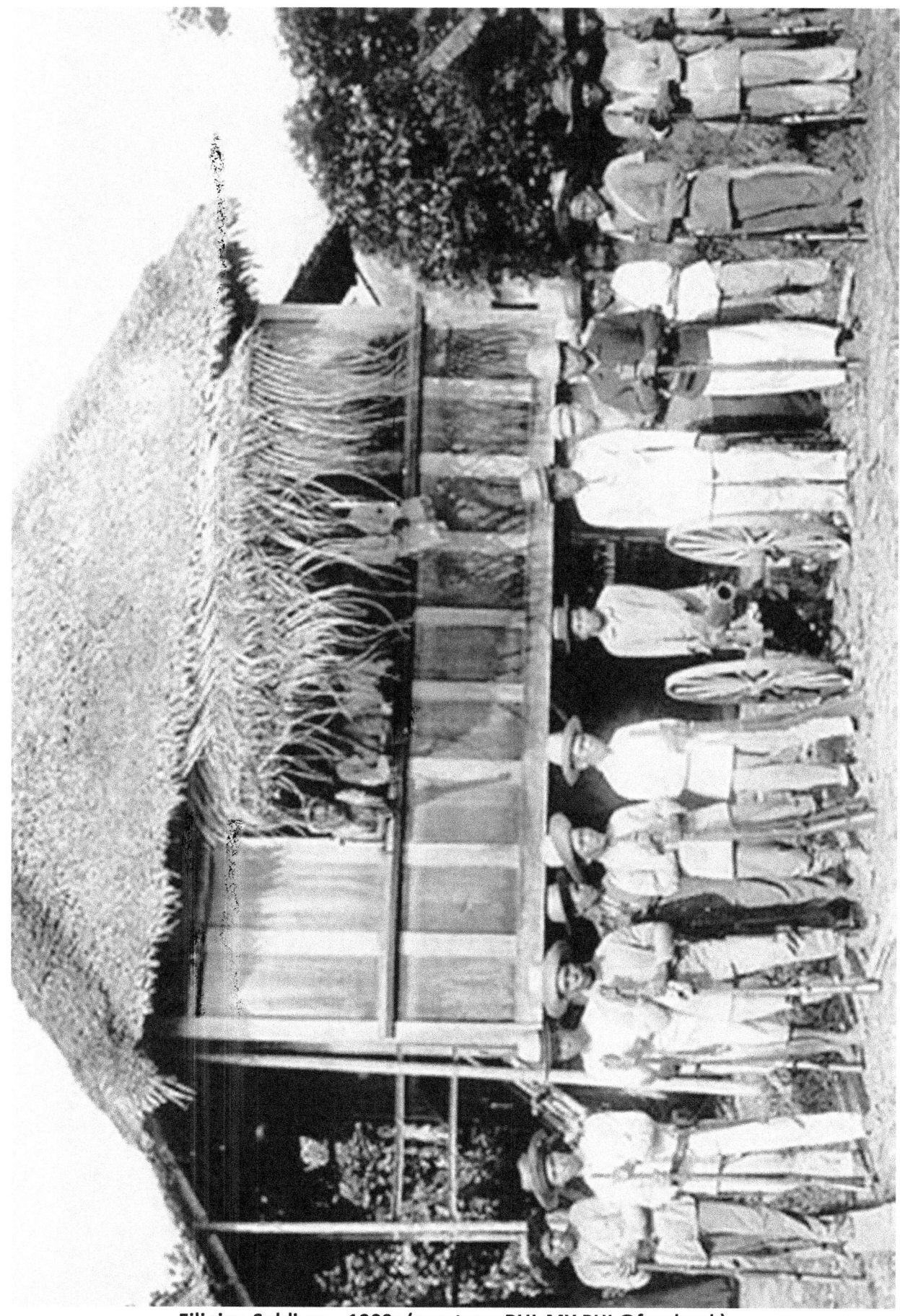

Filipino Soldiers – 1900s (courtesy: PHL MY PHL@facebook)

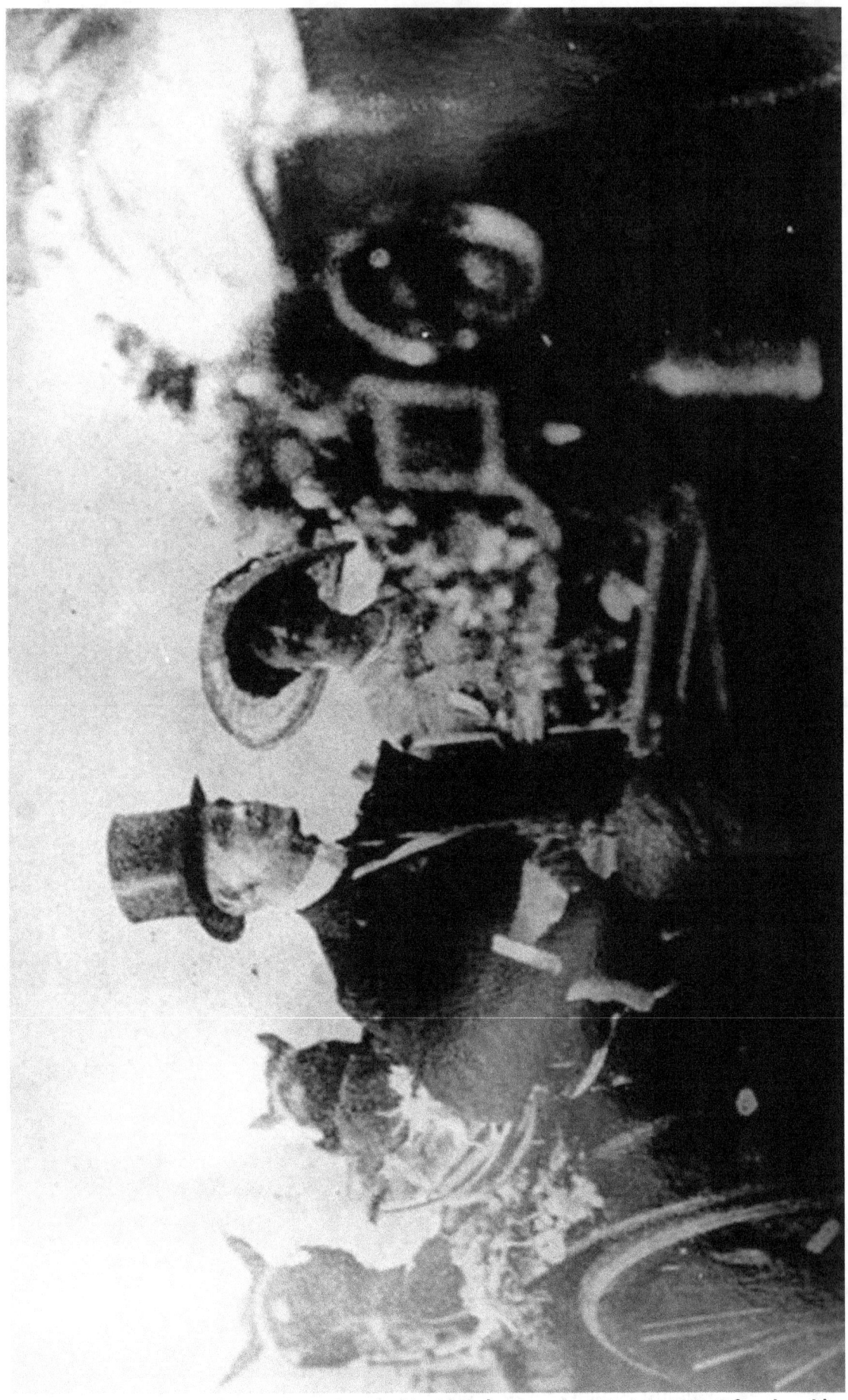

Francis Burton Harrison – Gov. General in Phil. (courtesy: PHL MY PHIL@facebook)

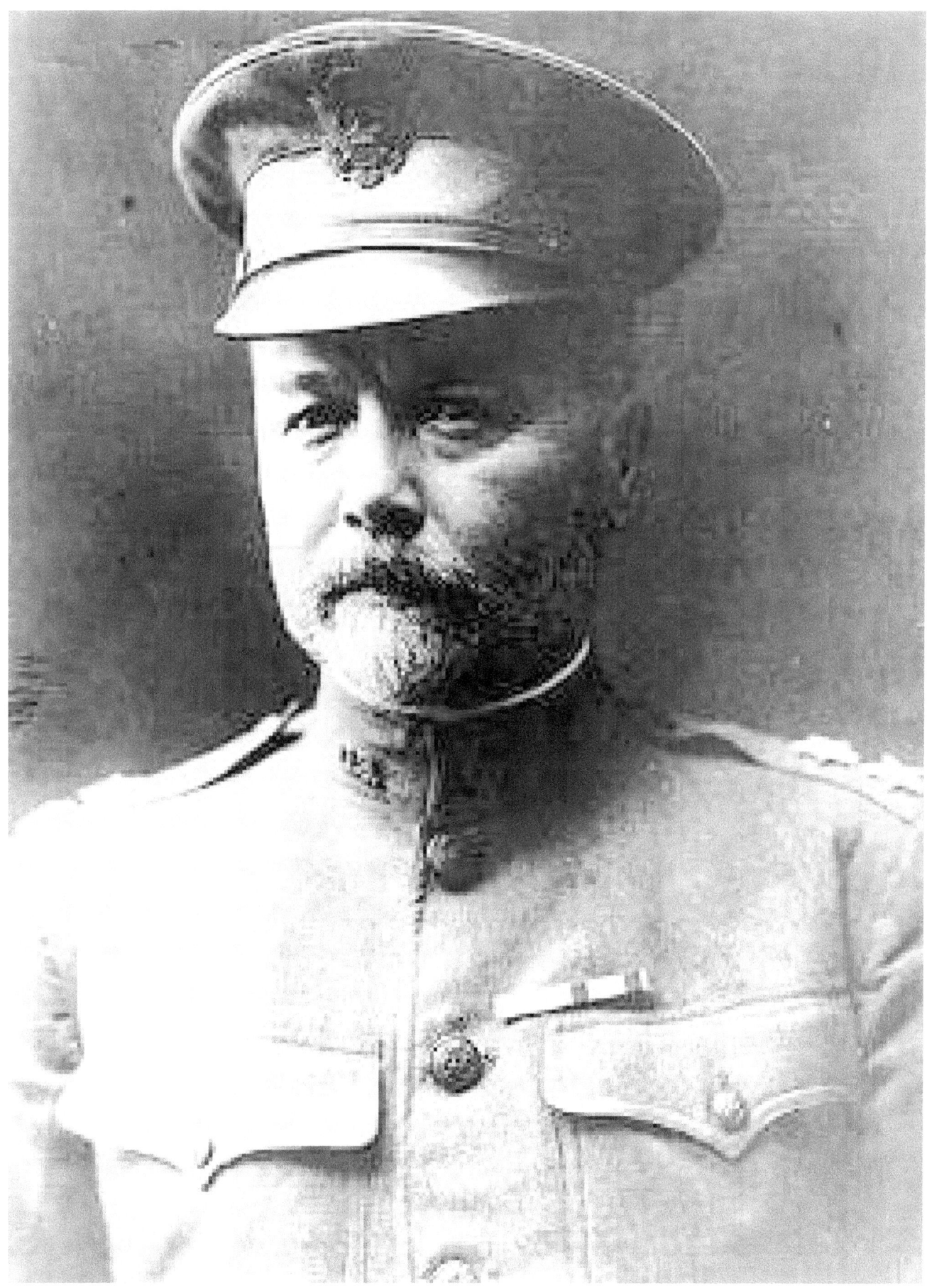

Gen. Frederick Funston – Took Gen Aguinaldo Surrender in Isabela (courtesy: PHL MY PHL@facebook)

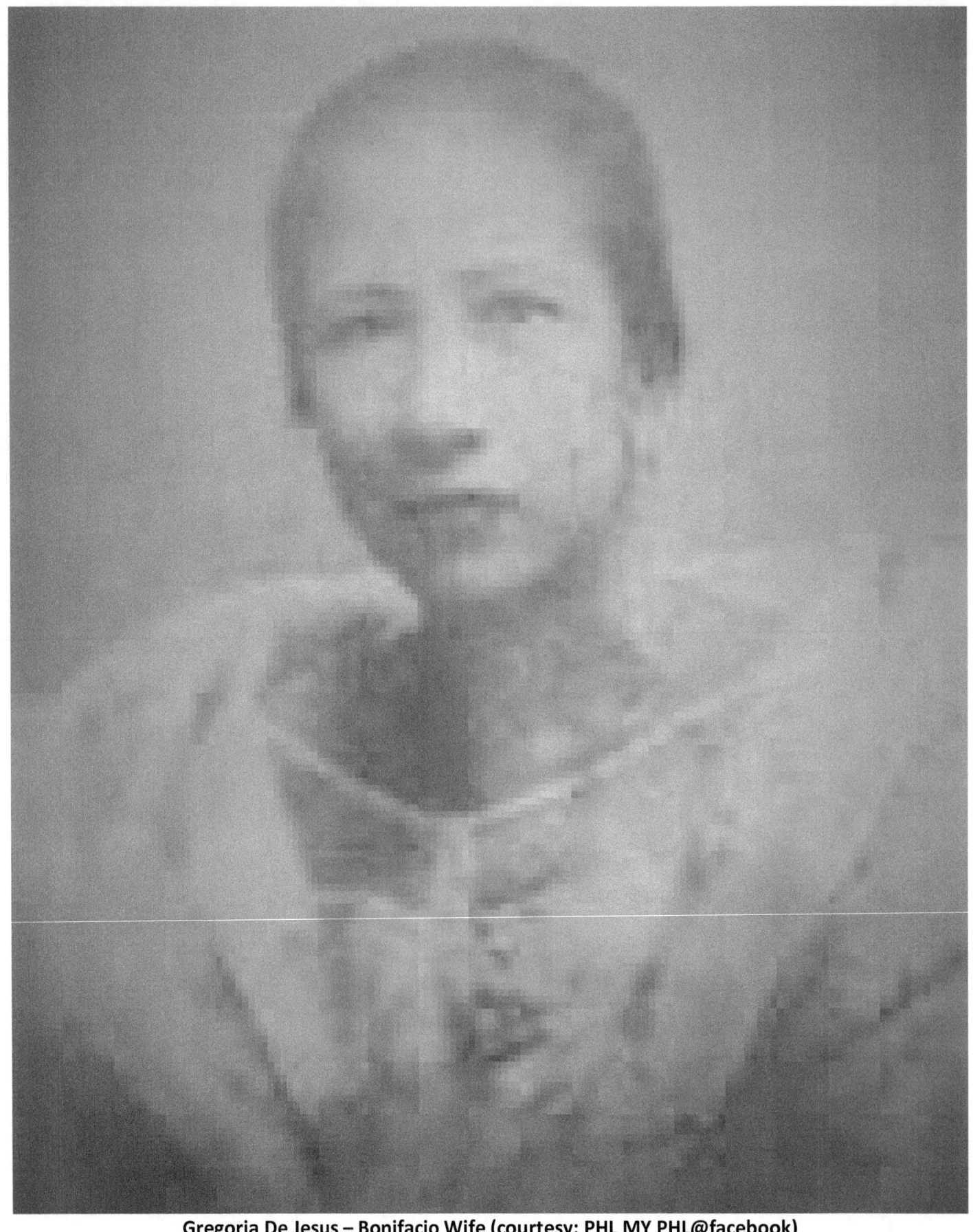

Gregoria De Jesus – Bonifacio Wife (courtesy: PHL MY PHL@facebook)

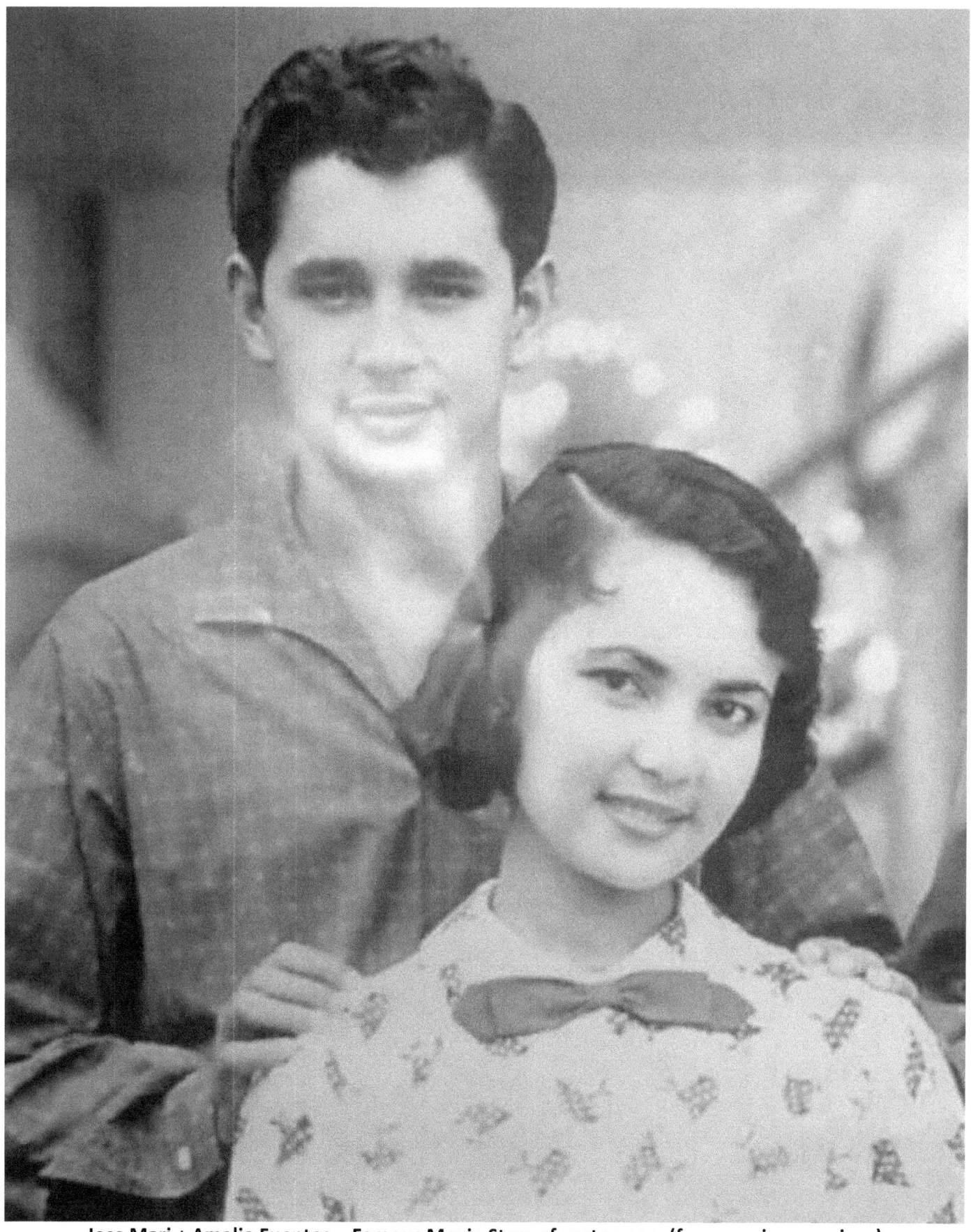

Jose Mari + Amalia Fuentes – Famous Movie Stars of yesteryears (from movie magazines)

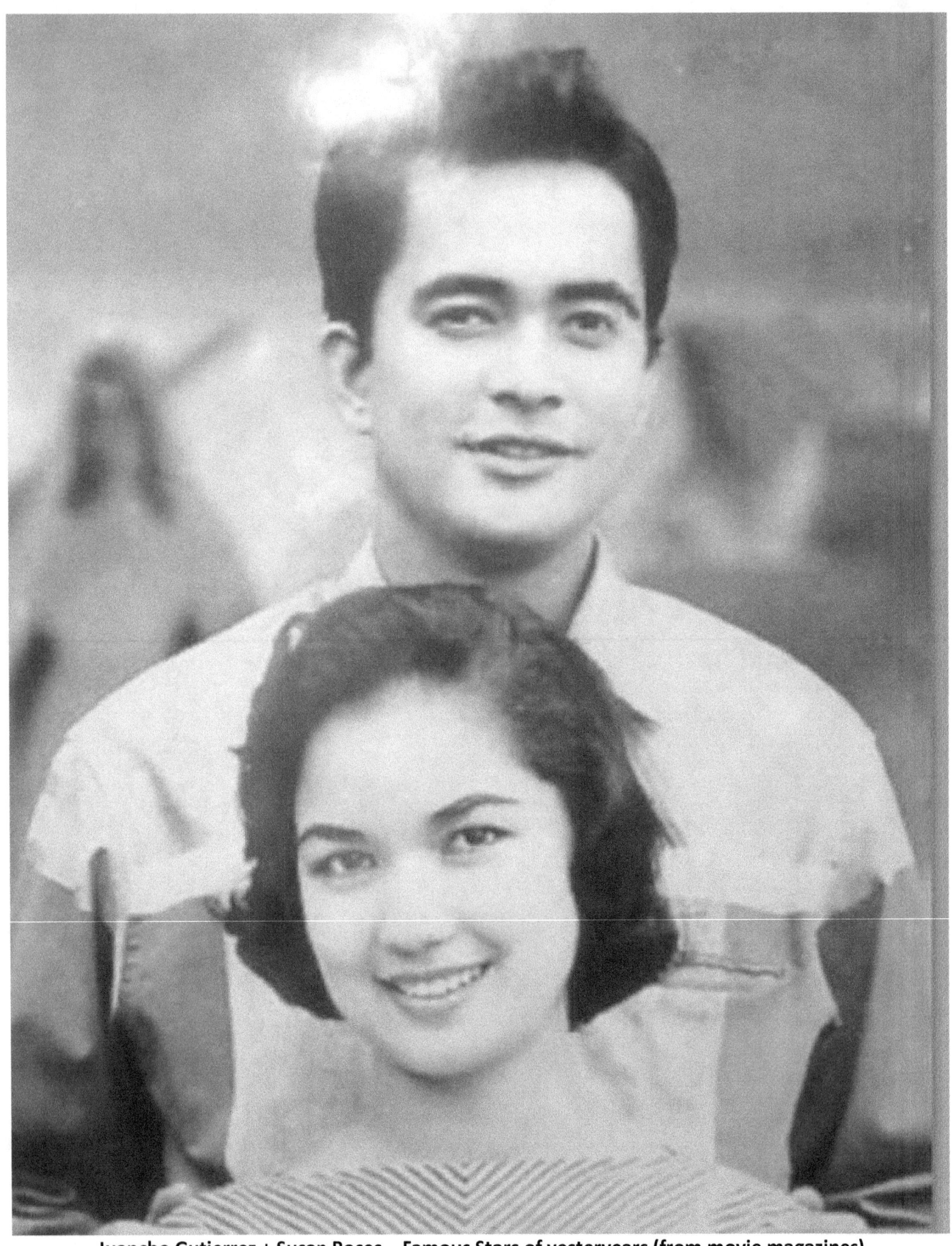

Juancho Gutierrez + Susan Roces – Famous Stars of yesteryears (from movie magazines)

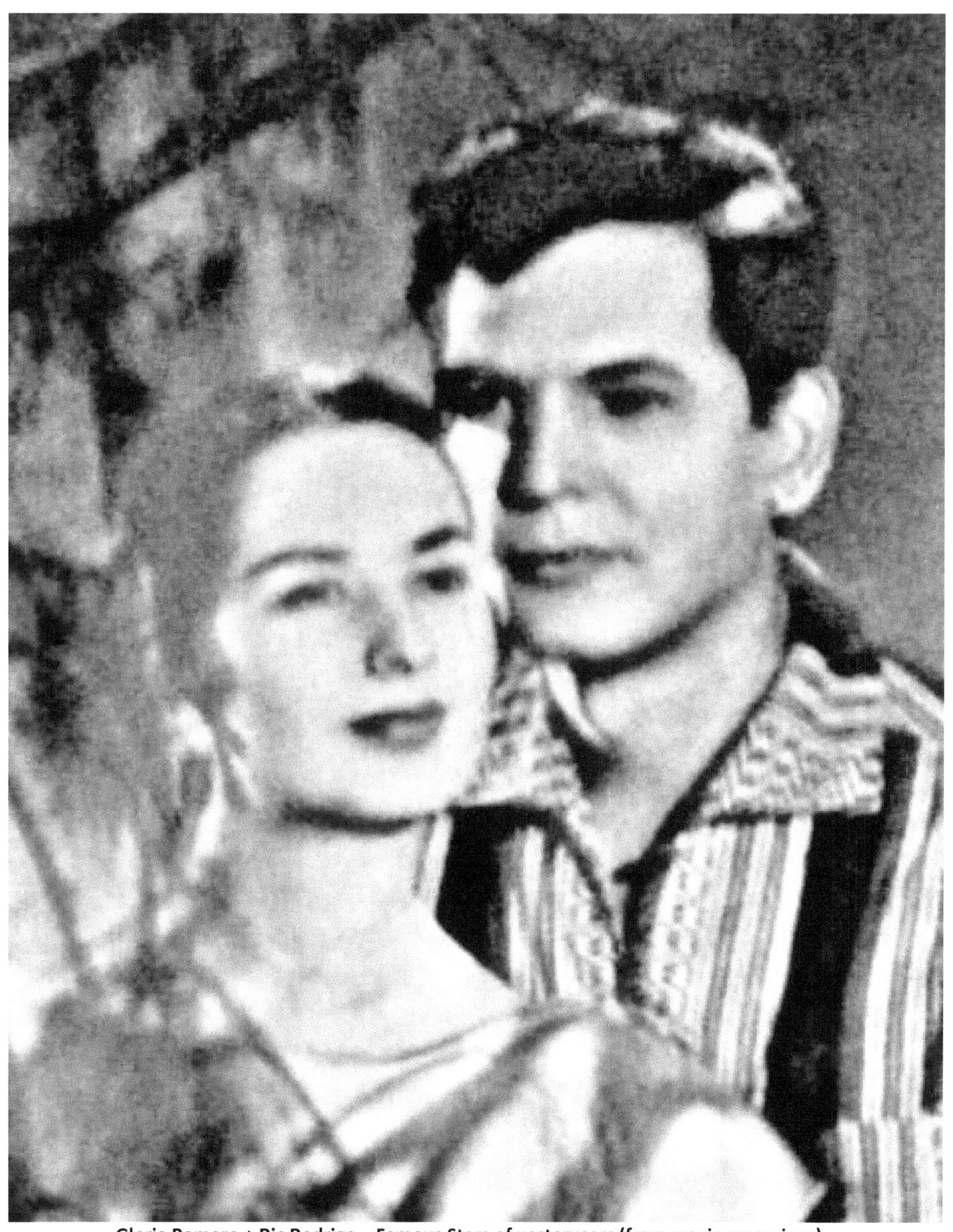

Gloria Romero + Ric Rodrigo – Famous Stars of yesteryears (from movie magazines)

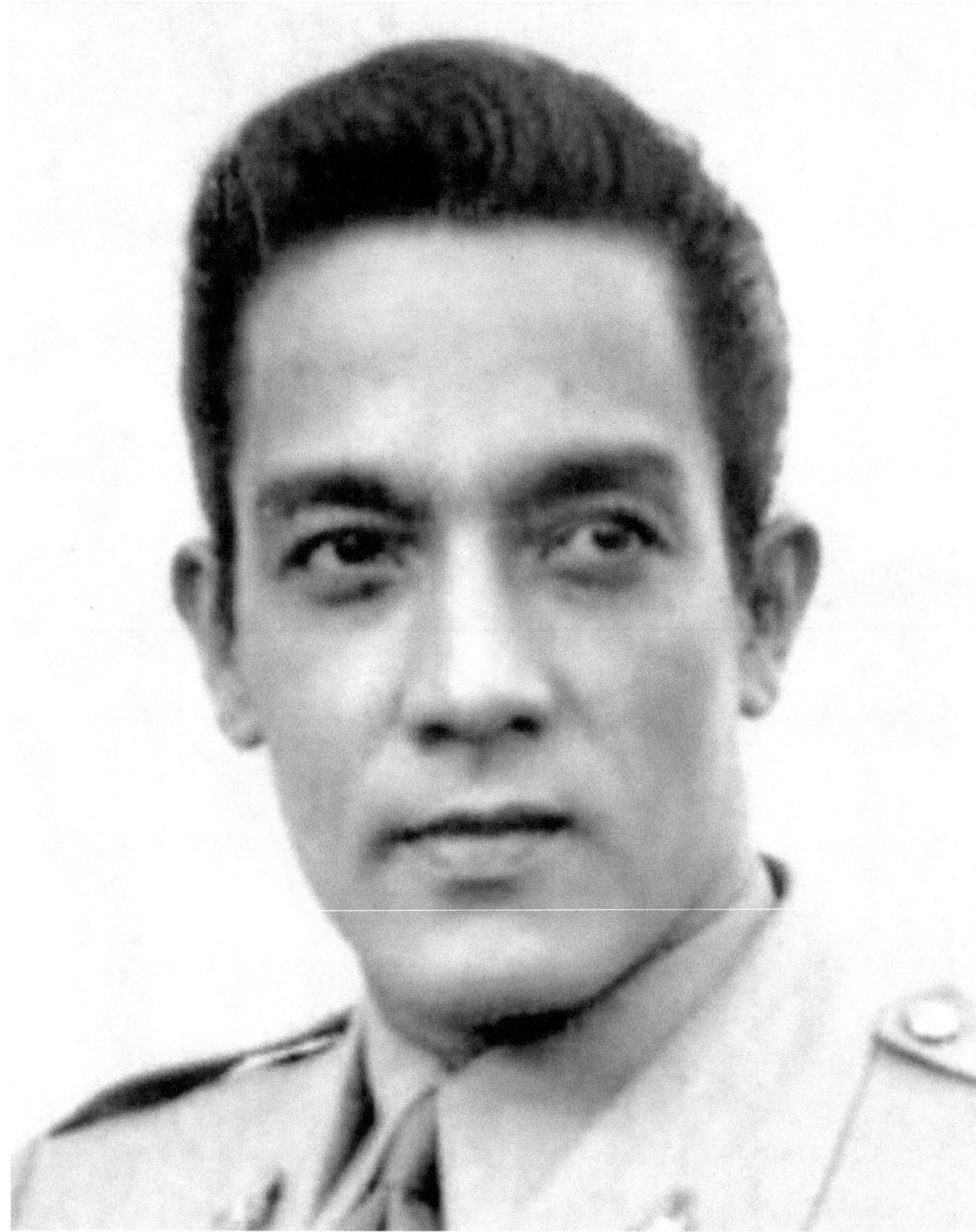

Leopoldo Salcedo – Famous Star of yesteryears (from movie magazines)

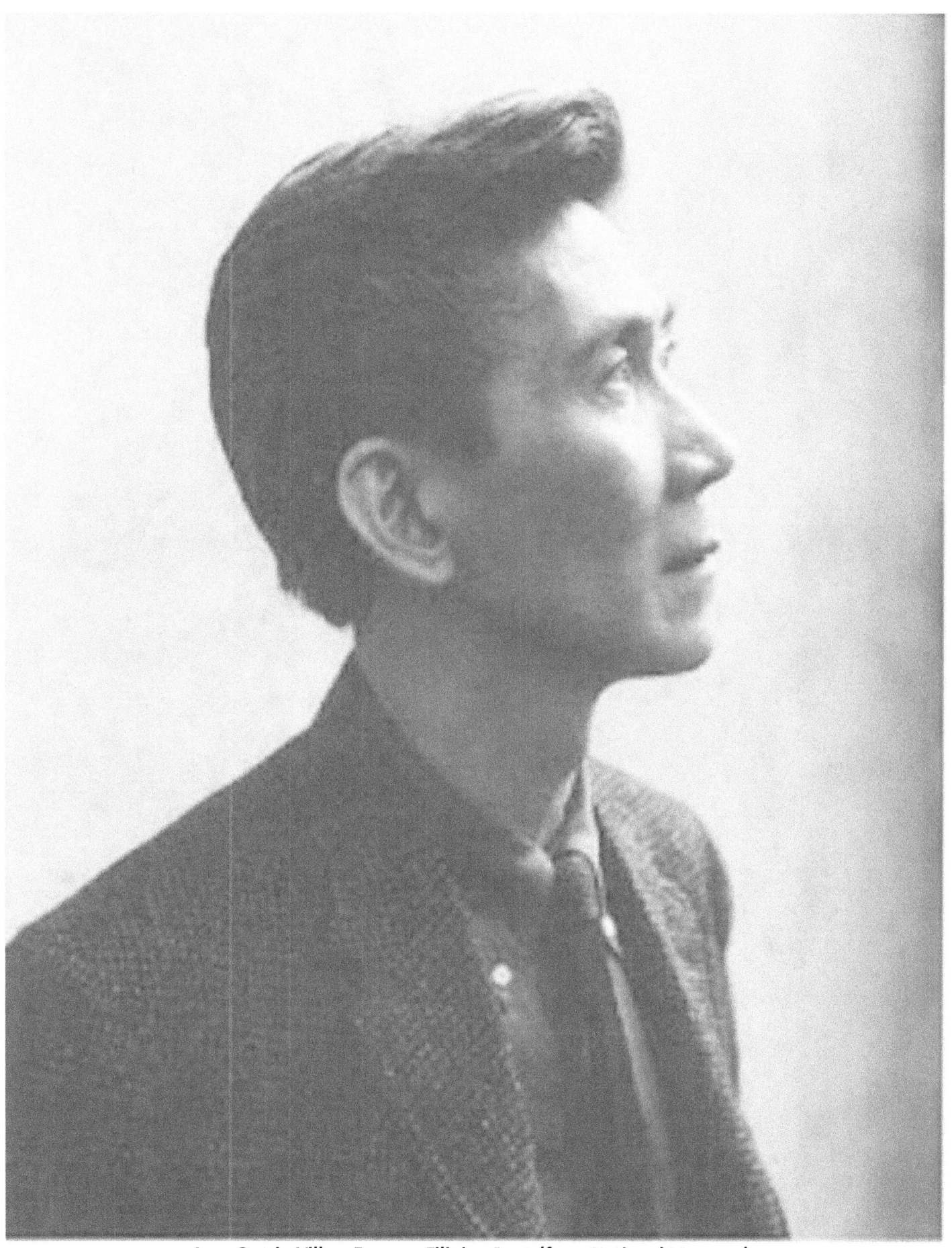

Jose Garcia Villa – Famous Filipino Poet (from National Museum)

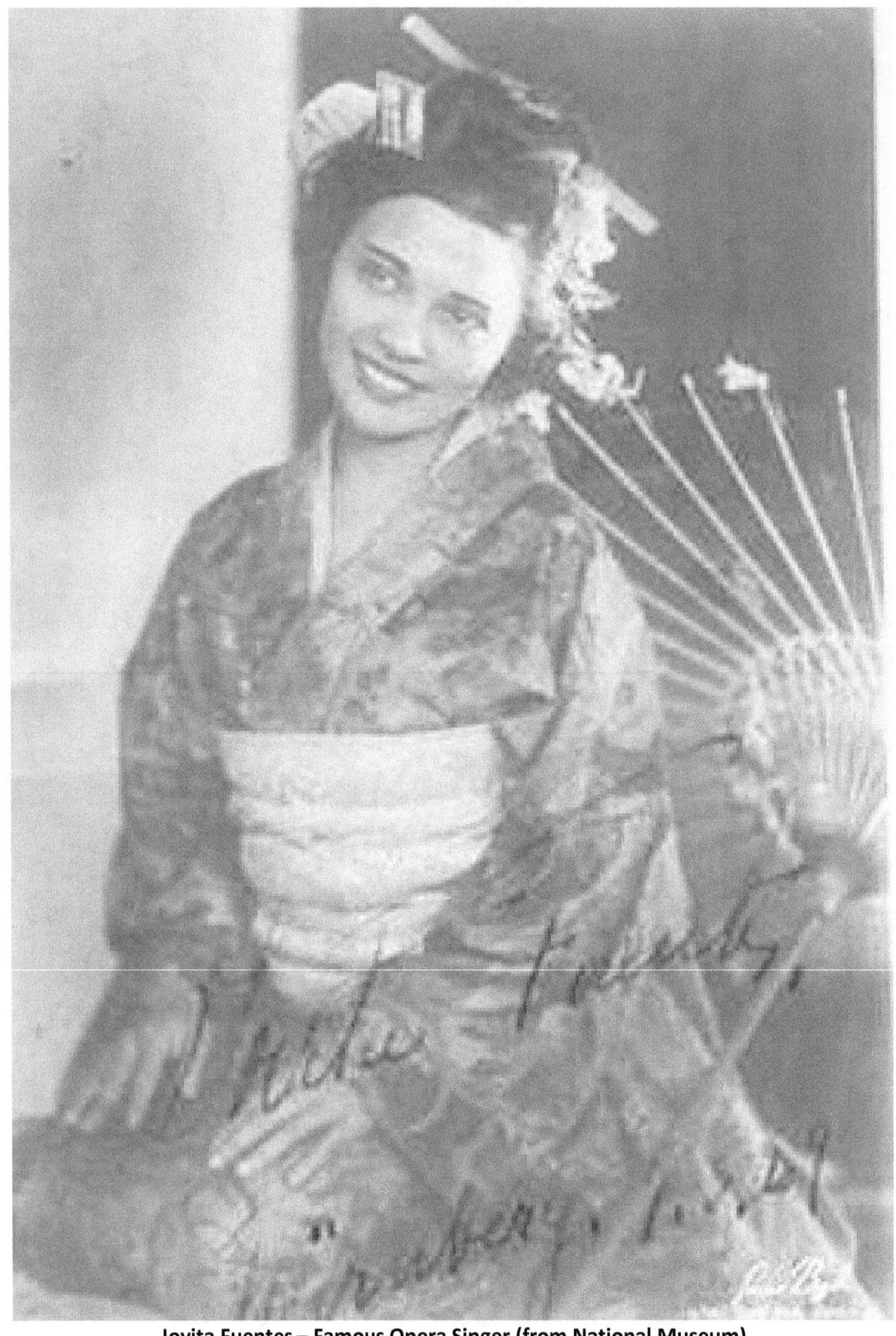

Jovita Fuentes – Famous Opera Singer (from National Museum)

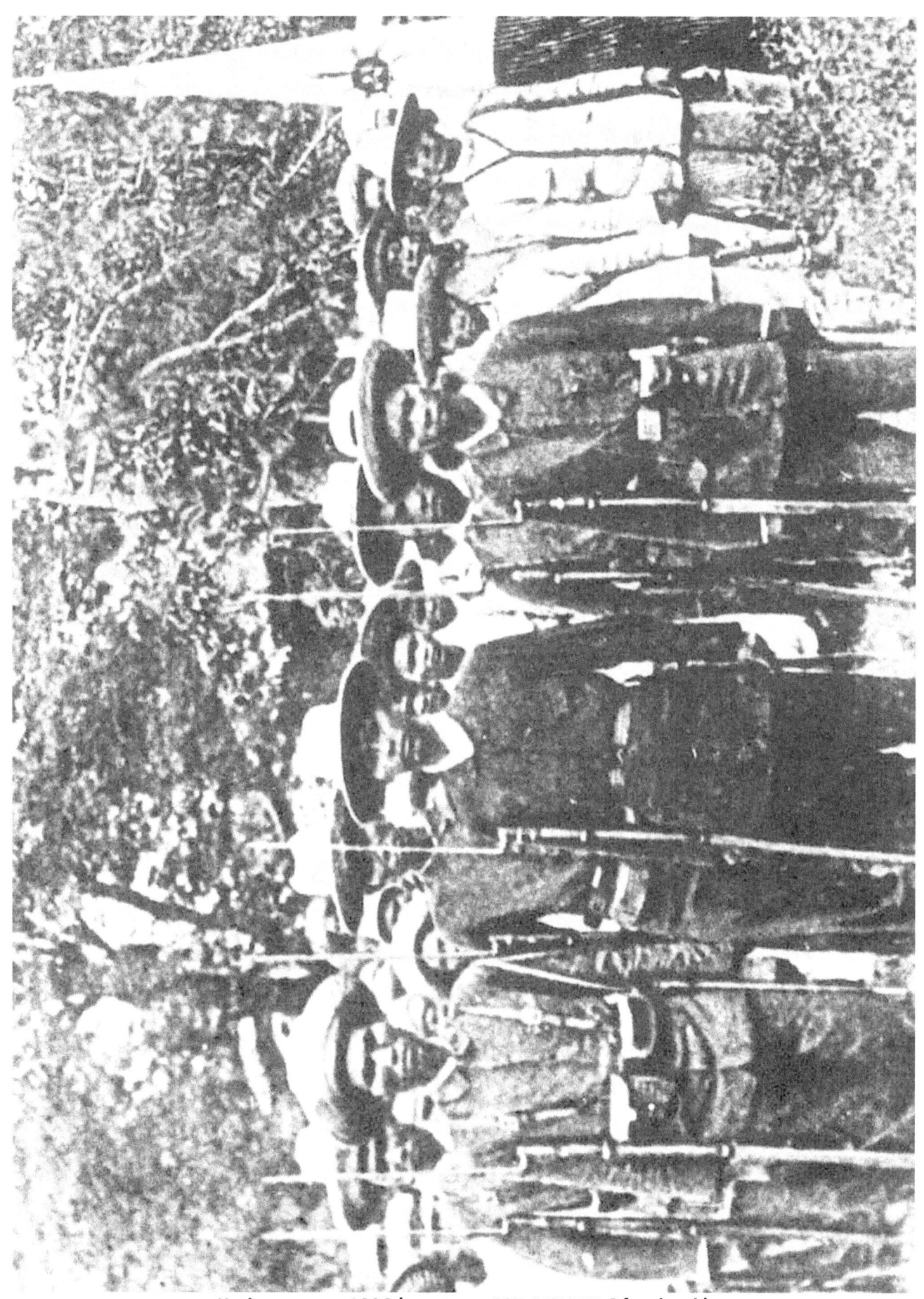

Katipuneros – 1896 (courtesy: PHL MY PHL@facebook)

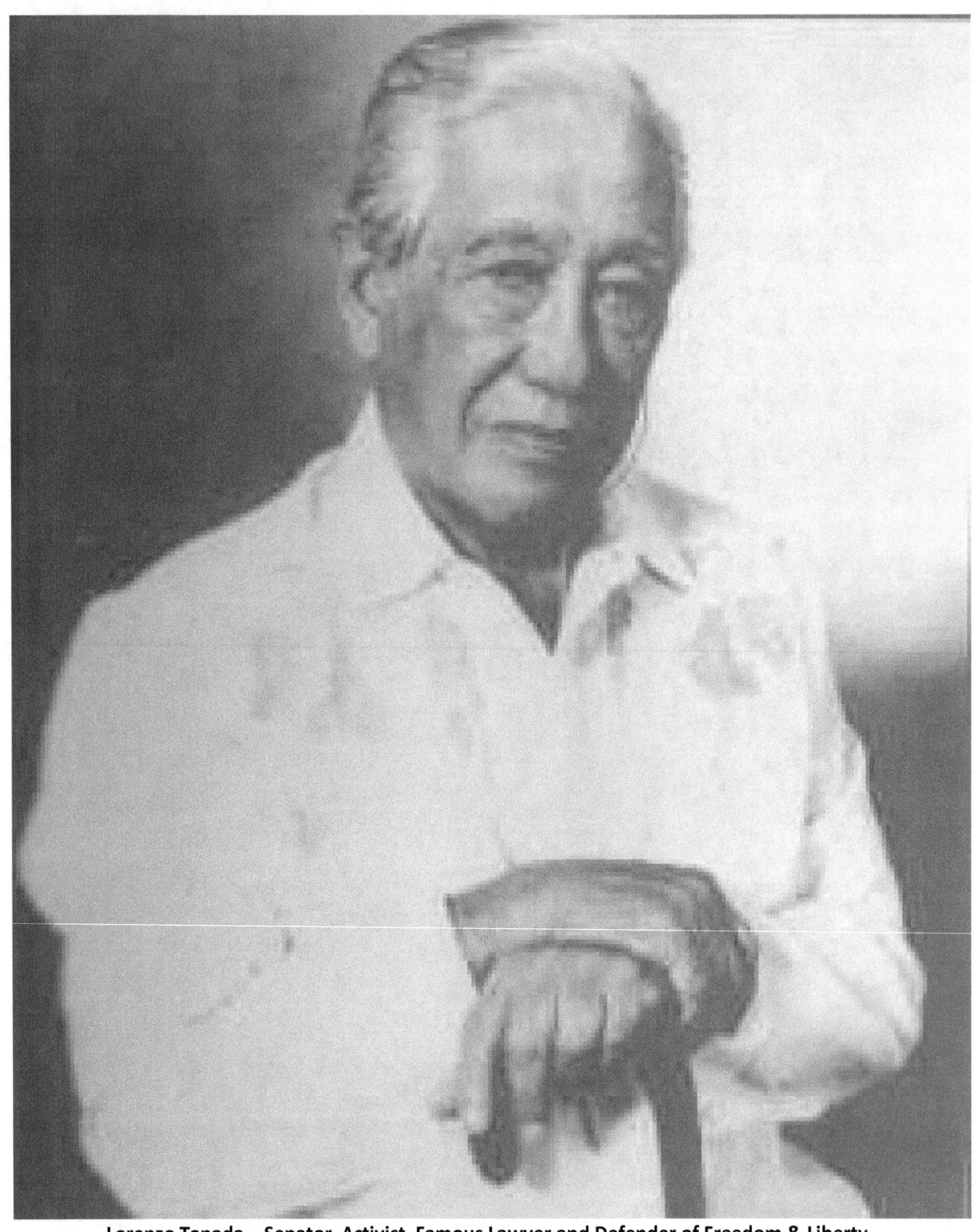

Lorenzo Tanada – Senator, Activist, Famous Lawyer and Defender of Freedom & Liberty
(courtesy: PHL MY PHL@facebook)

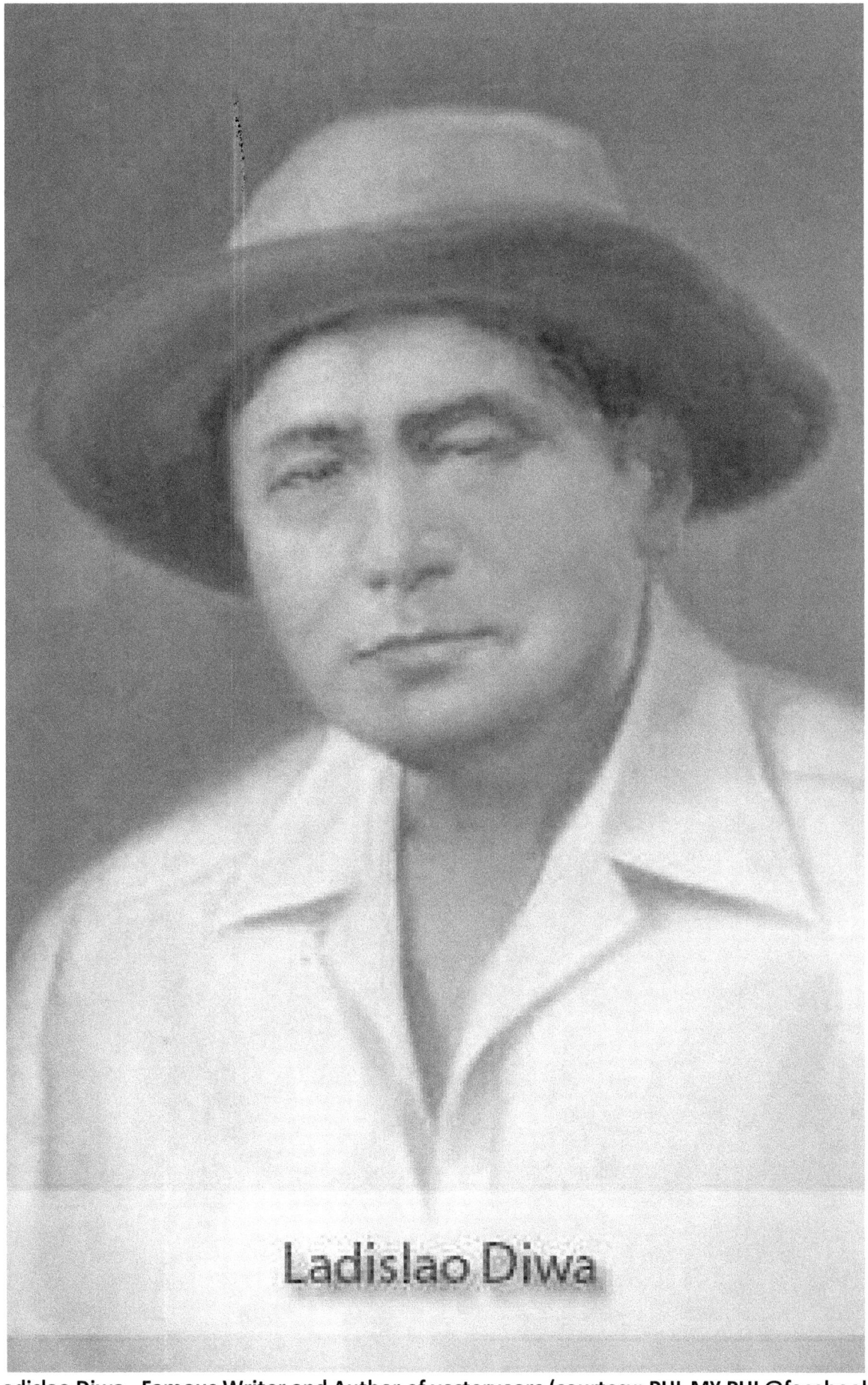

Ladislao Diwa

Ladislao Diwa - Famous Writer and Author of yesteryears (courtesy: PHL MY PHL@facebook)

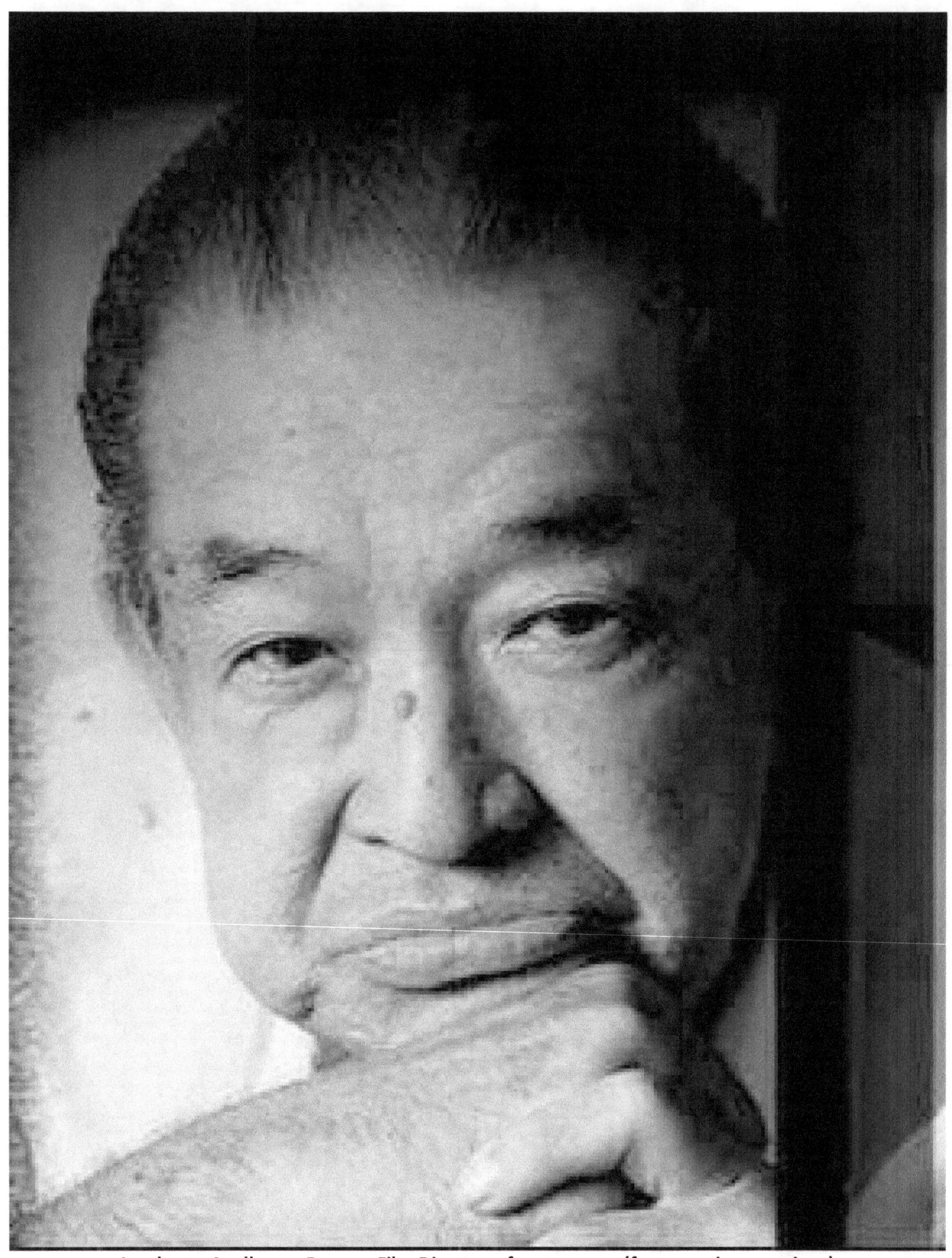

Lamberto Avellana – Famous Film Director of yesteryears (from movie magazines)

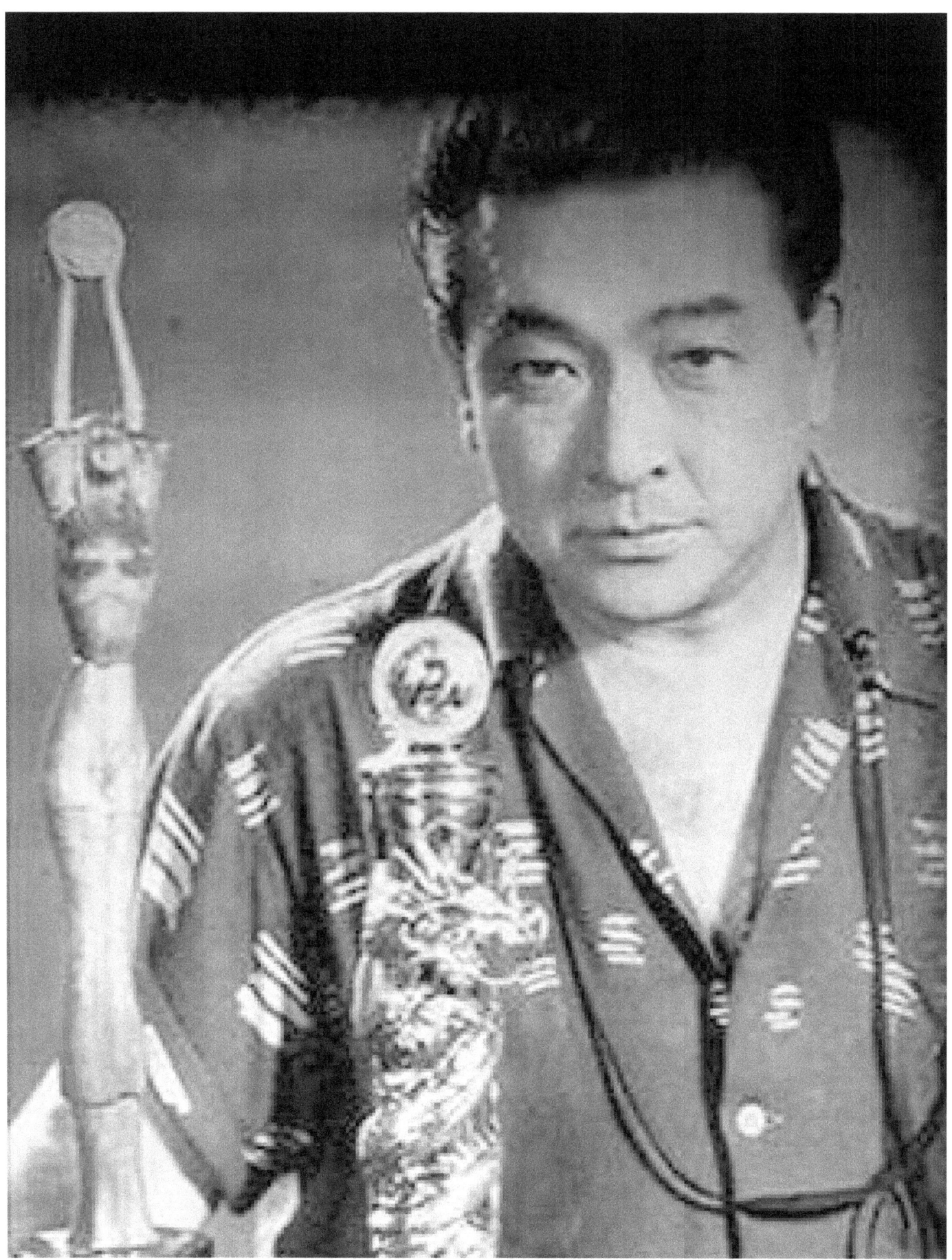

Lamberto Javellana – Famas Awardee as Director (from movie magazines)

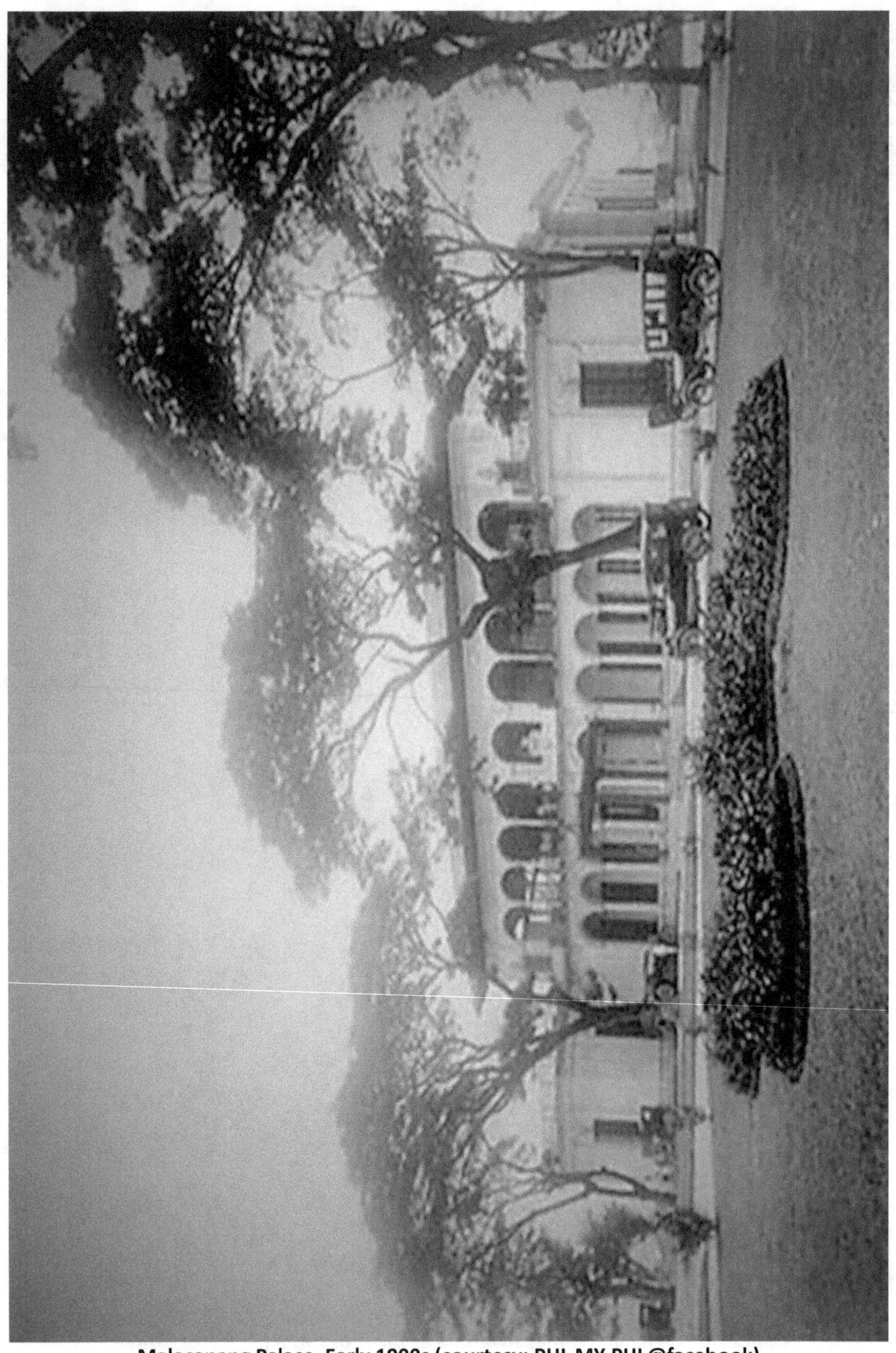

Malacanang Palace, Early 1900s (courtesy: PHL MY PHL@facebook)

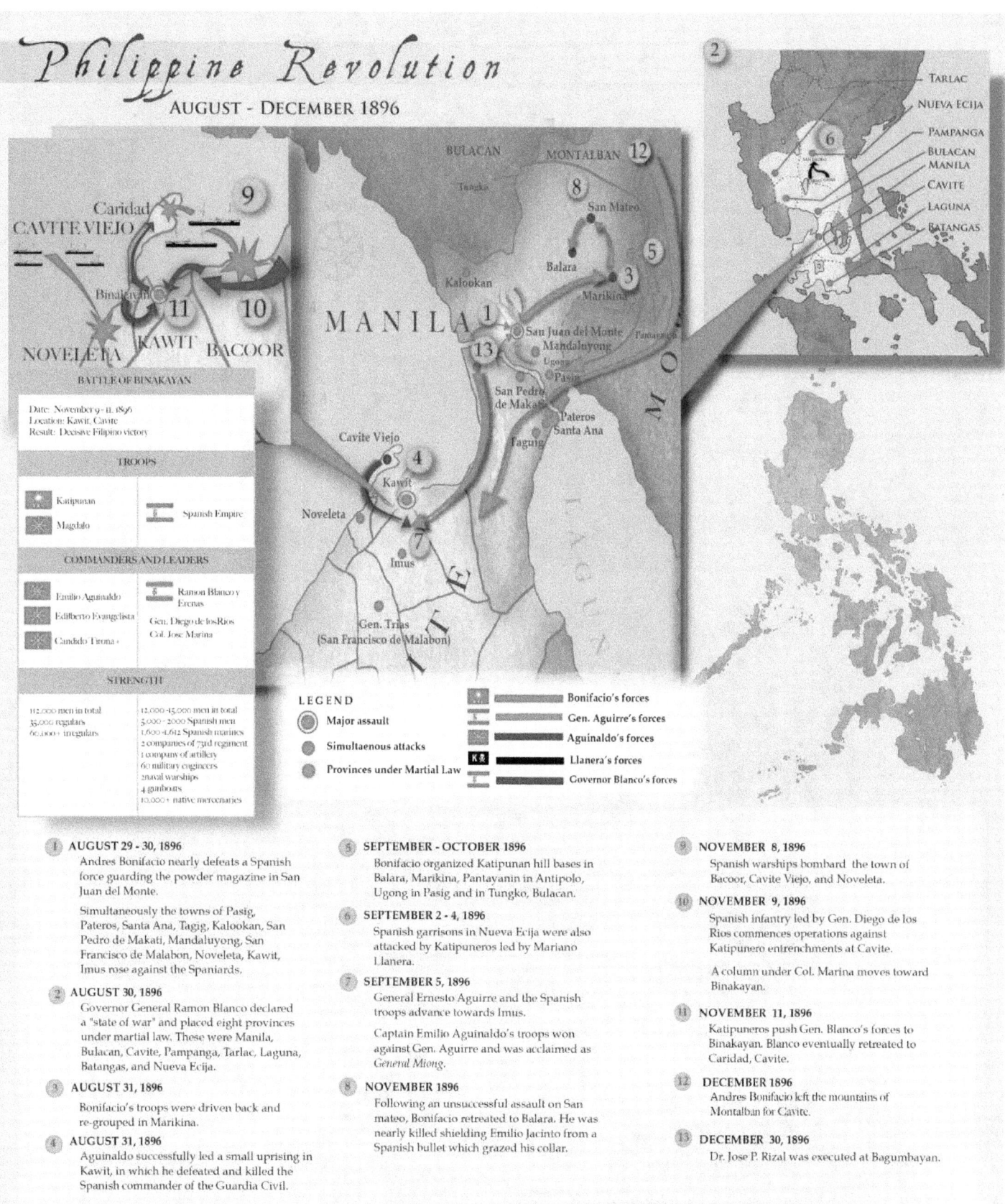

Philippine Revolution
AUGUST - DECEMBER 1896

BATTLE OF BINAKAYAN

Date: November 9 - 11, 1896
Location: Kawit, Cavite
Result: Decisive Filipino victory

TROOPS

| Katipunan | Spanish Empire |
| Magdalo | |

COMMANDERS AND LEADERS

Emilio Aguinaldo	Ramon Blanco y Erenas
Edilberto Evangelista	Gen. Diego de los Rios
Candido Tirona +	Col. Jose Marina

STRENGTH

112,000 men in total	12,000 -15,000 men in total
35,000 regulars	5,000 - 7000 Spanish men
60,000+ irregulars	1,600 -4,612 Spanish marines
	2 companies of 73rd regiment
	1 company of artillery
	60 military engineers
	2 naval warships
	4 gunboats
	10,000+ native mercenaries

LEGEND

- Major assault
- Simultaenous attacks
- Provinces under Martial Law

- Bonifacio's forces
- Gen. Aguirre's forces
- Aguinaldo's forces
- Llanera's forces
- Governor Blanco's forces

① AUGUST 29 - 30, 1896
Andres Bonifacio nearly defeats a Spanish force guarding the powder magazine in San Juan del Monte.

Simultaneously the towns of Pasig, Pateros, Santa Ana, Tagig, Kalookan, San Pedro de Makati, Mandaluyong, San Francisco de Malabon, Noveleta, Kawit, Imus rose against the Spaniards.

② AUGUST 30, 1896
Governor General Ramon Blanco declared a "state of war" and placed eight provinces under martial law. These were Manila, Bulacan, Cavite, Pampanga, Tarlac, Laguna, Batangas, and Nueva Ecija.

③ AUGUST 31, 1896
Bonifacio's troops were driven back and re-grouped in Marikina.

④ AUGUST 31, 1896
Aguinaldo successfully led a small uprising in Kawit, in which he defeated and killed the Spanish commander of the Guardia Civil.

⑤ SEPTEMBER - OCTOBER 1896
Bonifacio organized Katipunan hill bases in Balara, Marikina, Pantayanin in Antipolo, Ugong in Pasig and in Tungko, Bulacan.

⑥ SEPTEMBER 2 - 4, 1896
Spanish garrisons in Nueva Ecija were also attacked by Katipuneros led by Mariano Llanera.

⑦ SEPTEMBER 5, 1896
General Ernesto Aguirre and the Spanish troops advance towards Imus.

Captain Emilio Aguinaldo's troops won against Gen. Aguirre and was acclaimed as *General Miong.*

⑧ NOVEMBER 1896
Following an unsuccessful assault on San mateo, Bonifacio retreated to Balara. He was nearly killed shielding Emilio Jacinto from a Spanish bullet which grazed his collar.

⑨ NOVEMBER 8, 1896
Spanish warships bombard the town of Bacoor, Cavite Viejo, and Noveleta.

⑩ NOVEMBER 9, 1896
Spanish infantry led by Gen. Diego de los Rios commences operations against Katipunero entrenchments at Cavite.

A column under Col. Marina moves toward Binakayan.

⑪ NOVEMBER 11, 1896
Katipuneros push Gen. Blanco's forces to Binakayan. Blanco eventually retreated to Caridad, Cavite.

⑫ DECEMBER 1896
Andres Bonifacio left the mountains of Montalban for Cavite.

⑬ DECEMBER 30, 1896
Dr. Jose P. Rizal was executed at Bagumbayan.

1896 Philippine Revolution Chart (courtesy: PHL MY PHL@facebook)

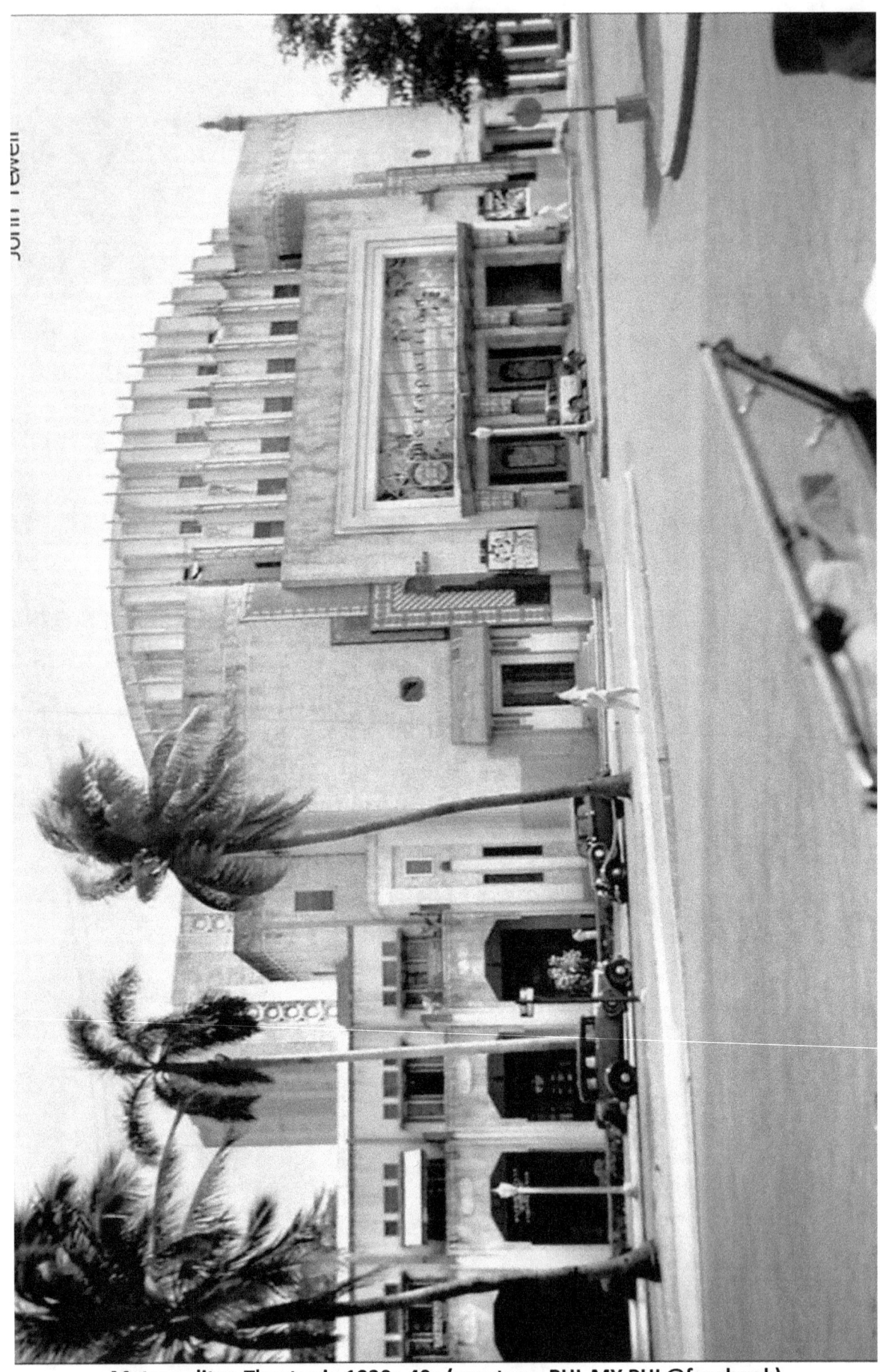

Metropolitan Theatre in 1930s-40s (courtesy: PHL MY PHL@facebook)

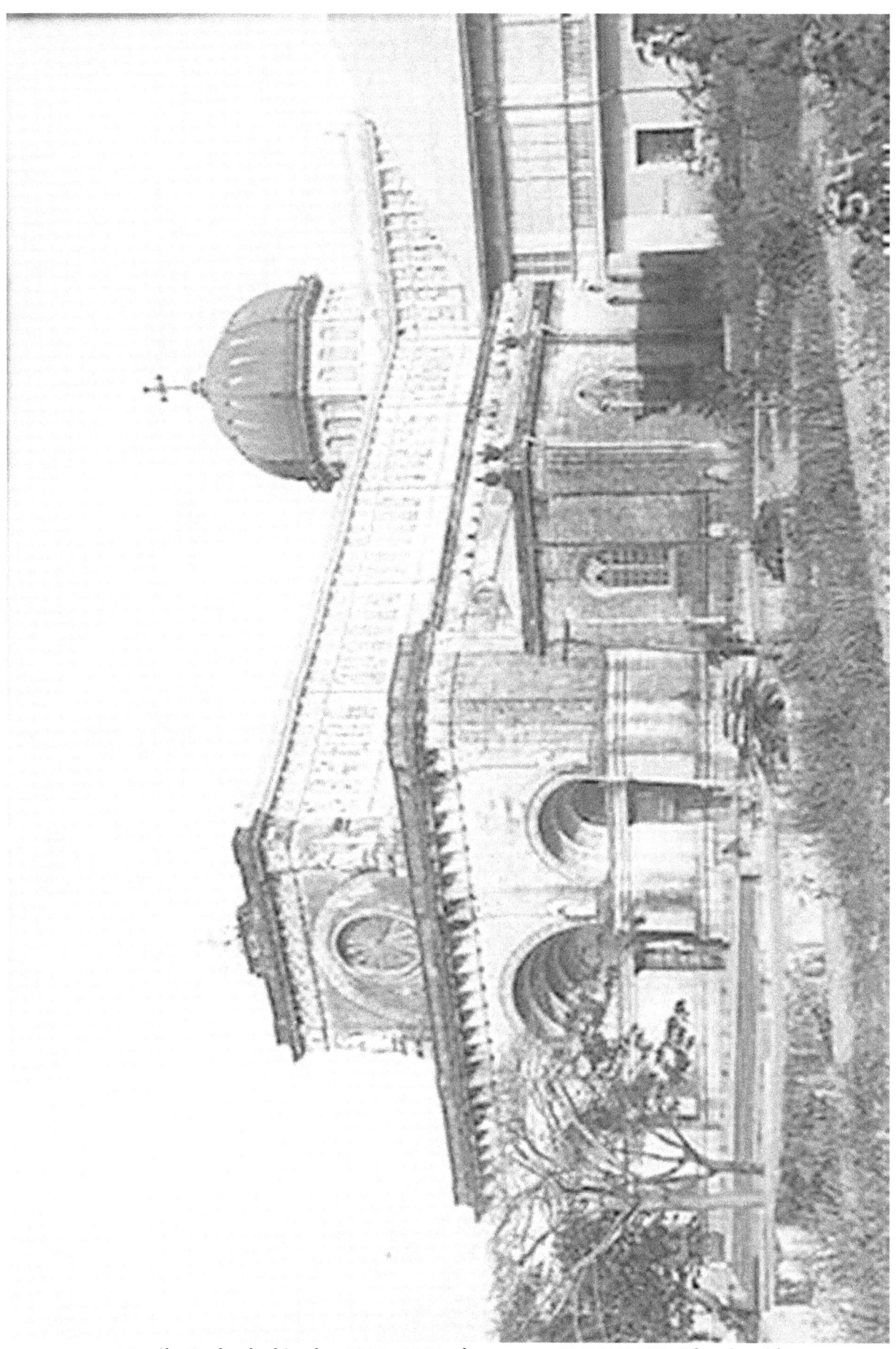

Manila Cathedral in the 1800=1900s (courtesy: PHL MY PHL@facebook)

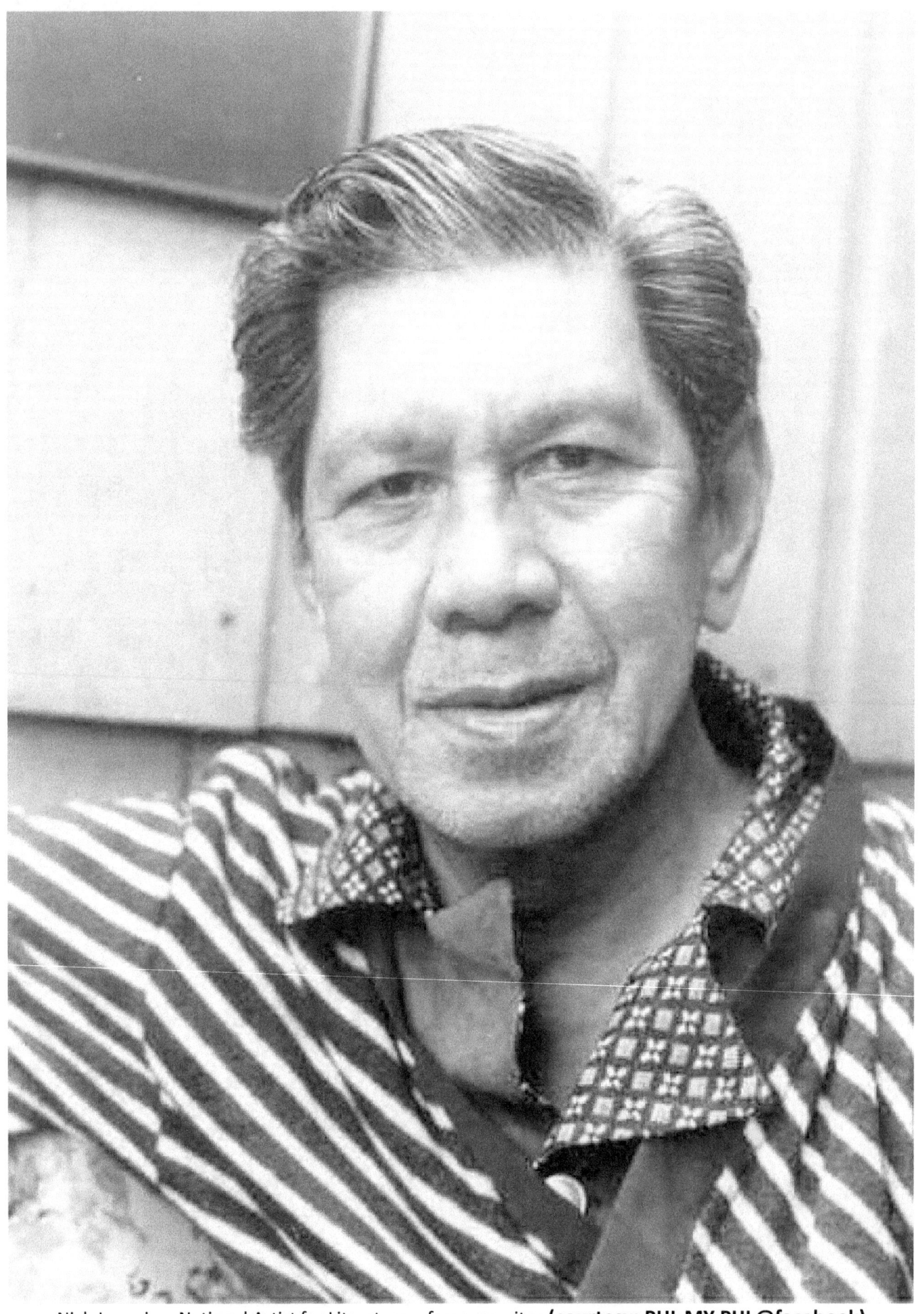

Nick Joaquin – National Artist for Literature – famous writer **(courtesy: PHL MY PHL@facebook)**

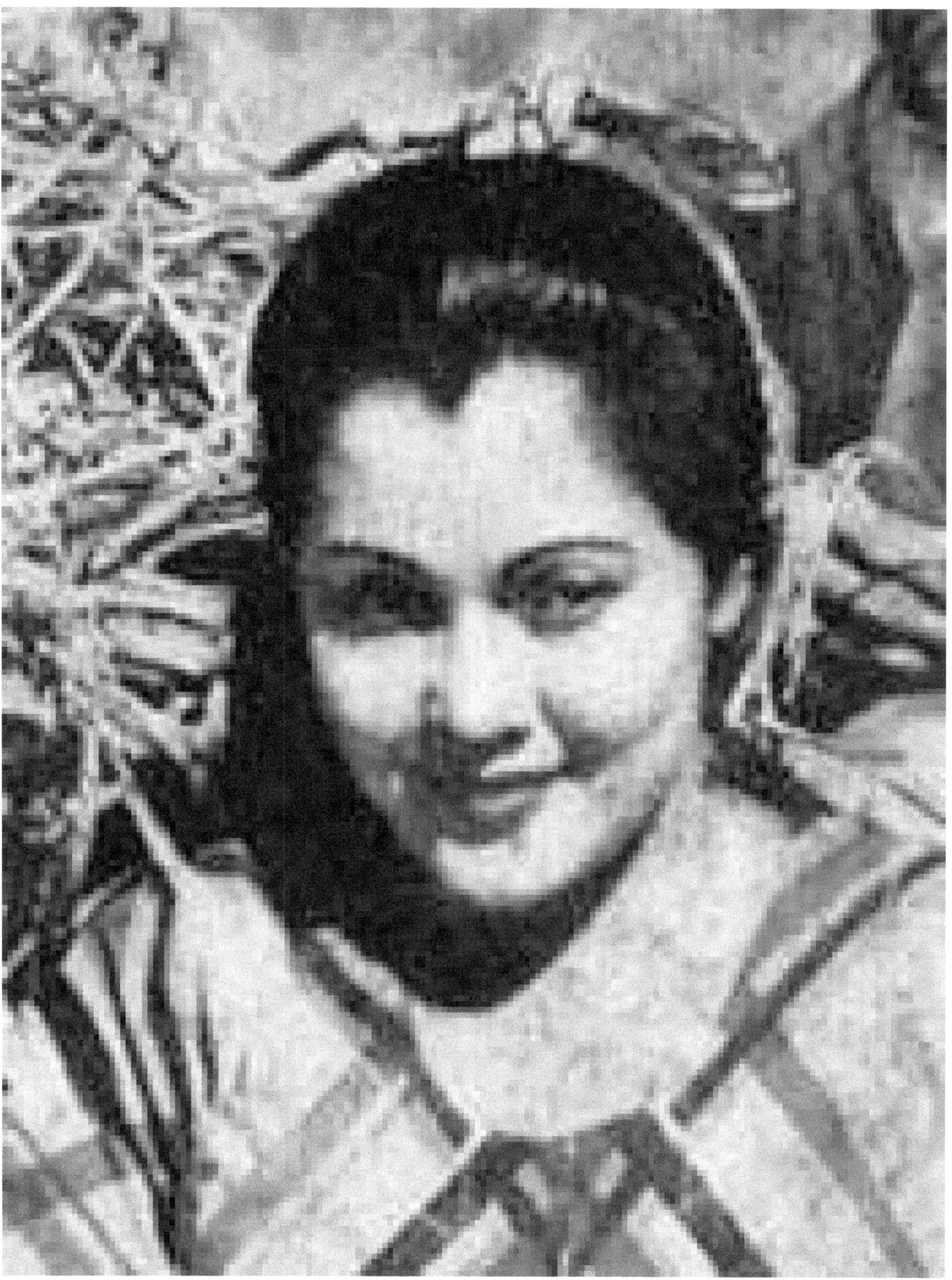

Norma Blancaflor – Famous star of yesteryears (from movie magazines)

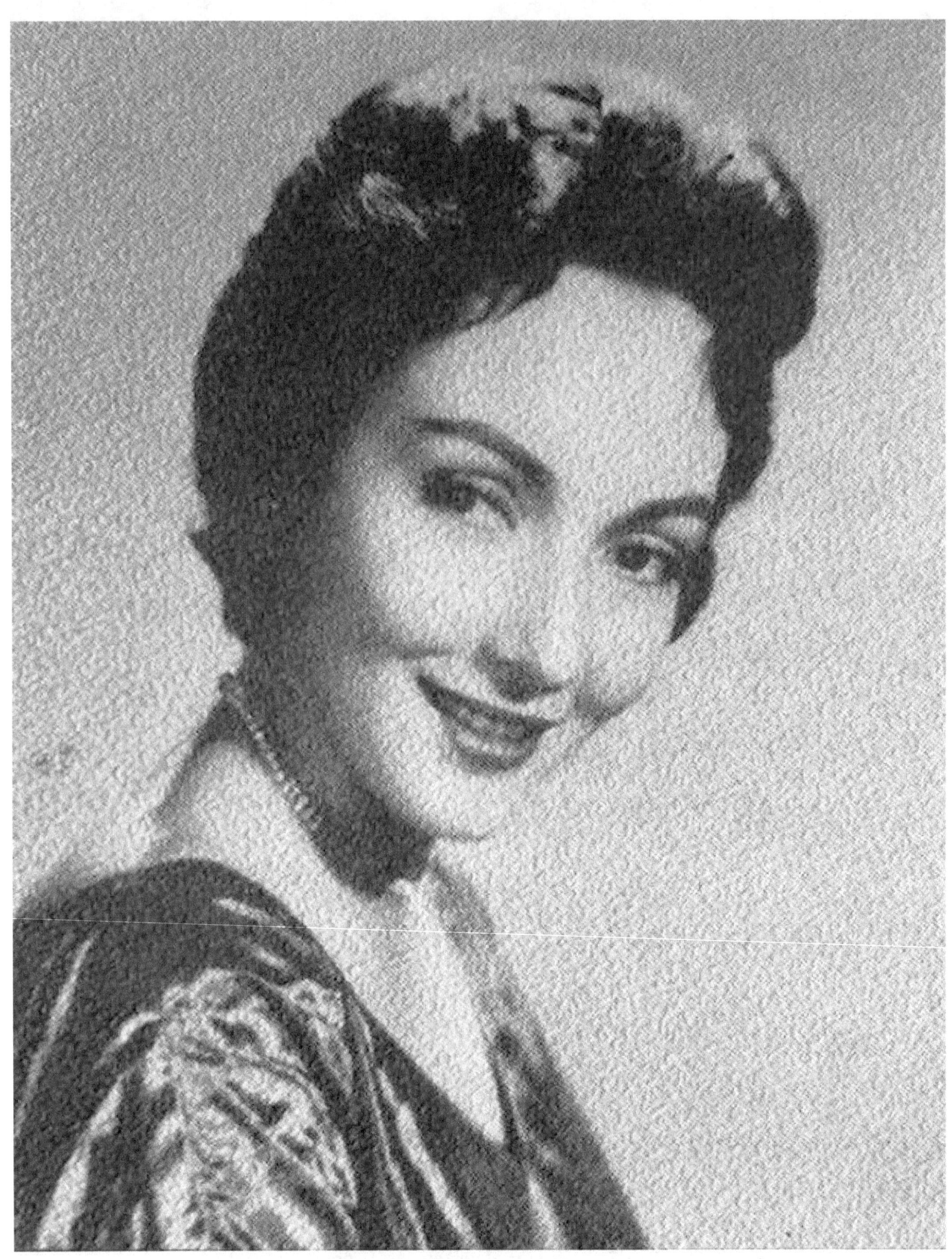

Paraluman – Famous star of yesteryears (from movie magazines)

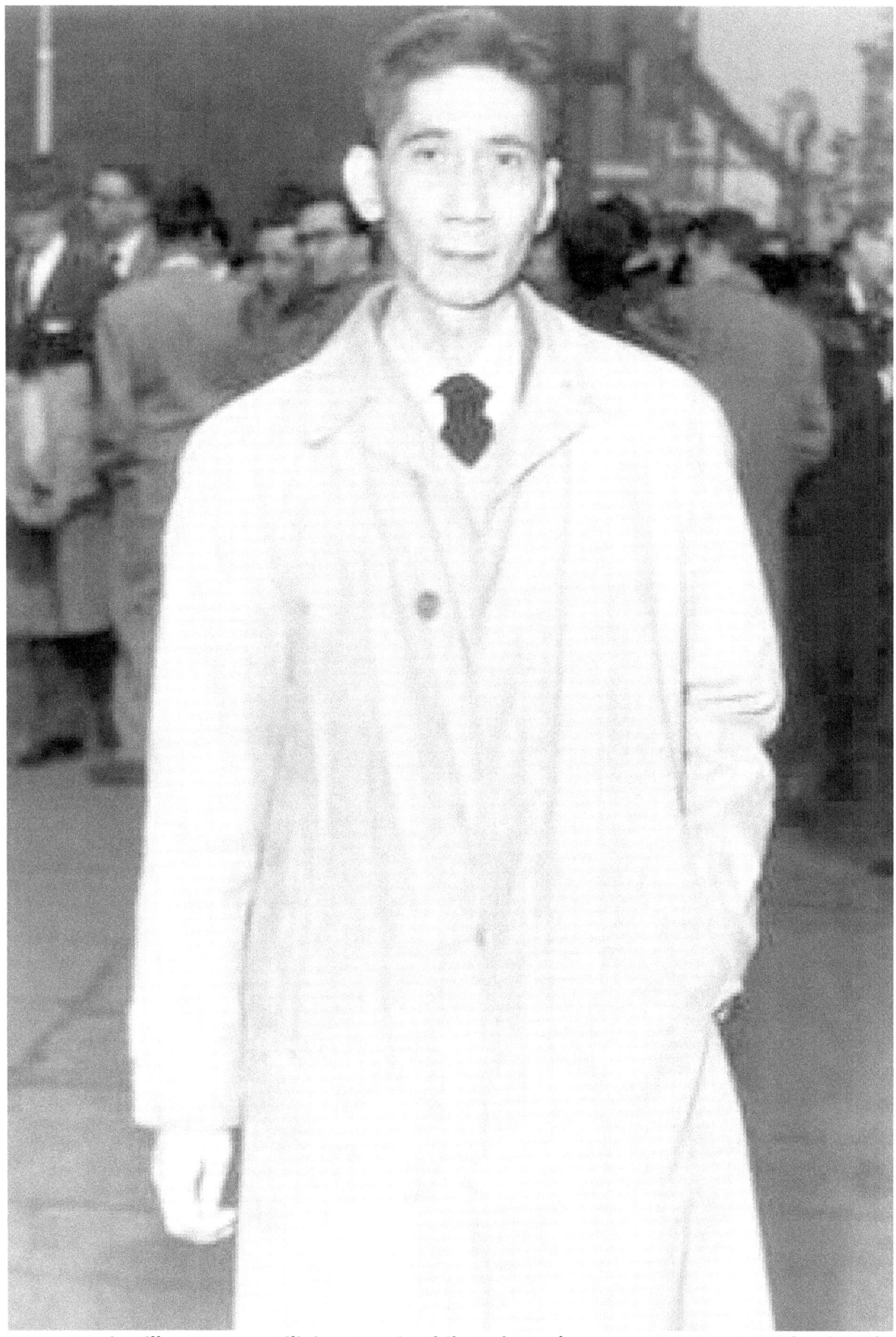

Jose Garcia Villa – Famous Filipino Poet in Phil. And USA (courtesy: PHL MY PHL@facebook)

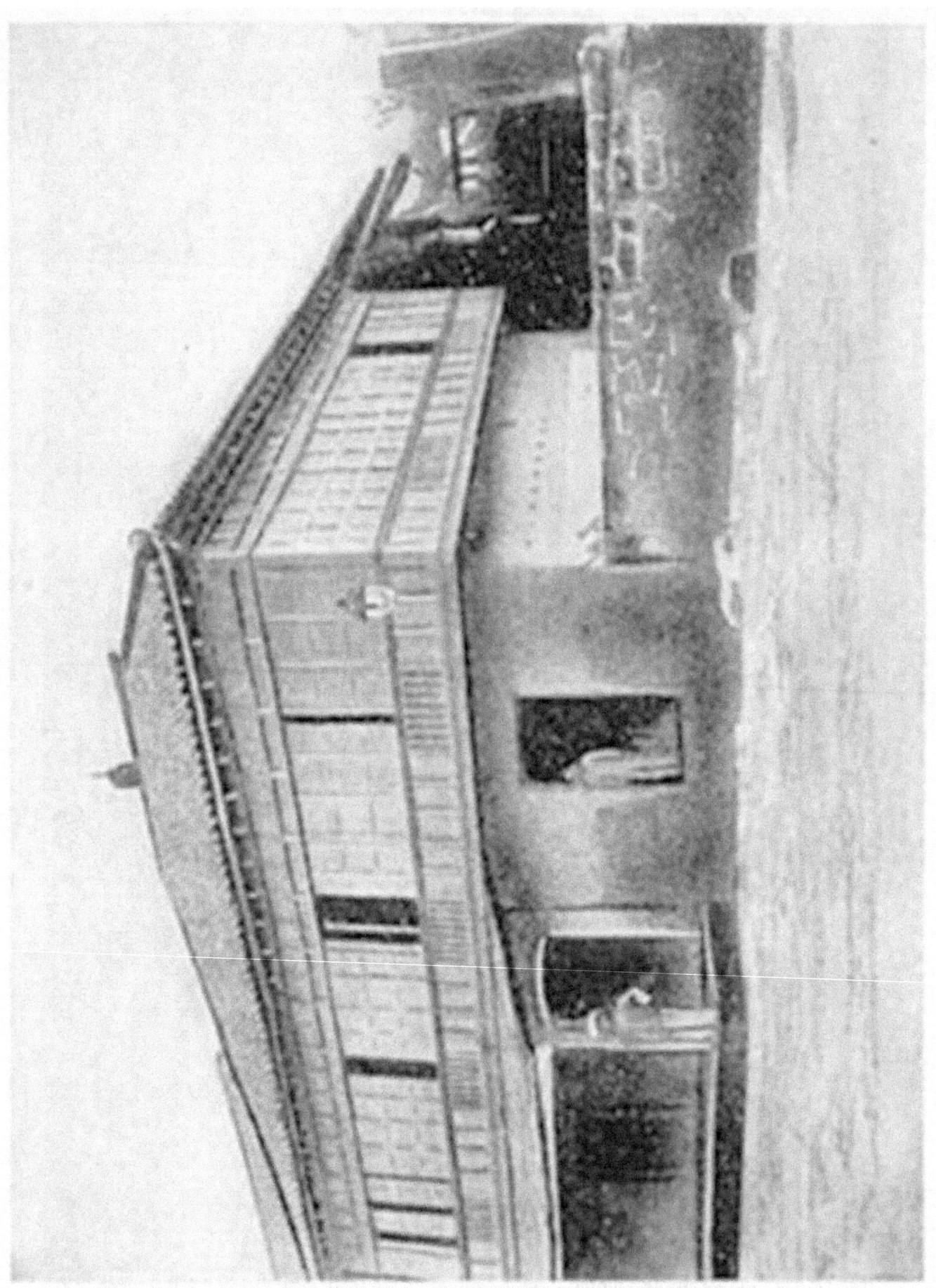

Original Rizal Home, his birthplace in Calamaba, Laguna, 1800s-1900s (courtesy: PHL MY PHL@facebook)

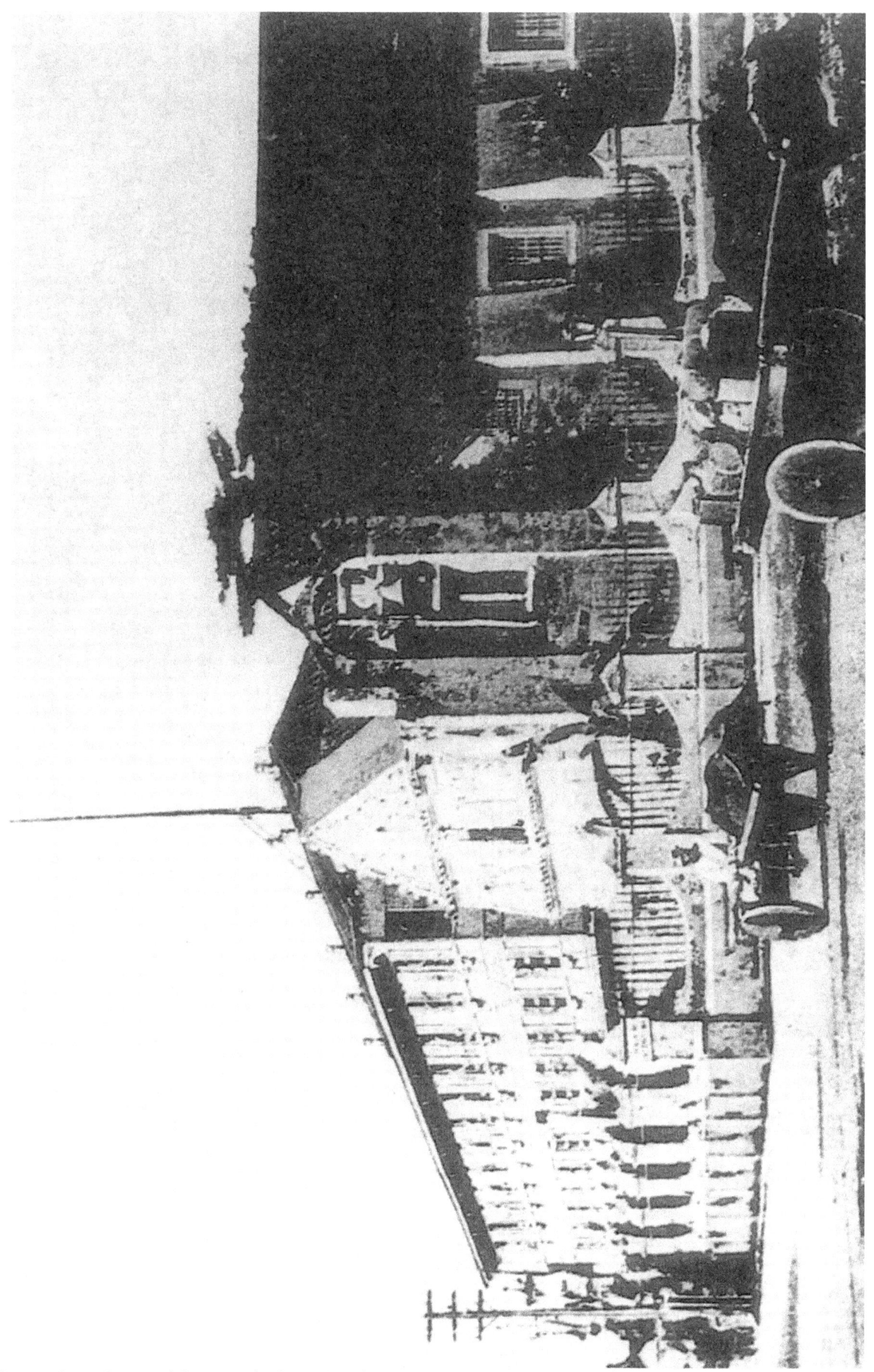

San Carlos University – Oldest Catholic School in Cebu, Visayan Region (courtesy: PHL MY PHL@facebook)

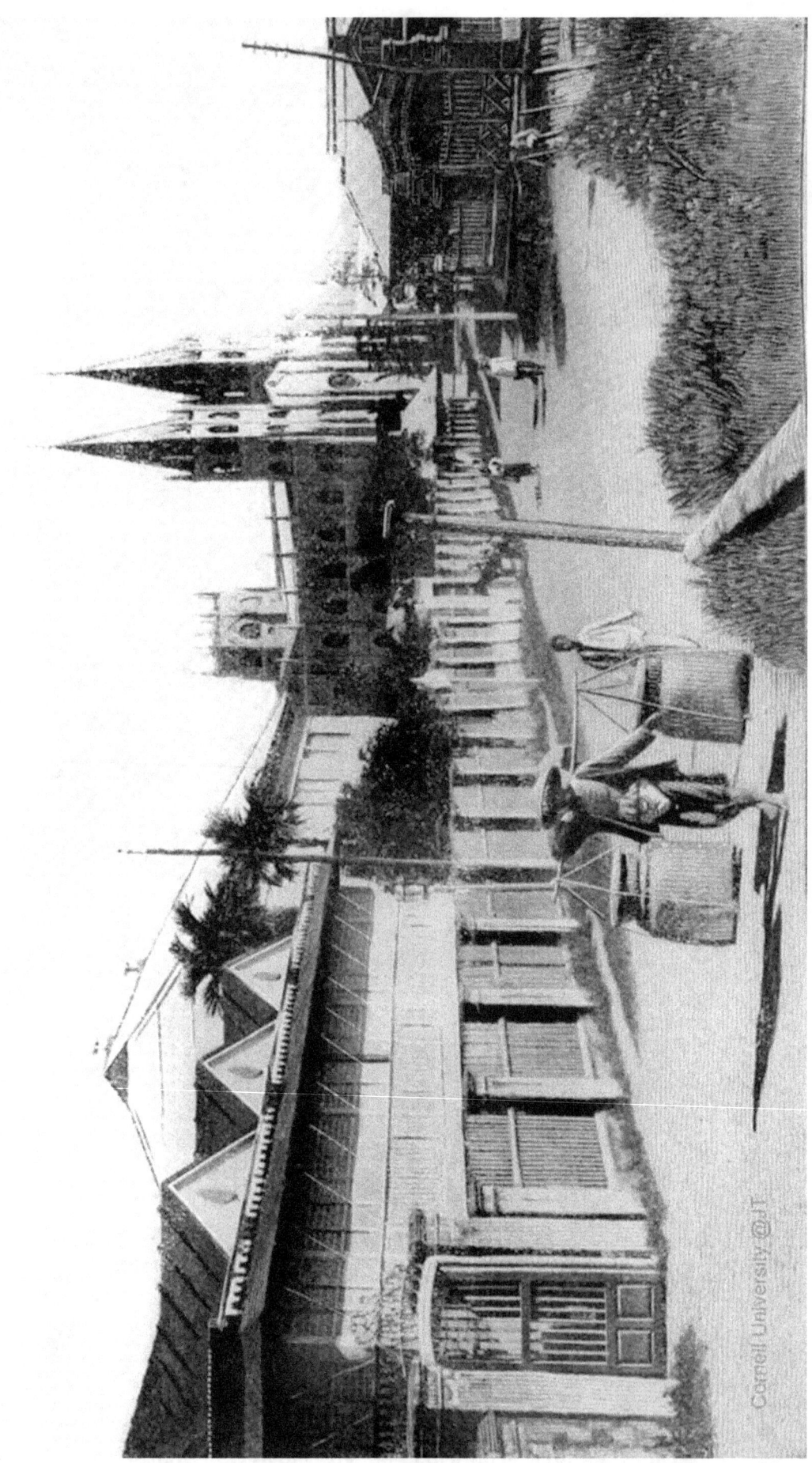

San Sebastian College in Manila, circa 1880 (courtesy: PHL MY PHL@facebook)

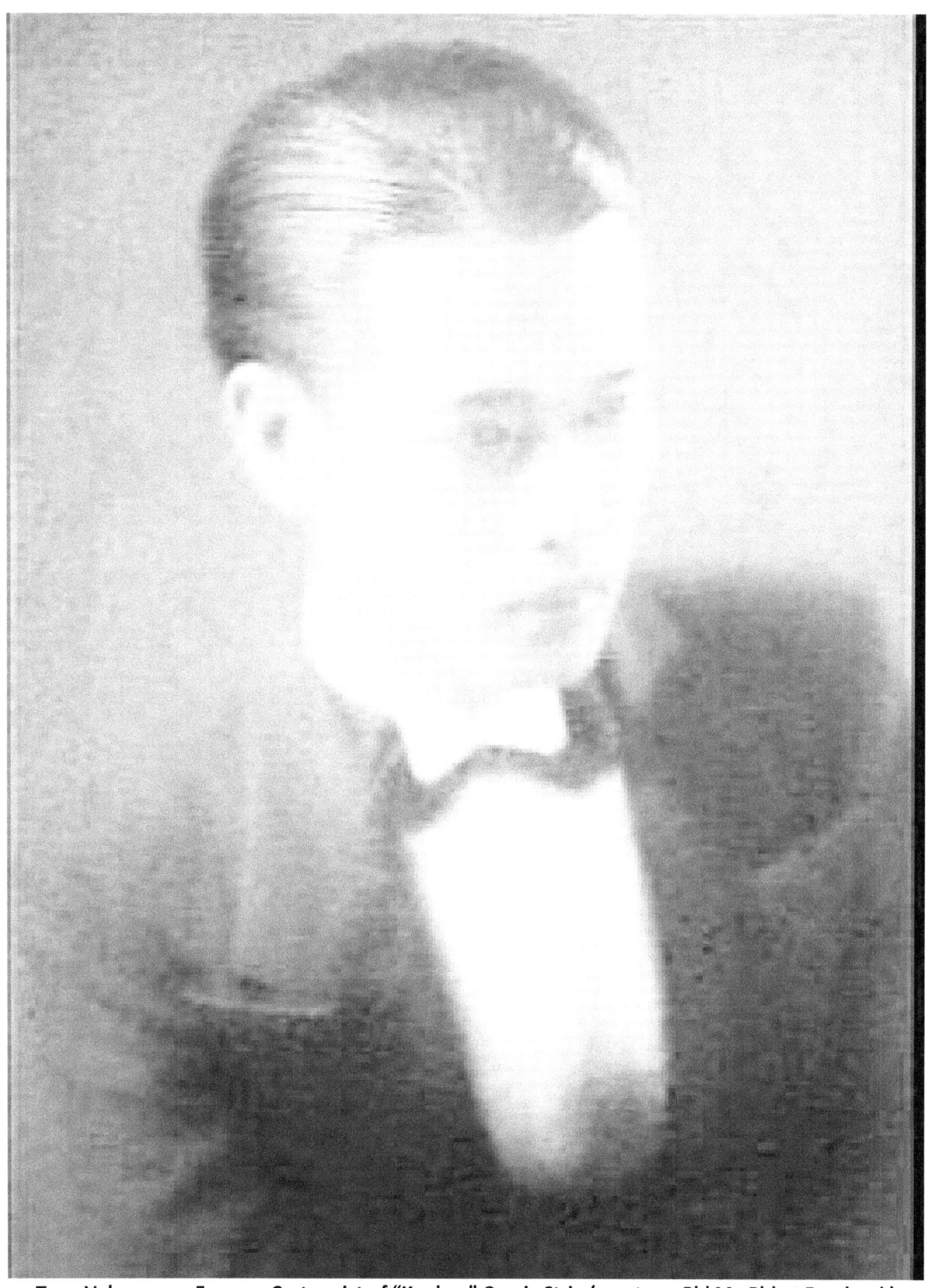

Tony Velasquez – Famous Cartoonist of "Kenkoy" Comic Strip (courtesy: Phl My Phl at Facebook)

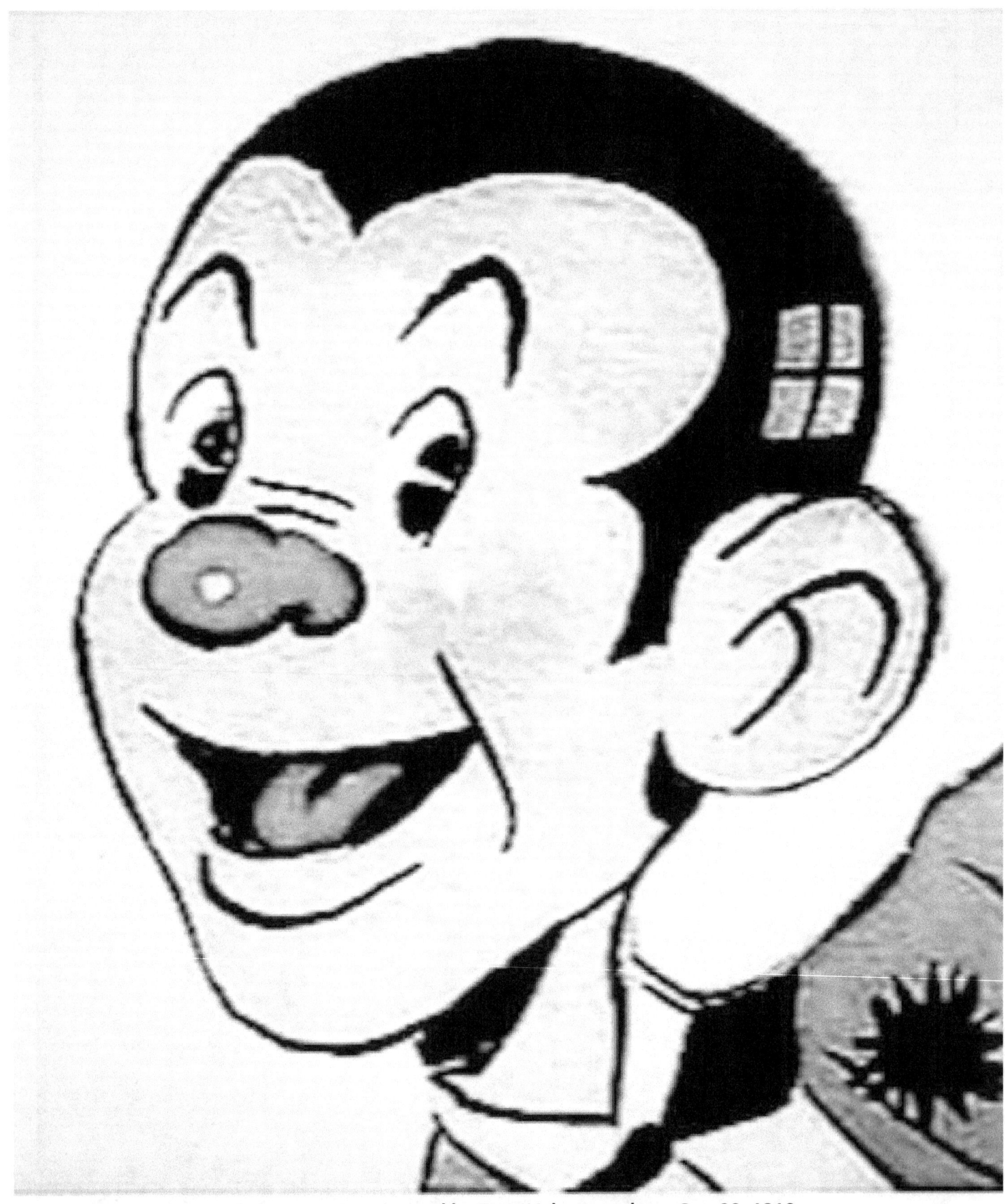

**KENKOY COMICS – Created by Tony Velasquez, born Oct. 29, 1910
(courtesy: Phl My Phl at Facebook)**

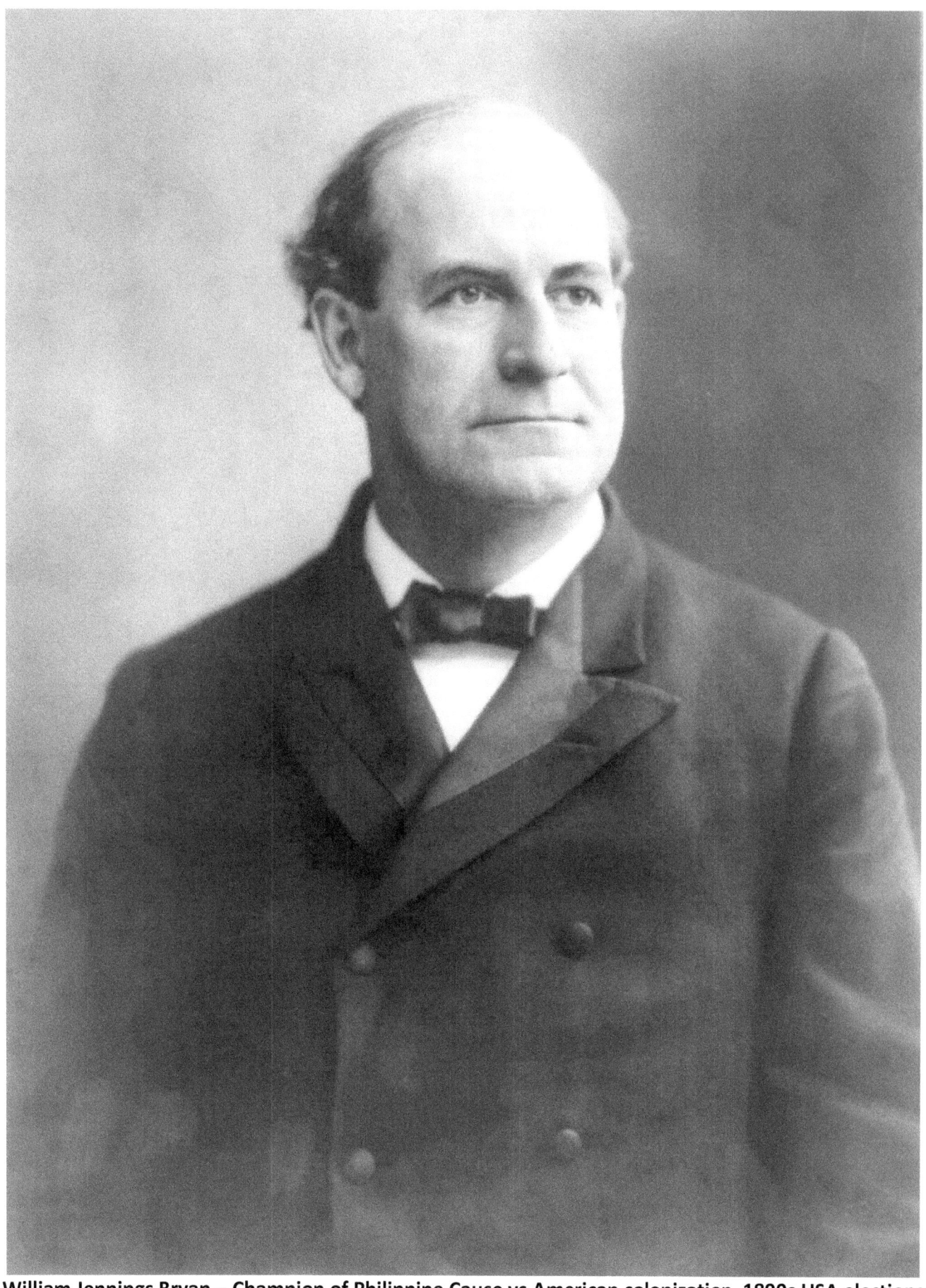

**William Jennings Bryan – Champion of Philippine Cause vs American colonization, 1890s USA elections
(courtesy: Phl My Phl at Facebook)**

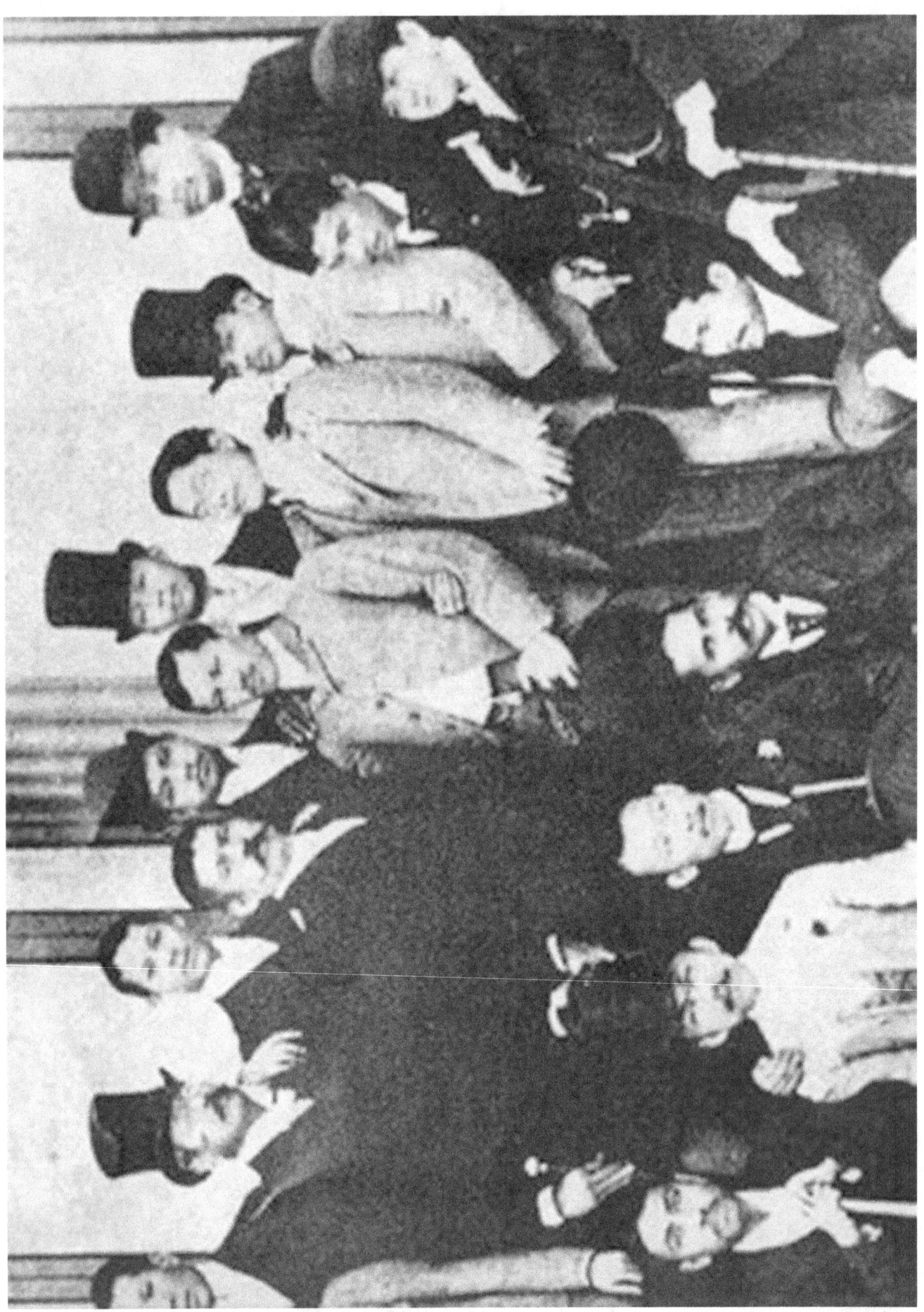

Marcelo Del Pilar and Jose Rizal with compatriots in Madrid (courtesy: Phl My Phl at Facebook)

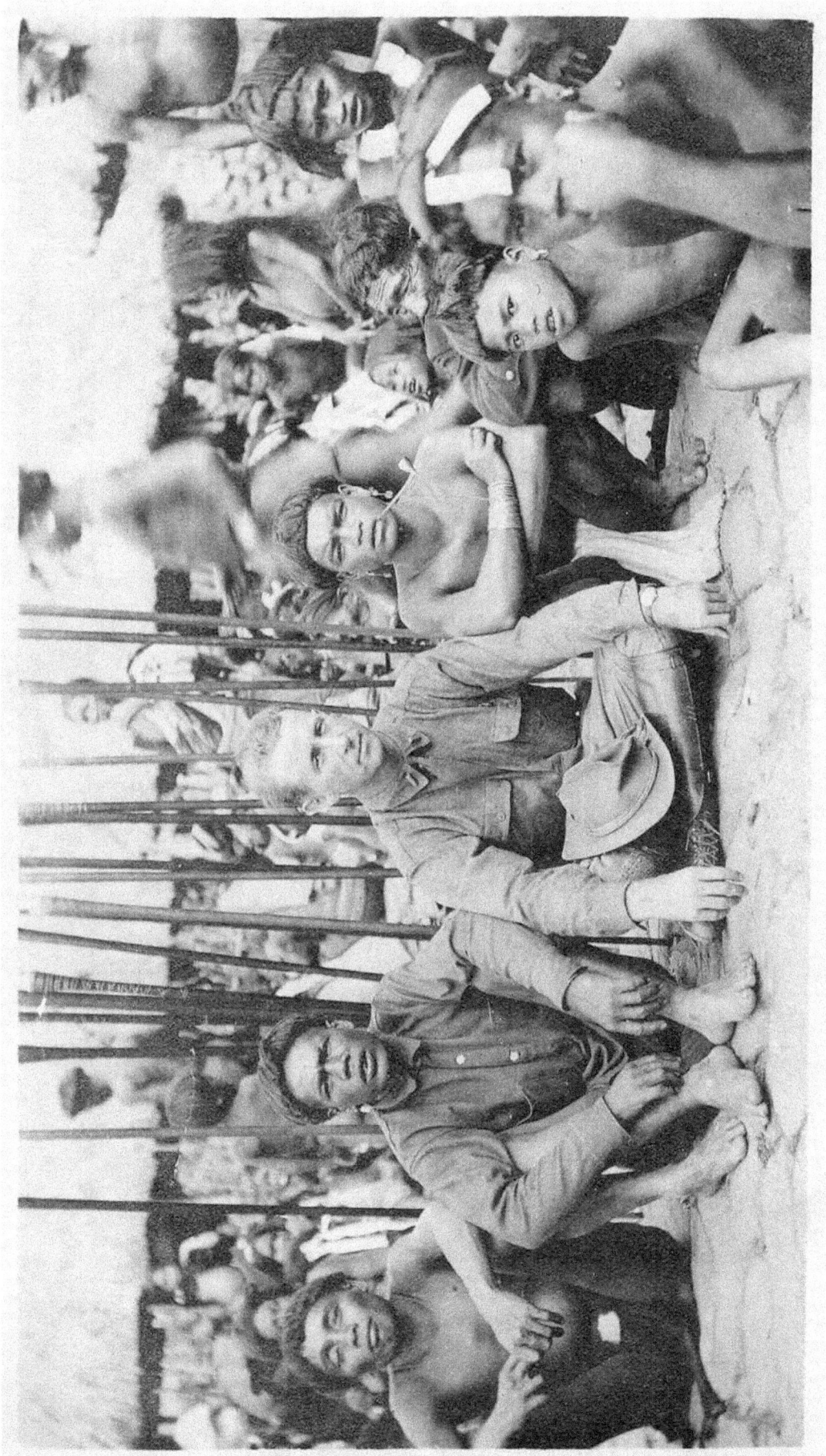

Mangyans of Mindoro, 1900s + American Soldier (courtesy: Phl My Phl at Facebook)

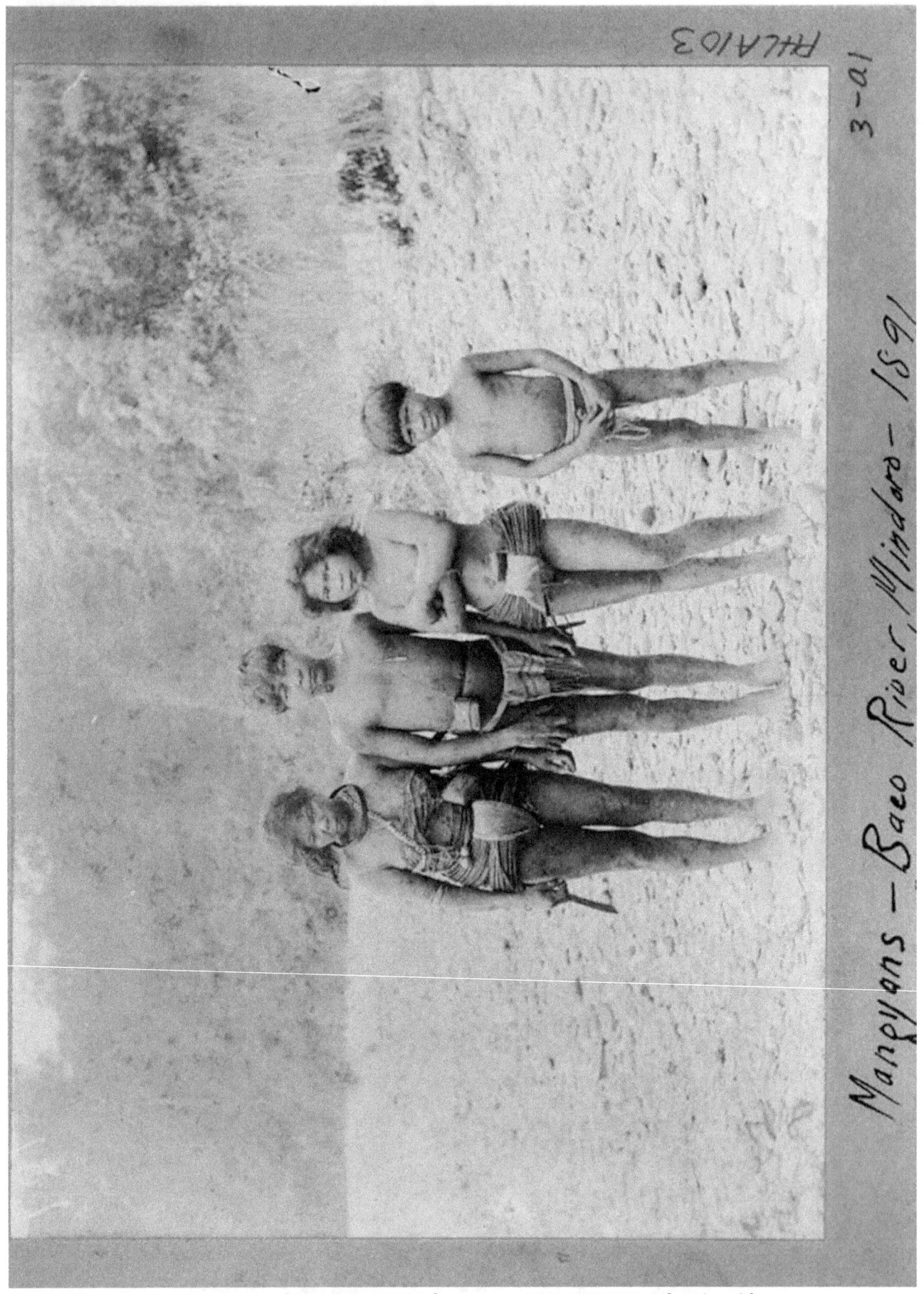

Mangyans – Baco River, Mindoro – 1891

PHLA103

3-01

Mangyans of Mindoro, 1891 (courtesy: PHL MY PHIL@facebook)

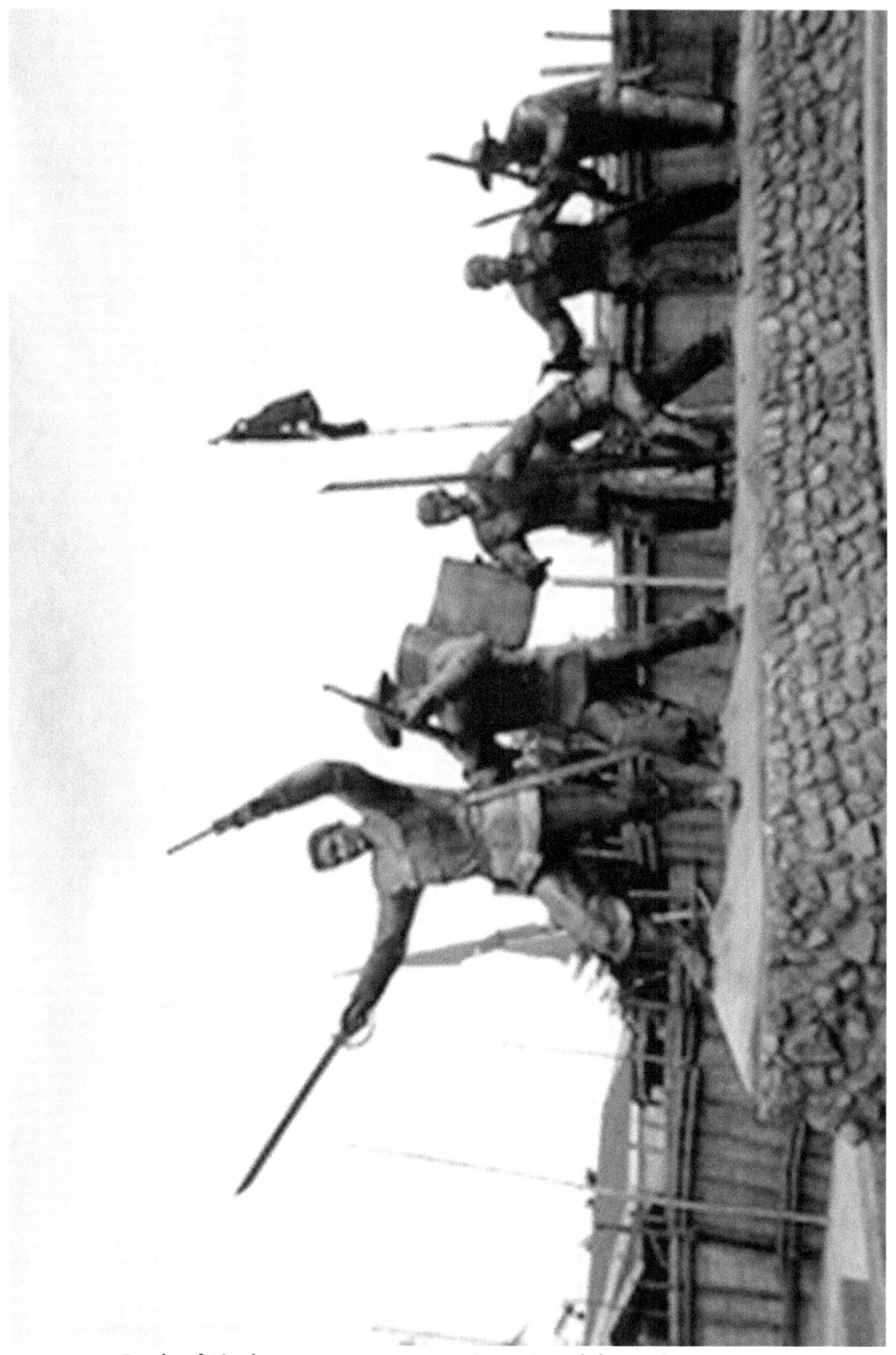

Battle of Binakayan Monument, Kawit, Cavite, Phil. Revolution, 1896

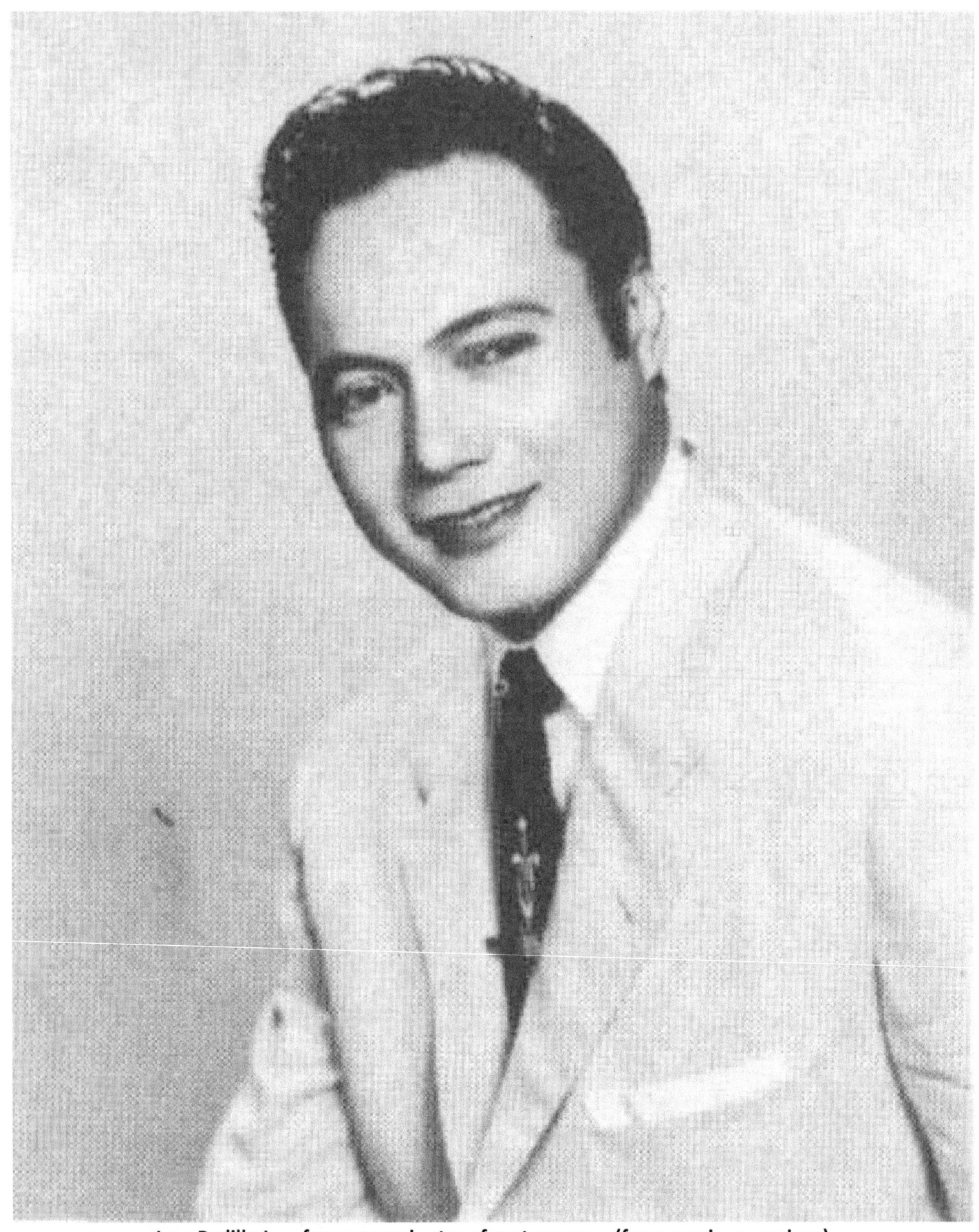

Jose Padilla Jr. = famous movie star of yesteryears – (from movie magazines)

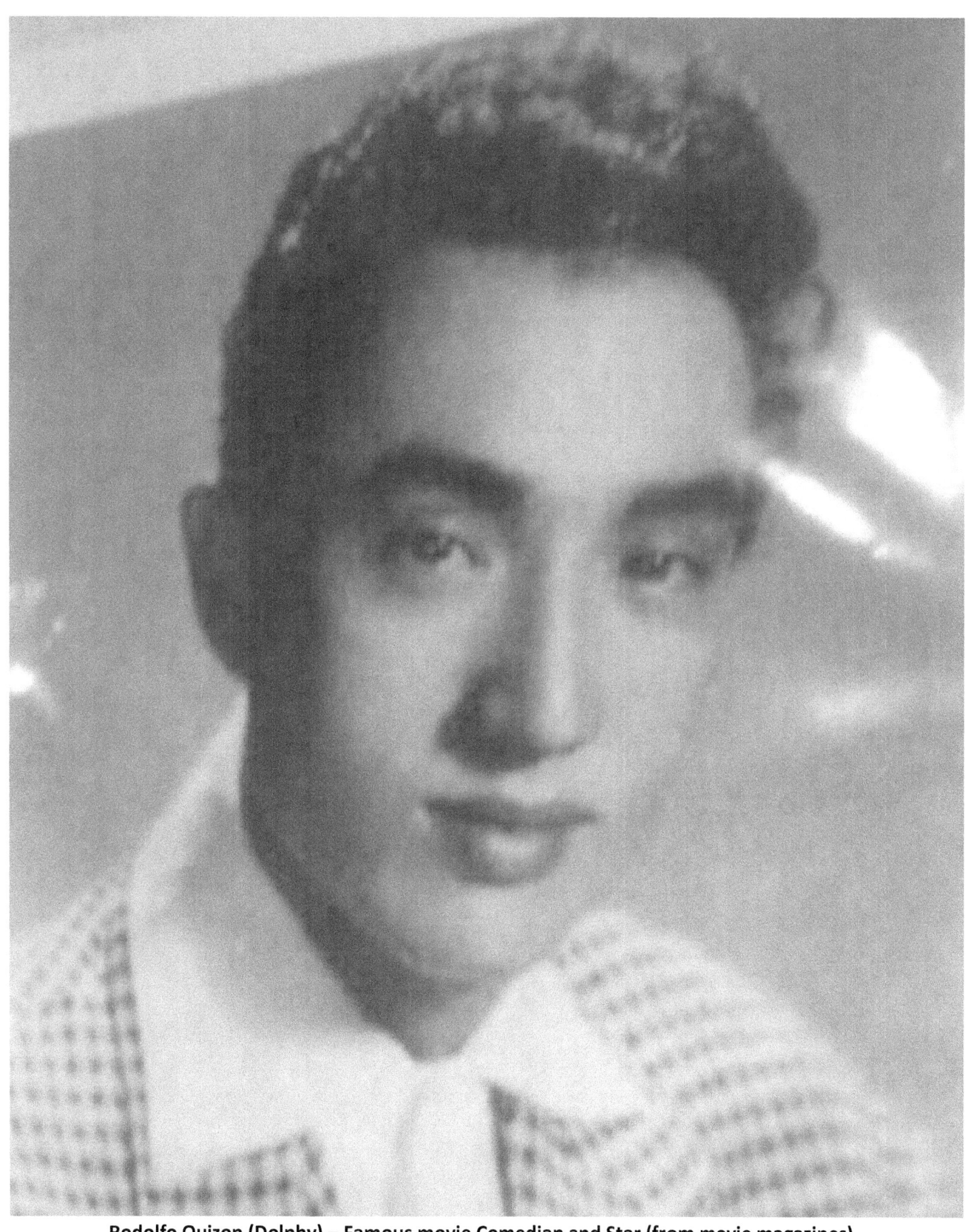

Rodolfo Quizon (Dolphy) – Famous movie Comedian and Star (from movie magazines)

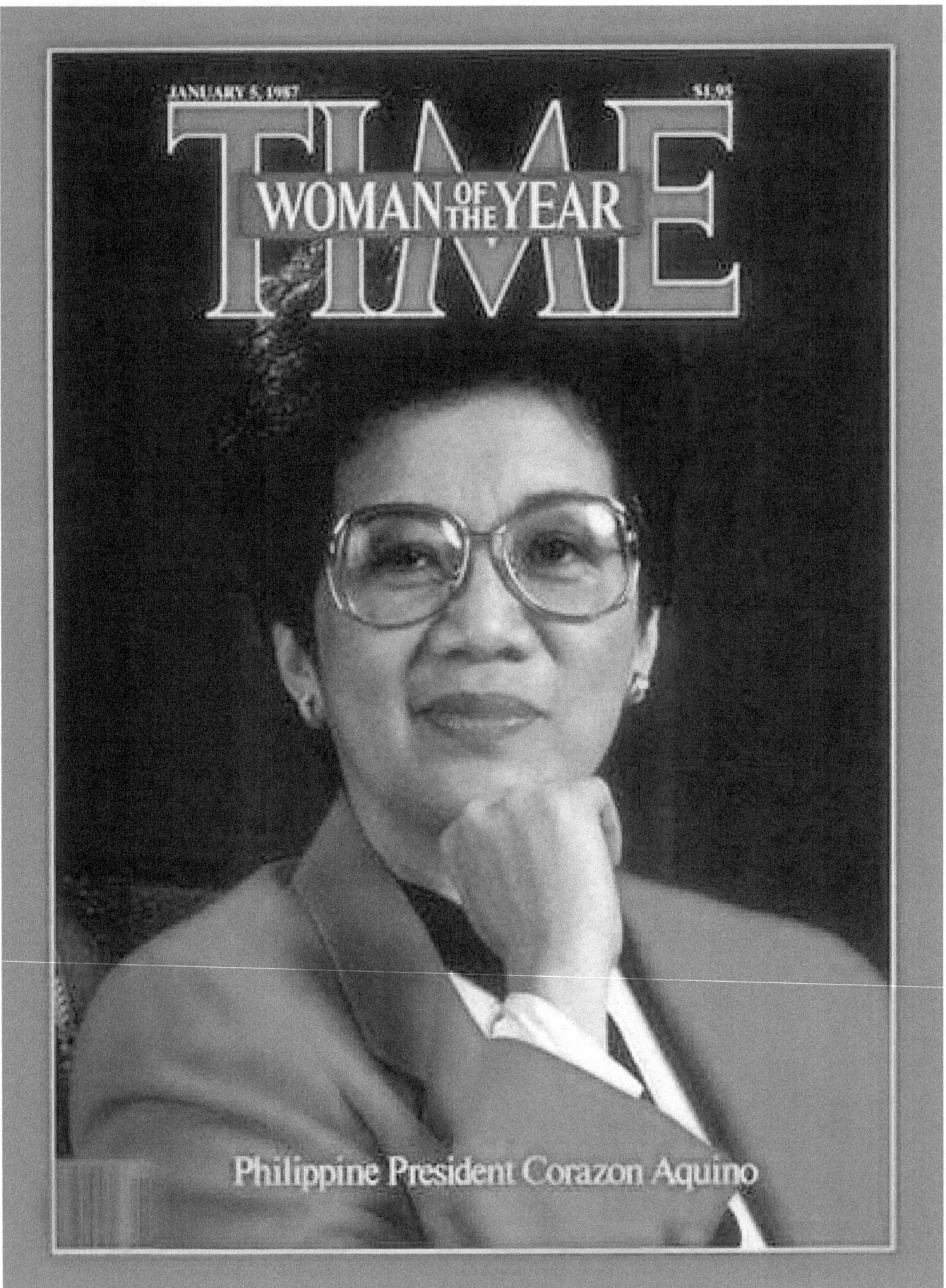

President Cory Aquino – Time's Woman of the Year, 1987

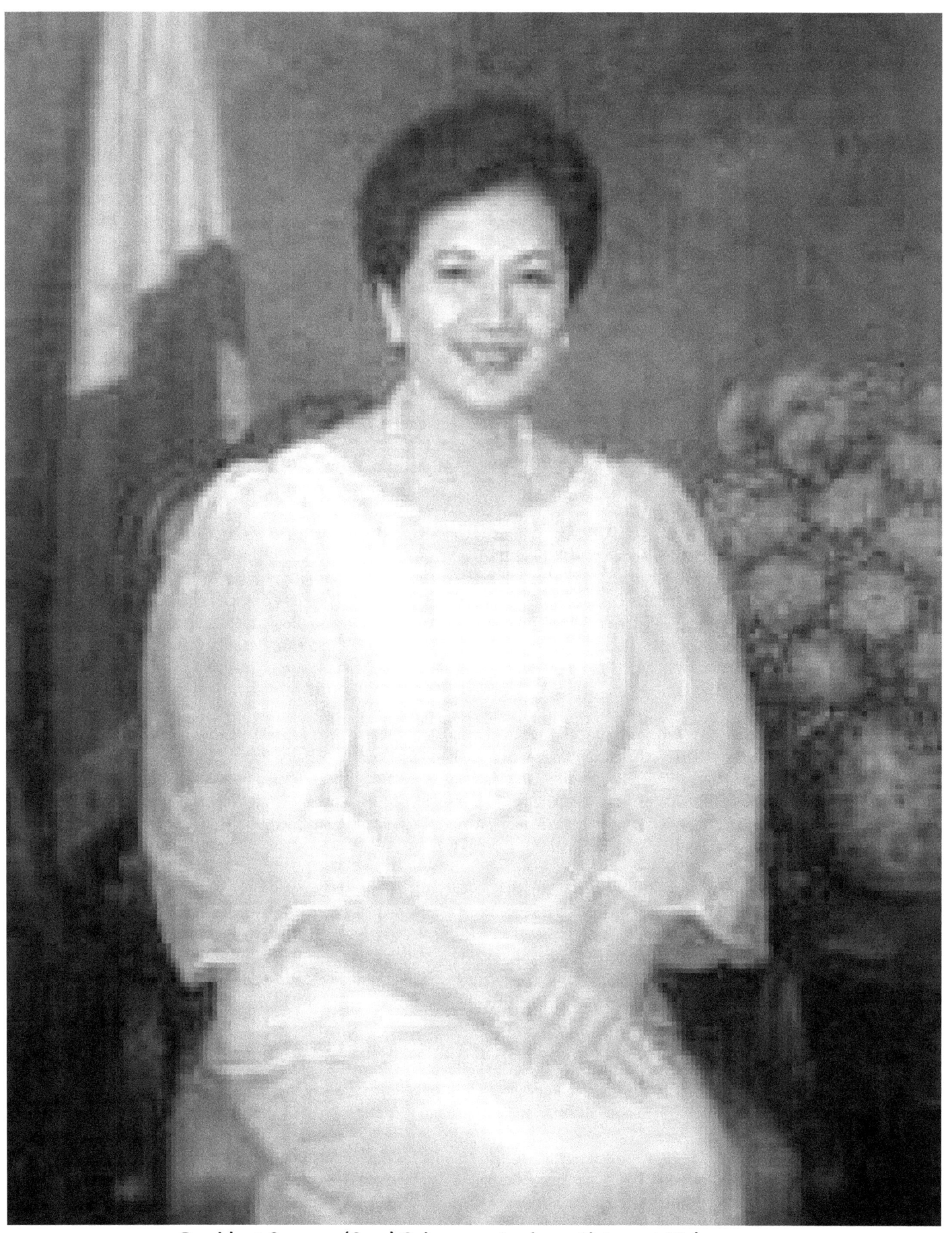

President Corazon (Cory) Cojuangco Aquino – Picture at Malacanang

Self-Publisher - Tatay Jobo Elizes
Printed, February, 2016, in the United States of America under ISBN codes below.
ISBN-13: 978 - 1523714896   +   ISBN-10: 1523714891

Book List - Buy online as paperback or kindle - Contact: job_elizes@yahoo.com, tatay@usa.com
Websites: http://tinyurl.com/mj76ccq + www.jobelizes.webs.com + www.tatayjobo.com

Writings 1 Book, 2012 , Articles by Bambi Harper + Butch Jiimenez + Dr. Phil Stack + Noel Alegre + Toto Causing +_ Melanie Ferrer + Susie Barbieri _ Rodel Ramos + Sylvia Salvador + Tatay Jobo Elizes + + Writings 2 Book, 2012, Artices by Gov. Grace Padaca + Melanie Aquino + Toto Causing + Rodel Rodis + Cesar Torres + Joey Concepcion + Charity Guides + Cesar Lumba +_ Casiano Mayor Jr. + Sonny Coloma + Anonymous.+ +

Writings 3A Book, 2012, Articles by Norman Madrid + Dr. Rene Azurin + Ernie Delfin + Toto Causing + Dr. Jose Abueva + MarVic Cagurangan + Casiano Mayor Jr + Rod Garcia + Roy Gaane + Tatay Jobo Elizes + + Writings 3B Book, 2012, Articles by Ceres Busa + John Reyes + Bert Guiang. + + Writings 4A Book, 2012, Articles by Dr Jose Abueva + Col. Dennis Acop + Fred Natividad + Irineo P. Goce, KaPule2 + Miguel Reynadlo + Marjorie Ann Elizes Reyes+ +

Writings 4B Book, 2012, 1. Mi Ultimo Adios (My Last Farewell), *Dr. Jose P. Rizal* + 2. Aling Pagibig Sa Tinubuang Bayan, *Gat. Andres Bonifacio* + Articles by Irineo P. Goce or KaPule2 + + Writings 5 Book - "Best Hopes" 2010 (About President P-Noy), Articles by Tony Meloto + F.SionilJose + Juan L. Mercado + OFWs Letter + Marcelo Tecson + Cesar Torres+ Perry Diaz + Dr. Philip S. Chua + Ernie Delfin + Atty. Ted Laguatan + Frank Wenceslao Jaileen F. Jimeno + Tatay Jobo Elizes + +

Writings 6 Book, 2010 + I. SONA - State Of Nation Address - English - *Pres. Benigno Aquino III* + II. **SONA** - State of Nation Address - Pilipino - *Pres. Benigno Aquino III* + III. **First 100 Days** peech - Pilipino - *Pres. Benigno Aquino III* + *Artiucles by Bert Guiang + Tony Meloto + Felicito or Tong C. Payumo + Cesar Lumba + Flor Lacanilao + Juan DelaCruz or Txtmanika + Dr. Ramon Marquez + Joey Jamito + Percival Cruz + Rod Garcia + Orion Perez Dumdum + Sarah Raymundo.* + + Writings 7 Book, 2010 - My Vintage Pics - Pictorials & Family, Tatay Jobo Elizes + + Writings 8 Book, 2010, Articles by Gel Santos Relos + Ms.Mike Portes + Jose Ma. Montelibano + Tony Meloto + Dr. Philip S. Chua + Dr. Cesar D. Candari + Dr. Eliseo Serina + Greg B. Macabenta + Irineo P. Goce or KaPule2 + Percival Cruz + Juan DelaCruz or Textmani + Demosthenes B. Donato. + +

Writings 9 Book, April 2011, Articles by Judge Simeon dumdum Jr + Gemma Cruz Araneta + Larry Henares Jr + Tony Joaquin + Allen Gaborro + Atty. Toto Causing + Mar-Vic Cagurangn + Emily Espanol Derry, Poet + Elyn Jean Felarca, Poet + Naysan A. Albaytar + Laura Wade, Blogger + Perter Allan Mariano + Marge Trajeco-Aberasturi + Julia Carreon Lagoc + Irineo P. Goce or KaPulle2 + Anonymous. + + Writings 10 Book, July, 2010, Articles by Atty.Ted Lagutan + Percival C. Cruz + Allen Gaborro + Peter Allan Mariano + M.L. Munoz + Alvib T. Tabaniag + Resty Odon + Dr. Phili S. Chua + Dr. Cesar D. Candari + Anonymous. + +

Writings 11 Book, August, 2011 + 1, SONA In English and Filipino, by President Benigno Aquino III (P-Noy) + 2, Telltale Signs: SONA and the Dogfight Over Spratlys, by Rodel Rodis + Atty. Ted Laguatan + Tatay Jobo Elizes + Jeremiah M. Opiniano + OFW Journalists + Bob & Carol Hammerslag + Roger P. Olivares + Rob Ceralvo + Anonymous + Irineo P. Goce or KaPule2 + Random. + + Writings 12 Book, April 2012 + Articles By Orion Perez Dumdum + Julia C. Lagoc + Honorio M. Cruz, MD + Ben Gonzales, MD + Mar-Vic Cagurangan + Marisa Lerias + Gerry Partido + Dr. Cesar D. Candari + Erwin De Leon + Jovelyn B. Revilla + Tatay Jobo Elizes + +

Writings 13 Book, July 2012 + Articles by Raymundo E. Narag + M.L. Munoz + Sonia Barbara gl Munoz + Pamela Joy Agtoto + Percival C. Cruz + Tatay Jobo Elizes + Jhakie Eslit Bayobay + Reygel Saplad Perales. + + Timely Writings 14, 2013 + Articles by Cesar F. Lumba + Eugenio Pulmano + Late Jesse Robredo + Antonio Nievera + Alvin T. Tabaniag + Kevin L. Nadal + Anonymous + Fred Natividad + Anonymous + Ellen Tordesillas + Lat Capt. Rene N. Jarque + +

Timeless Writings-15 (TW15), 2014 + Articles by SC Justice Antonio T. Carpio + Atty Dodel Rodis + Atty. Ted Laguatan + Sona by Pres. Benigno Aquino III + F. Sionil Jose + Dr. Philipi Stack + Racz Kelly, Padilla + Bert Armada.+ + Timeless Writings-16 (TW16), 2014 + Articles about The Martyrs of Camarines Norte + by Rodel Rodis + R.A.Gubalane + Robert Bernardo + Pres. Aquino's SONA 2014 + + Timeless Writings-17 (TW17), 2014 + Articles by Rodel Rodis+ Jose P. Rizal+ Irineo Goce+ Julia Lagos + Alvin Tabaniag+ Ragubalane + Red Butterfly+ Cesar Torres + + Timeless Writings-18 (TW18)

+ Articles by Rodel Rodis + Raul Manglapus + Ragubalane + Allen Gaborro + Manuel Vergara + + Timeless Writings-19 (TW19) + Articles by Atty. Ted Laguatan + Romely Bacsain + Charlie Chaplin + Orlando Carvajal + Allen Gaborro + Rodel Rodis + Primitivo Mijares + Krip Yuson + + Timeless Writings-20 (TW-20) + Excerpts from Primitivo Mijares Book, Conjugal Dictatorship + +

Solo Authored Books: + + +

Book A, Turning Points, *Job Elizes Sr,1968 (Reissue 2009)* + + + Book B, Be Considerate For Once, *Tatay Jobo Elizes (Jr), 2013* Book C, Piglets Unlimited - Wealth, *Tatay Jobo Elizes, 2009* + + + Book D, Out of the Misty Sea We Must, *Cesar Lumba, 2010* + + + Book E, Fulfilled – *Gonzales Reynaldo, Editor, 2010* + + + Book F - Reflections - *Bert Guiang, 2010* + + + Book G, Writings 7 - My Vintage Pics, *Tatay Jobo Elizes, 2010* +

Book H, May Bagwis Ang Pag-ibig, *Percival C. Cruz* + + + Book I, Letters To Matrimony, *Irineo P. Goce, Ka Pule2, 2011* + Book J, Songs I Wish You Knew, *Soledad R. Juan, 2011* + + + Book K, Make My Day, *Larry Henares Jr., 1993, Re-issue 2011* + Book L, Our Guerrero Family, *Tatay Jobo Elizes, 2010* + + + Book M, Handy Jokes, *Tatay J. Elizes, 2011* + Book N, FaveArt 1, *Tatay Jobo Elizes, 2011* + +

Book O, Beyond idle thoughts, *MLMunoz, Sept,2011* + + + Book P, Cracks In The Armor, *Mariano Ngan, Oct 2011* + + + Book Q, FaveArt 2, *Tatay Jobo Elizes, 2011* + + Book R, Balitang Kutsero, *Perry Diaz, Jan 2012* + + + Book S, FaveArt3, *Tatay Jobo, 2011* + + + Book T, FaveArt4 ,2012, *Tatay Jobo* + + + Book U, Stack Family Journals, *Phil & Fe Stack, 2012* + + + Book V, Emily, An Adoption Journey, *Romerl Elizes, 2012* + + +

Book W, Hermes Alegre Art Gallery, *TJ & Hermes, 2012* + + + Book X, Masaya Din, Malungkot Din, *Jovelyn B. Revilla, 2012* Book Y, Tiis, Sipag At Tiyaga, *Raquel Delfin Padilla, 2012* + + + Book Z, Until I Meet You, *Jhackie Eslit Bayobay, 2012* + + + Book AA, Buhay At Pag-ibig, *Argel Lucero Tamayo, 2012* + + + Book AB, Hail to the Second Best, *Dr. Philip Stack, 2012* + + + Book AC, Life Bus, *Mommy Joyce Pineda-Faulmino, 2012* + + + Book AD, My Candid Musings, *Monette Dioquino Calugay, 2012* + Book AE, Tickets to Life, *Maria Lourdes Jesalva, 2012* + + + Book AF, The Dove Files, *Mike Portes, 2012* + + + Book AG, Nursing Vignettes, *Jocelyn Cerrudo Sese, 2012* + Book AH, Poor Ba Us, *R.A. Gubalane, 2012* + + +

Book AI, Summer Idyll, *Avelina Gil, 2012* + + Book AJ, Legacy (Pamana), *Rachel Astrero, 2012* + + Book AK, Narratives Old & New, *Avelina J. Gil, 2013* + + Book AL, Buhay Saudi, *Adele J. Esic, 2013* + + Book AM, Buhay Ofw Atbp, *Jessica Napat, 2013* + + Book AN, Mga Tula Ng Buhay, *Angelita C. Esguerra, 2013* + + Book AO, Not by Bread Alone, *Judge Lily V. Magtolis, 2013* + + Book AP, Jokes Collection-2, *Tatay Jobo Elizes, 2013* + + +

Book AR, *My Writings Sometimes, Tatay Jobo Elizes, 2013* + + Book AS, Sa 'Yo Na Ako, *Shayne A. Martinez, 2013* + + Book AT, My Kin's Family Trees, *Tatay Jobo Elizes, 2013* + + Book AU, Rizal Family Tree & Others, *Tatay Jobo Elizes, 2013* + + Book AV, Make My Day-2, Nice & Nasty, *L. Henares, 2013 (1993)* + + Book AW, Make My Day-3, Cecilia, Love, *L.Henares, 2013 (1993)* Book AX, Handy Lyrics-1, *Tatay Jobo Elizes, 2013* + +

Book AY, Ang Biblos, *Rev. Dr. Eugenio Guerrero, 2014 (1929)* + + Book AZ, Make My Day-4, *Sweet & Sour, L. Henares, 2014 (1993)* + + Book BA, Life's Journey, True Stories, *Dr. Phil Stack, 2014* + + Book BB, Gerry Gil Writings, 2014, Danny Gil + + Book BC, Mr. President, *Hermie Rotea, 2014* + + Book BD, Nostalgic Pics *1, Tatay Jobo Elizes, 2014* + + Book BE, MakeMyDay-5, Saints & Sinners, *Henares, 2014 (1993)* + +

Book BF, MakeMyDay-6, Villains & Heroes, *Henares, 2014 (1993)* + + Book BG, Nostalgic Pics 2 (ElizesClan), *TatayJE, 2014* + + Book BH, MakeMyDay-7, Tough & Tender, *Henares, 2014(1993)* + + Book BI, MakeMyDay-8, Light & Shadow, *Henares, 2014(1993)* + + Book BJ, MakeMyDay-9, Give & Take, *Henares, 2014(1993)* + + Book BK, MakeMyDay-10, ToBeOrNotToBe, *Henares, 2014(1993)* +

Book BL,Emily Forever In Love, Poems,*Emily Espanol Derry, 2013* + + Book BM, The Sinatra Songbook, *Henares, 2014* + + Book BN, The Gaborro Reader, *Allen Gaborro, 2010* + + *Book BO,* Ramon H. Lopez - *Art Gallery, 2014* + + *Book BP,* Philippines Via Old Pics-1, *Tatay Jobo, 2014* + + Book BQ, Ronna Manansala - *Art Gallery, 2014* + + Book BR, Philippines Via Old Pics-2, *Tatay Jobo, 2014* + + *Book BS,* Being Good-A Medley Of Love, *Dr. Phil Stack, 2014* + + Book BT, Lifestream Fisherman, A Filipino Odyssey, *Paul Dalde, Jul2014* + + Book BU, Kristina Reed Manansala, Art Gallery-1, *August 2014.*+ +

Book BV, Hermes Art Gallery-2, *Sep2014,* + + Book BW, Fave Art-5, *Tatay Jobo, Sep2014* + + Book BX, Cash & Credits, Make My Day-11, *Larry Henares, Sept 2014* + + Book BY, Rise & Fall, Make My Day-12, *Larry Henares, Oct 2014* + + Book BZ, Swans & Swine, Make My Day-13, *Larry Henares, Oct 2014* + + Book CA, Touch & Go, Make My Day-14, *Larry Henares, Oct 2014* + + Book CB, Life & Death, Make My Day-15, *Larry Henares, Oct2014* + +

Book CC, Kiss & Bite, Make My day -16, *Larry Henares, Oct 2014* + + Book CD, Good & Evil, Make My Day-17, *Larry Henares, Oct2014* + + Book CE, Beast & Beauty, Make My Day-18, *Larry Henares, 2014* + + Book CF, Beggar & King, Make My Day-19, *Larry Henares, Oct 2014* + + Book CG, Trash & Treasures, Make My Day-20, *Larry Henares, Oct 2014* + + Book CH, Wear & Tear, Make My Day-21, *Larry Henares, Oct 2014* + + Book CI, Why Blame the President, *Irineo P. Goce, Oct 2014* + +

Book CJ, Angel & Devil, Make My Day-22, *Larry Henares, Oct 2014* + + Book CK, Pretty Ugly, Make My Day-23, *Larry Henares, Oct 2014* + + Book CL, Salvation & Damnation, Make My Day-24, *Larry Henares, Oct 2014* + + Book CM, Don Daniel Maramba, *Larry Henarez & Edith Perez de Tagle, Oct 2014* + + Book CN, Hilarion G. Henares, *Larry Henares & Edith Perez de Tagle, Oct 2014* + +Book CO, FaveArt-5 ++ Book CP, FaveArt-6, Book CQ, FaveArt-7, Book CR, FaveArt-8 *(All FaveArt books by Tatay Jobo), 2014* + +

Book CS, Minsan May Isang Puta, *Ms.Mike Portes, 2014* + + *Book CT, Ramblings A, Danny Gil, 2014* + + *Book CU, Ramblings-B, Danny Gil, 2014* + + *Book CV, Grace Esmeralda Album, by her, 2014* + + *Book CW, Secrets of a Romantic Man, Dr. Phil Stack, 2014* + + *Book CX, Ramblings-C, Danny Gil, 2014* + + *Book CY, Ramblings-D, Danny Gil, 2014* + + *Book CZ, Ramblings-E, Danny Gil, 2014* ++ *Book DA, Tenacious Nurse-1, Gretheline Bolandrina, 2014* + + *Book DB, Tenacious Nurse-2, Gretheline Ramos-Bolandrina, 2015* + + *Book DC, Of Words I Have Found, Dan Jimenez (danmeljim), 2015* + + *Book DQ, PhilippinesViaOldPics-4, Tatay Jobo Elizes, Jan2016* + +

Book DD, Tanjay East Coast Magazine, Issue 1, Feb 2015 + + *Book DE, Tanjay East Coast Magazine, Issue 2, April 2015* + + *Book DF, Catechism Manual, Dr. Latorre, April 2015* + + *Book DG, Tanjay East Coast Magazine, Extra Issue 2A, April 2015* + + *Book DH, Wedding Album, Anita & Barry, May 2015* + + *Book DI, Tanjay E. Coast Magazine, Poconos, May 2015* + + *Book DJ, Baptism Guidebook, Dr. Latorre, May 2015* + + *Book DK, Chita, a Memoir, Tony Joaquin* + + *Book DL, A Journey Unto Peace, Dr. Phil Stack, June2015*+ + *Book DM, Jokes Collection-3, Tatay Jobo Elizes, July2015* + + *Book DN, Jokes Collection-4, Tatay Jobo Elizes, Aug2015* + + *Book DO, Jokes Collection-5, Tatay Jobo Elizes, Sep2015* + + *Book DP, Beautiful Lie, Joecel Jayme, Jan2016* + + *Book DR, Conjugal Dictatorship, Primitivo Mijares (1976), Reprint Jan 2016,* + + *Book DS, Phil Via Old Pics-5, Tatay Jobo, Feb2016* + +

Permission had been granted by the author/authors to print their books under my free self-publishing service. They own copyrights to their works. Interested reader may request free reading of any of my booklist via online reading or ebook. Just email me.

Why I   Publish Books By Tatay Jobo Elizes

Writings are timeless and they act as mirrors of history. I publish writings as they remain relevant anytime. I am offering these services free of charge because of the availability of print-books-on-demand (POD) system nowadays. I have acquired the knowledge the hard way. I am now in a position to help publish writings of anybody. I can produce the book, but it's not entirely free of cost on my part. I merely assume the cost.

Why put your writings in a book? And not just in the internet? I recommend that writings be retained in a hard copy or in book form or printed form for posterity. The book will always be there among your collections or libraries. Not all use the internet. The internet access has its technical problems. Writings in the internet may be erased erroneously. Free storage is hard to access. Paid storage may be returned or lost.

For those looking for a publisher, especially if you have a novel or many essays, I can produce the paperback book under your own authorship at no cost. I can produce art books, family tree books, family albums/pictorials, biographies, joke books, songhits books, travelogues, reunions, in color or black & white.

Notes about this picture book

This book can be displayed as coffee table book for family and guests. Each picture can be cut and framed. Just buy more books. This book is suitable for libraries and schools in Philippines and Pinoys abroad. It's a perfect reference material for study of history and heroes. It's suitable as gift for any occasion. It's a collector's item. Heirs of those persons and pictures shown may want to own this book for their own families.

www.ingramcontent.com/pod-product-compliance
Lightning Source LLC
Chambersburg PA
CBHW080706190526
45169CB00006B/2259